CLIENT SCIENCE

Advice for Lawyers on Counseling Clients through Bad News and Other Legal Realities

Marjorie Corman Aaron

OXFORD
UNIVERSITY PRESS

OXFORD
UNIVERSITY PRESS

Oxford University Press, Inc., publishes works that further
Oxford University's objective of excellence in research, scholarship, and education.

Oxford New York
Auckland   Cape Town   Dar es Salaam   Hong Kong   Karachi   Kuala Lumpur   Madrid
Melbourne   Mexico City   Nairobi   New Delhi   Shanghai   Taipei   Toronto

With offices in
Argentina   Austria   Brazil   Chile   Czech Republic   France   Greece   Guatemala
Hungary   Italy   Japan   Poland   Portugal   Singapore   South Korea   Switzerland
Thailand   Turkey   Ukraine   Vietnam

Published by Oxford University Press, Inc.
198 Madison Avenue, New York, New York 10016

Oxford is a registered trademark of Oxford University Press
Oxford University Press is a registered trademark of Oxford University Press, Inc.

Library of Congress Cataloging-in-Publication Data

Aaron, Marjorie Corman.
Client science : advice for lawyers on counseling clients through bad news and other legal
realities / Marjorie Corman Aaron.
  p. cm.
Includes bibliographical references and index.
ISBN 978-0-19-989190-0 ((pbk.) : alk. paper)
  1. Attorney and client—United States. 2. Communication in law—United States.
3. Attorney and client—United States—Psychological aspects. 4. Attorney and client—
Social aspects—United States. 5. Practice of law—United States—Psychological aspects.
6. Practice of law—Social aspects—United States. 7. Interpersonal communication. I. Title.
KF311.A923 2012
340.02'3—dc23   2011048707

9 8 7 6 5 4 3 2
Printed in the United States of America on acid-free paper

Note to Readers
This publication is designed to provide accurate and authoritative information in regard to the
subject matter covered. It is based upon sources believed to be accurate and reliable and is intended
to be current as of the time it was written. It is sold with the understanding that the publisher is not
engaged in rendering legal, accounting, or other professional services. If legal advice or other expert
assistance is required, the services of a competent professional person should be sought. Also, to
confirm that the information has not been affected or changed by recent developments, traditional
legal research techniques should be used, including checking primary sources where appropriate.

(Based on the Declaration of Principles jointly adopted by a Committee of the
American Bar Association and a Committee of Publishers and Associations.)

You may order this or any other Oxford University Press publication
by visiting the Oxford University Press website at www.oup.com

For Elliot and Devora Corman

And in memory of Samuel M. Corman

Contents

Acknowledgments

Collectively, my students in the 2L Client Counseling course at the University of Cincinnati College of Law have been the most important instigators of this book. I owe a great debt to each student who endured the course's "Final Counseling Skills Exercise" with my coaching, no doubt often clumsy, less-than-sensitive, too directive, or too vague. Without the variety and number of student struggles, patience, forbearance, and willingness to try it again, this book would not have been possible.

It has been a privilege to work with extraordinary actors who have played the client role in more than 700 of these Final Counseling Skills Exercise sessions. Melinda (Mindy) Seibert, John Bromels, and Jeff rey Groh must appear at the top of the screen: Mindy as the longest running, ever convincing and inventive client; John for his perceptive and constructive interventions on voice, facial expression, and gesture; and Jeff for his articulate reflections on why the client would feel and respond as he did. In the early years, my students and I also appreciated the sensitivity of actors David Hughes, Linda Crystal, and Deondre Means. More recently, we are fortunate to have worked with Denise Dal Vera, Annie Fitzpatrick, and Rob Jansen, who introduced fresh ways to understand the client. In Michigan, our clients were adeptly played by Tricia Klapthor, Gordon Granger, and Adam Schaeffer. I am also grateful for CCM Professor Rocco Dal Vera's teaching on the power of story arcs, character narratives, and the way internal actor (and lawyer) belief and emotion generate shifts in body, gesture, and voice, with profound impact on the listener.

Much appreciation, respect, and recognition are due to people whose insights, comments, hard work, and generosity have contributed to the research and writing process.

At the University of Cincinnati College of Law, I am deeply grateful to Dean Louis Bilionis for encouraging and supporting this book project. I also owe great gratitude to the Harold C. Schott Foundation for underwriting several summer research stipends and research assistants.

Taking a longer historical perspective, thanks are due to A. J. Stephani, then director of the Weaver Center for Law and Psychiatry, for joining me to design and teach an initial, short client counseling elective. The students' appreciation for that course and our recognition of how difficult it was to articulate what was good and bad client counseling (and why) propelled serious teaching focus on the topic.

In 2003, then Dean Joseph Tomain earned full credit for convening then-Associate Dean Barbara Watts, Director of the Center for Professional Development Mina Jefferson Jones, Professor Marianna Bettman, and me to brainstorm about infusing practice into the curriculum. That led directly to client counseling as a required 2L course. We became the course teaching team and coaches for the Final Counseling Skills Exercise that first year, with the invaluable assistance of then-student, now-colleague and friend Patricia Foster. All credit for administrative juggling over the years goes to our longtime faculty assistant Toni McGuire, Registrar Charlene Carpenter, and web wizard Connie Miller. Most recent credit goes to our new faculty assistant Mindy Lawson for her deft management of the course administration in 2011–2012.

Each year, I am thankful to Dean Bilionis and Associate Dean Nancy Oliver, and the College of Law faculty, for continuing to value and support 2L Client Counseling and its labor-intensive Final Counseling Skills Exercise.

My intelligent and resourceful research assistants must be named: Tre Ronne, Nathaniel Simpson, Jonathan Norman, Jonathan Amitrano, Keith Pfeffer, James Tanous, Joseph Morgalis, and Bradley Rudinsky. Particular gratitude is owed to Tre Ronne, who stuck with this project for many semesters and was an early, invaluable critical reader and source of encouragement as well as indefatigable source locator and footnote scrutinizer. Brad Rudinsky earns extra credit for the dedication, thoroughness, and energy needed to finish the final manuscript and endnote challenges.

I spent the 2011 spring semester at the University of Michigan Law School. Full professional admiration and appreciation are due to Michigan Law research librarian Seth Quidachay Swan and the Michigan Law student research assistants he supervised, for working through countless research questions and incomplete notations, and supplying wondrously complete references.

At the University of Cincinnati's College of Law Library, now so ably managed by Director Kenneth Hirsh, I thank James Hart, Susan Boland, and Victoria Fleischer for ever-prompt responses to my queries and requests and for guiding my research assistants in fruitful directions.

Much appreciation is owed to those who encouraged this project early on, including: Michael Watkins, Shawna Slack, Dwight Golann, Amy Glass, Joanna Jacobs, Janet Martinez, Sharon Press, Daniel Bowling, and Richard Paszkiet, and other publications committee members of the American Bar Association Section on Dispute Resolution.

I am grateful to the many law professor colleagues, students, attorneys, and others who have commented upon chapter drafts and subtitles, including: Jacob Cogan, Daniel Donnellon, Joseph Heyd, Cathleen Kuhl, Doloris Learmonth, Sean Mangan, Ken Patel, Seth Schwartz, and Carl Stich. Two colleagues (whom I count as friends) have spent far too much time on this manuscript, earning an abundance of extra credit: Professor Richard Reuben of the University of Missouri at Columbia; and Russ Bleemer, editor of *Alternatives*, published by International Institute for Conflict Prevention and Resolution. Richard's contribution is long and deep, from co-teaching workshop versions of Client Counseling with me over many years, to reading too many early, terribly unpolished chapters. I am forever indebted to Russ Bleemer for his immediate, contagious, and constant enthusiasm for all that I sent him. Russ so graciously and quickly read each chapter, always providing invaluable comments along with continued affirmation of the project's value for lawyers and clients.

Finally, and most profoundly, I thank those who have patiently and lovingly sustained me in this long endeavor: my husband, David Aaron; my sons Joshua and Elisha Aaron; all members of the Corman and Aaron families; and so many treasured friends. Of course, David deserves the endurance prize, for gracefully fulfilling the spousal listener obligation at all hours, and granting me limitless time and freedom to work.

Long ago, my parents, Devora and Elliot Corman, explained one of their criteria in choosing a child's name: it must look dignified on a book cover. I thank them for that, and for the love and confidence they have expressed in me since the day I was born.

Marjorie Corman Aaron
Cincinnati, Ohio
January, 2012

Preface

Clients!!!!

Many years ago, while teaching a law school negotiation class, I asked a student how he would explain his rather strange negotiated agreement to his client. He responded with a blank look: "Who?" I began building short segments on talking with and getting authority from clients into my negotiation course. I was astonished to see how much law students struggled to counsel even their classmate clients.

Upon reflection, this should not have been surprising. As a mediator of civil cases, I have seen countless ill-counseled clients. Extremely intelligent, skilled advocates can be terribly uncomfortable in the counselor's role—unclear, insensitive, or less-than-candid. Even lawyers generally adept as counselors struggle with so called "difficult clients."

As a mediator, I have long suspected that a greater percentage of the difficult clients find their way to mediation. A mediator can assist communication with difficult clients whose legal circumstances are grim. After all, when the lawyer explains the case will likely end on summary judgment, he risks the client's suspicion or accusation of less than zealous advocacy. There's no tension between the mediator's straight talk and the lawyer-as-advocate.

Mediators too become frustrated when clients opt to "walk off the cliff" despite our best efforts to explain their lawyers' analysis, talk through choices, and lay out the negotiation problem. Real clients are just not easy!

Back to a law professor's focus on the serious, too often unexamined challenges of client counseling. At the University of Cincinnati College of Law, one curricular idea led to another. The faculty voted. Client counseling became a required course for 2Ls.

I created the course with a series of simulation exercises designed to introduce specific client counseling challenges. Individual coaching, feedback, and video recording are highly valued teaching tools. Thus, at the end of the course, each student is recorded and coached in a "Final Counseling Skills Exercise" with actor-clients. The exercise requires student-lawyers to give actor-clients bad news of unanticipated risks and explain complex law and process for that news to make sense. Success is declared when: the student-lawyer obtains the client's authority to settle for far less than previously contemplated; the client perceives the lawyer as highly competent; and the client feels strong trust and rapport and would recommend that lawyer to a friend. Whenever I describe this exercise to lawyer colleagues, they groan with empathy for the students. "Yes, that's the hardest thing a lawyer has to do. . . . And we must do it."

When I coached the first actor-clients for that first semester's Final Counseling Skills Exercise sessions, I thought I knew the skills and strategies it required. And I thought students would perform well, if they had paid attention during the course. After all, I had so cleverly planted the course lessons into the exercise.

Over seven years of coaching students in their search for effective phrasing, order, timing, emphasis, and delivery, I've come to respect the deep difficulty of the exercise. I've watched the vast majority of students struggle to explain summary judgment in a way the client can understand. I've seen actor-clients completely misunderstand an explanation I thought was clear as a bell. I've felt the palpable tension between a lawyer's need to deliver bad news straight and his client's need for an advocate-protector.

I've observed how the failure to pause—and pause for quite a while—between sentences and paragraphs leaves a client unable to process an explanation or his own emotion, and thus completely unable to hear what comes next. I've come to recognize that discussion of settlement numbers is a nearly separate arena fraught with distinct problems in client communication. I've also observed how failure to respond to a client's expressed regret or feelings of powerlessness causes frustration and alienation.

Full credit for my ability to observe, reflect, understand, and offer insight from this exercise is due to the tremendously intelligent, talented, thoughtful, and dedicated actors with whom we've been privileged to work. One amazing characteristic of great actors is that the scene is fresh every time. They are "in the moment" with each new student lawyer.

With these actors as clients, we tried, tested, and stumbled upon phrasings that seemed to work better. Students and professor learned from them why the client reacted so negatively to what we heard as simply accurate word choice. We came to understand how and why ordering the message impacted the client's ability to process it. We learned the power of story-telling over statistics, how suspicion arises, and why meaning matters as much as logic.

Sometimes, after just a few minutes, the actor-clients would announce their complete trust and confidence in certain student lawyers. Others inspired the opposite reaction. We attempted to articulate why. What are the manifestations of presence, of trust, of perceived competence? Sometimes, the actor-client and I would see that some aspect of delivery undermined a student-lawyer's effectiveness, even if his or her phrasing was fine. The actors taught their student-lawyers as they taught me technical aspects of delivery: how voice, body movement, and gesture can diminish or enhance perceived confidence, competence, trust, and rapport.

I began to realize that the most practical and valuable lessons from the Final Counseling Skills Exercise were not written, at least not in a single accessible source for lawyers. A few summers ago,

I set out to change that. First, I wrote a "thought draft" of all we had learned. I then worked with various research assistants to see if social science supported that draft. Not surprisingly, it did, on all counts. The result is this book. The title, "Client Science," proudly reflects that it is supported by academic empirical and experimental research, as well as observation, reflection, and trial and error in more than 700 simulated client counseling sessions at the University of Cincinnati College of Law and 24 sessions at the University of Michigan Law School.

By this endeavor, I hope to serve the legal profession and its clients well.

About the Author

Marjorie Corman Aaron is Professor of Practice and Director of the Center for Practice at the University of Cincinnati College of Law, teaching courses in client counseling, negotiation, mediation, mediation advocacy, and decision analysis. She received the College of Law's Goldman Prize for Excellence in Teaching in 2010, and a University President's Excellence Award in 2006. In the spring of 2011, she taught client counseling and negotiation as a Visiting Professor at the University of Michigan Law School.

Professor Aaron was formerly the Executive Director of the Program on Negotiation at Harvard Law School where she was a lecturer in negotiation. She also served on the Harvard Business School faculty team that designed its MBA negotiation curriculum.

Aaron has been an active mediator, arbitrator, and trainer in negotiation and dispute resolution for more than twenty years. In private dispute resolution practice in Boston with ENDISPUTE, Inc. (now JAMS) and more recently in Cincinnati, she has mediated disputes involving general commercial contracts, employment, age and gender discrimination, business torts, products liability, personal injury, complex construction and design claims, corporate partnership, environmental claims and allocation issues, real estate and business valuation, real estate trusts, and medical, legal and other professional malpractice.

She also designs and teaches workshops on negotiation, mediation, client counseling, decision analysis, and presentation skills for law firms, corporations, and other organizations and has authored numerous chapters, articles, and case simulations in her field.

A sustaining academic member of the CPR Institute for Dispute Resolution, and a member of CPR's ADR Training Faculty, Professor Aaron previously served on the Ohio Commission on Dispute Resolution and Conflict Management, the Ethics Commission of the CPR Institute for Dispute Resolution, and the Conference and Publications Committees of the ABA Section on Dispute Resolution.

A graduate of Princeton University and Harvard Law School, Aaron first practiced as a litigator at Goodwin Procter in Boston and as an Assistant District Attorney in Plymouth County, MA.

INTRODUCTION

A lawyer finds it painful to watch his client jump off a cliff, relying upon flimsy wings and lucky winds. Too often, the lawyer is bound to jump alongside his client and pick up the pieces. There's little solace in knowing the wings were the best any lawyer could have constructed, given the materials available. The client's greater pain will come in the crash with reality at ground level. Shattered, angry, bitter, or incredulous, had the client ever fully contemplated such an ending and its consequences?

Some lawyers sigh sagely or shrug resignedly about "difficult clients," "clients who just can't see reality," or "clients who resist our advice in their best interests."

A lawyer's obligation is to inform his client of the law and its consequences. Once informed, the client has decision-making authority. Ultimately, to jump or not, and in which direction, is the client's choice. A lawyer can't block a client's foolish but lawful jump. Strong advocacy can only seek to influence the landing.

Does the lawyer meet the obligation to inform by explaining the laws of physics and the glider wings' vulnerability to harsh weather, wind shear, high wires, and eagle claws? Myth, optimism, stories of others taking flight, and aversion to weak surrender before the cliff's edge all propel the client forward. After all, he has seen others glide over the canyon chasm, against the odds, in so many movies.

Was the client fully informed if he heard the lawyer's words of caution and risk, but never understood the physics at work? What if the client did understand the lawyer's explanation of the laws of physics but never really believed they would apply to *his* flight? Is it a well advised client who understands the reality of physics but feels compelled and perhaps protected by the jump's cosmic meaning?

I suggest that the answer is "not necessarily," on all counts. Clients are fully informed only when they understand and accept the legal realities: the opportunities, risks, and consequences of law and process in their circumstances. Clients are fully informed only when they feel full trust and confidence in their lawyers' advocacy, competence, motive, and respect. Absent a strong lawyer-client relationship, a client may comprehend the lawyer's words but reject their validity.

Emotion and psychology inevitably shape and arguably distort perception, understanding, memory, and meaning. Thus, client realization of full information may require clearing emotional and psychological interference. It may require the client to recognize that causes, effects, and meanings of our actions are often self-generated, multiple, and malleable. The only fully "fully informed" client is one who can step back, seeing what his lawyer sees and understanding what his lawyer knows—a client who has fully integrated the lawyer's information, explanation, and advice.

Having set the bar high for what is a fully informed client, this book offers insight and advice for lawyers to meet that bar. After all, shouldn't lawyers aspire to the highest level of practice in client counseling?

Like all professionals, no matter what the outcome, a lawyer should consistently reflect: What might I have done differently? What more could I know about communicating? How could I have counseled more effectively against that needless fall or missed opportunity or, at the very least, better prepared my client for the consequences?

Before a sigh and a shrug about difficult clients, some probing questions are warranted: Was this client *impossibly* difficult? Unfathomable? Unreachable? Or, while no doubt a challenging client and tough circumstances, could another lawyer have more skillfully facilitated his reaching a wiser decision? We invoke the image of professional mentors or muses and wonder how they might have worked with this client.

In some sense, this book's purpose is to expiate lawyers' frustration and self-recrimination when, despite their counsel, the client nevertheless jumps off a cliff or walks out the door (likely to jump off the same cliff with another lawyer). As professionals, we can only achieve the possible. When a trial ends in an unwelcome verdict, a mediation ends in impasse, a business negotiation ends without a deal, or a client consultation ends badly, a lawyer's ruminations naturally begin.

However if, upon *fully* self-critical reflection, you find no lapse in knowledge, strategy, or skill that another lawyer could have employed, you have earned the right to sound and guiltless sleep. You were informed by the science—the research and observations discussed in this book. You employed the communication strategies and techniques appropriate for the client in this case. You did the best you could, and no other lawyer could have done better.

One clarification is due in the name of respect for clients' self-determination and limits to their lawyers' responsibilities. A lawyer does not fail every time a client rejects his advice. Nor does the lawyer have license to impose his own values or preferences upon his clients. Consider a family business dispute giving rise to a client's minority shareholder claim against her father. The lawyer might abhor the idea of suing one's father under any imaginable circumstances. The client might hold different values, viewing family ties as unchosen and severable. Despite knowing potential financial, legal, and family consequences, the client may decide to file suit. The lawyer has not failed; a fully informed client has exercised decision-making authority.

The lawyer's obligation is merely to ensure that, before jumping, the client's eyes are wide open to the panorama, the distance, the fragility of the flying machine, and the cost of the aftermath. That is hard enough.

Which would you like first, the good news or the bad news? Arguably, where bad news informs all that follows, it should come first. Thus, the book's first chapter, "Bad News and the Fully Informed Client," addresses the lawyer's most difficult challenge: to deliver bad news the client wasn't expecting to hear, obtain full client comprehension of legal complexities, and counsel the client toward a wise decision. Delivering bad news and its legal explanation risks client confusion, incredulity, denial, and shaken faith in the lawyer-messenger. Understandably, the lawyer seeks to maintain client loyalty, trust, and confidence. The first chapter takes on this most difficult task and yields practical advice for conveying bad news, where the law is complex and its impact severe, and these realities constrain what is a wise decision.

If the first chapter is the punch line, the rest are substantial commentary, parsing the components of effective communication for lawyers as counselors. Climbing the most difficult mountain requires the full set of gear, most careful strategy, and highest skill. Thus, when discussing bad news or difficult legal realities, lawyers are advised to draw upon all that is offered. Not all expeditions require us to ascend Mt. Everest. However, given the ubiquity of emotion, psychology, complexity, and myth in law and legal process, these chapters will also benefit client counseling sessions less fraught with obvious difficulty.

As its title suggests, the second chapter, "Translating the Terrain" recommends that lawyers consider communicating with clients about law and process as a translation task far beyond occasional Latin phrases. It derives translation strategies that enable lawyers and their clients to see the same picture of the legal circumstances.

"Meaning Truths" moves to the more profound social, philosophical, political, and identity-based meaning and values we ascribe to decisions, actions, and consequences in our legal system. It suggests why a client may say he "gets it"—fully *understands* the lawyer's translation of the legal jargon—but seems to *disbelieve* that reality. This chapter is also written for the client who sees that a decision makes rational sense, but remains troubled by its meaning within her personal and social narrative.

The fourth and fifth chapters, "Emotional Effects and Affecting Emotions" and "Predictable and Potent Psychology," address emotion and psychology as inevitable influences on human decision-makers.

It's arguably artificial to draw a sharp line between emotion and psychology. After all, a psychologist will admit that emotion—the way we feel about a data set or a decision—impacts our thinking, interpretation, evaluation, reasoning, and conclusions. And a therapist will call upon cognitive psychology to understand and shape emotional responses.

From the feeling side of the line, the "Emotional Effects" chapter focuses on emotion in lawyer-client interactions as well as emotion arising from the underlying legal problem that brought the client to his lawyer's office in the first place. "Emotional Effects" gleans from the science of emotion and prescribes ways for lawyers to reduce their clients' negative emotions. Even if legal circumstances are dire, a lawyer may use these prescriptions to build client rapport, trust, and positive emotion. This leads to better client decisions and, incidentally, stronger client loyalty.

"Predictable and Potent Psychology" looks at the way lawyers and clients evaluate information and make decisions, presenting relevant findings from social and cognitive psychology. In general, this book assumes that the lawyer's analysis is impeccable, and the challenge lies in its communication. However, this chapter provides evidence that *all of us* are susceptible to psychological tendencies leading to faulty analysis and poor decisions. It suggests ways for a lawyer to question memory, frame narratives, and reduce distortion in the client's decision-making process.

It might be said that the first five chapters address their titled topics—"Bad News and the Fully Informed Client," "Translating the Legal Terrain," "Meaning Truths," "Emotional Effects and Affecting Emotions," and "Predictable and Potent Psychology"—to yield insight and advice for lawyers on WHAT to say when counseling clients. The remaining chapters address HOW to say it: how best to communicate the lawyer's message, providing advice on voice, body language and gesture. Their goals are greater clarity when conveying complexity, enhanced client connection and trust, and perceived competence and authority, particularly in the face of bad news.

Have you ever sat in a client meeting and observed another lawyer speak the same words you used moments ago—but this time the client listens? Why do some people manage to keep a client's unquestioning loyalty and confidence despite direct, honest, and dire case assessments? Would another lawyer, delivering the same assessment, likely receive an angry, resistant client response? As trained actors learn and highly effective communicators demonstrate—whether in stand-up presentations or sit-down one-on-ones—the way we vocalize, stand, sit, and move determines our impact, often far more than the words chosen.

I am confident lawyers will bring professional perspective to reading the advice taken from actors, presented in the last several chapters (6 through 9), on how best to communicate the lawyer's message. Actors use voice, gesture, body movement, and facial expression to convince their audience that they are an assumed character—that the artifice is real. The lawyer's realm is reality. Unless a highly skilled actor, the lawyer's attempt to become someone else will be unconvincing. Even if it were possible, it seems wrong for a lawyer to seek to adopt an entirely different persona through voice, gesture, body posture or movement. Instead, these chapters are intended to enable lawyer-readers to more astutely observe their own and others' vocal patterns, gesture, and body language, and to experiment deliberately within their own ranges.

Opening the "how to say it" chapters, "Choices in Voice" presents research findings, observation, and advice on using voice for greater clarity, connection, confidence, and professional authority. It suggests strategic shifts in vocal speed, pausing, and pitch that can profoundly impact how we listen, what we learn, and how we are heard. The next chapters all address choices in physicality. "Choreography of Counsel" discusses body position, posture, and motion directly applicable to lawyer-client counseling, as well as other legal professional contexts. "A Gesture to Clarity" focuses on specific ways lawyers can use gesture to enhance client understanding of complex concepts. The final chapter, "Channel Navigation

Notes," examines gesture and movement in that narrow channel of space between seated lawyer and client; it yields advice for strengthening feelings of connection and trust. As is true for the entire endeavor, the goal is straightforward: a fully informed and loyal client.

Note

* Singular pronouns in English are inevitably gendered, as are individual lawyers and clients. To avoid the awkwardness of using "his or her" and "he or she," I have chosen to use gendered pronouns and to reference male and female lawyers and clients in a reasonably balanced way throughout the book

1

Bad News and the Fully Informed Client

"Bad news isn't wine. It doesn't improve with age."
— COLIN POWELL[1]

"Yet the first bringer of unwelcome news hath but a losing office."
— SHAKESPEARE, *Henry IV*[2]

Good News Paves an Easy Path

You just received notification from the clerk's office that the court granted your defense client's motion to dismiss; the plaintiff will not appeal. There's no ambiguity or uncertainty, and no need for advice on what to say. Call your client and give him the final, bottom-line great news.

Talking with clients about positive developments in an ongoing lawsuit or negotiation is a communication task that rarely threatens client trust or rapport. Imagine that, after researching an important legal question, you explain to your defense client that he is safe from personal liability and his company will likely escape liability as well. Or, after reviewing gathered evidence, you reassure your plaintiff-client that her causation evidence is rock solid. These clients are unlikely to focus on whether your presentation of legal process or case law is crystal clear or in perfect order. Where you must inform them of some minor, lingering concerns, they will listen and appreciate your earnest (and important) disclaimers that nothing is certain.

When discussing strengths in litigation or settlement position, you bask in your clients' approval. They are so pleased to hear confirmation that the law supports their view of what is right. With a positive frame of mind, they are open to brainstorming about next negotiation moves or potential witnesses. Rapport is easy. Just remember to hold onto caution and a bit of gravitas while sharing the clients' delight.

Perhaps Unnecessary, Free Advice for Delivering Good News

Do remember disclaimers—don't be overconfident and don't communicate overconfidence.

Do articulate the nature of the uncertainties and the risks, and make sure the client understands they are real, even if unlikely. It's good practice to put them in writing to the client after your meeting.

Do articulate the elements that form the basis of your favorable conclusion, emphasizing that if an element changes, your analysis and conclusion will change as well. That way, if and when a problematic document surfaces or a manager's deposition reveals unwelcome surprises, your client should understand their significance. Unless you have explained the reasons for your earlier optimistic analysis, the now less-than-happy client might think you are waffling or making excuses.

Difficult and Tricky Road to Bad News Delivered Well

On this less than sunny day, you represent a plaintiff facing a defense motion for summary judgment and, in a different case, a defendant who wants desperately to obtain summary dismissal of a personal fraud claim against him. While you could write (or have written) credible briefs supporting your clients' positions, you see a very low probability of success based upon your thorough review of the evidence, recent case law, and the judge's track record. You now strongly believe the plaintiff-client's case will be lost on summary judgment and the defendant-client will face the fraud claim at trial. You are not entirely optimistic about either client's chances of success at trial. You anticipate client anger, sadness, frustration, and resistance to this conclusion. When meeting with either one, your goals are that:

1) the client continue to *feel connection*, trust, and loyalty in his relationship with you, despite the bad news;

2) the client *fully understand* the bad news—your unfavorable conclusions, their basis in reasoned analysis, and how they impact his legal case and personal or business circumstances;

3) the client *maintain confidence in your competence*—the meeting would be unsuccessful if the client came to wonder whether a "better lawyer" would have reached a more favorable conclusion; and

4) the client continue to *believe you will zealously represent him*—the meeting would be unsuccessful if the client came to doubt whether you remain fully on his side and will fight for his cause.

If you are mindful and strategic, you can deliberately choose more effective ways to use your voice, order the presentation of bad news, difficult concepts, and unwelcome reasoning, and reduce client resistance to your message. This is not to diminish client choice: he is entitled to resist or reject his lawyer's advice regarding what choice to make. However, that choice should come only after the client is indeed fully informed and has fully integrated his lawyer's analysis of legal realities.

The next few sections of this chapter offer insight and advice directed toward the first two goals of client counseling when you must convey bad news: a continued positive client relationship, and a fully informed client. These themes are more fully developed in later chapters on meaning, emotion, psychology, voice, and gesture. This chapter concludes with advice specifically related to the third and fourth goals: maintaining client confidence in your competence and in your commitment to zealous representation.

Insights for Lawyers from Communication Scholars on Doctors

Profoundly bad news, or even profoundly good news, with potentially life-altering impact, can cause us to experience a rupture in the fabric of our everyday lives. Professor Douglas Maynard, of the University of Wisconsin, whose research has focused on the social psychological impact of good and bad news, writes that these cause us to "experience a breakdown, however momentary or prolonged, which requires realignment to and realization of a transfigured social world."[3] People receiving extremely bad news (and also extremely good news, though that is not my focus) report disorientation or confusion as they slip into "some new world."[4]

Most important, extensive research confirms that poor delivery of bad news can damage or destroy the relationship between the speaker and listener-recipient. When the listener feels bad news was communicated insensitively—too abruptly, after stalling, or without caring—tremendous and lasting anger or hurt will result, damaging or ending the relationship. On the other hand, sharing of bad news, done well, can enhance the relationship and sense of affinity. Social psychology thus identifies our challenge: how best to communicate bad news without doing harm to the social relationship and, in Professor Maynard's words, "how best to obtain recipients' *realization* (understanding and acceptance) of bad news."[5]

Professor Maynard and other scholars base advice to the bearers of bad news upon narrative data research primarily from the doctor-patient counseling and medically-related bad news, but also to some degree from family, employment, and lawyer-client contexts.[6] My experience and observation in two decades of mediating legal disputes and hundreds of counseling sessions with actor-clients confirms the value of that research and the wisdom of this advice. With that in mind, I offer the following specific suggestions for lawyers who, mindful of the obligation to fully inform their clients, seek to deliver bad news in ways that strengthen or at least maintain lawyer-client relationships, and facilitate clients' realization and acceptance.[7]

1) Be prepared—make sure you have all the important information and are ready to articulate it. Know what your own emotional responses are likely to be.

2) Arrange for private, comfortable surroundings and an in-person conversation, if possible. History is replete with examples of outrage at bad news delivered indirectly or impersonally (by telephone or worse, e-mail or voice-mail or, in the olden days, telegrams and "Dear John" letters).

3) **Forecast or preface the bad news up front, with sensitivity and expression of caring,** to foster your client's emotional readiness for what is to come. This suggestion comes with an important caveat: don't be too blunt with your *opening* words. Don't start with "your tumor is malignant," in the medical context, or "the judge threw out your case," in our legal realm.

4) After the preface, don't stall: don't delay communication of the bottom-line news by waiting until after complete delivery of lengthy and detailed explanations of law and process.

5) Be direct and scrupulously accurate—don't allow a natural instinct to "soften the blow" to deter you from conveying the reality of the circumstances, whatever they are.

6) Provide information at a pace comfortable for the client, in simple language, without jargon.

7) Attend to your client's emotion. Be caring and empathetic, not detached.

8) Allow time for your client to absorb and come to terms with the news.

The first two admonitions—be prepared, and arrange for comfortable private surrounding—are wise, but common sense. Most of us would be angered or upset if our physician hadn't prepared by informing herself about the medical consequences of a diagnosed condition before communicating the diagnosis, or if she wasn't prepared to articulate them in our meeting. We would not respond well to bad news conveyed in an elevator, waiting room, or hallway. An in-person discussion seems more kind than a phone call. And if a meeting can't be arranged, the voice-to-voice communication by telephone is better than an e-mail.

The suggestions in the latter half of the list—to be empathetic, speak without jargon at a comfortable pace, attend to emotion, and allow time and space to come to terms with the news—echo various other chapters in this book. It's nice to know that social psychologists' research and advice highlight their importance.

Academic research and consequent insight and advice are most valuable when they lead to counter-intuitive or uncommon practice. If so, then two pieces of the listed advice bear highlighting: **(1) forecast or preface the bad news up front—avoiding bluntness but without stalling;** and **(2) be direct and scrupulously accurate.** We weren't taught this in law school, and those of us who learned client counseling on the job, perhaps from a mentor, are likely to have witnessed the opposite in practice. Lawyers often fail to provide advance warning that bad news will follow an explanation of law and process; many avoid the true magnitude of the problem and its impact, "softening" through words that distort reality.

The balance of this chapter offers advice to lawyers on how to forecast and be unflinchingly direct and accurate when delivering bad news, as these are critical to your client's realization and acceptance and to the lawyer-client relationship.

Preface and Forecast Bad News; Neither Blunt nor Stalling Be

Imagine that you recently retained an expert to evaluate environmental hazards on your residential property, with an eye toward future sale. The moment you sit down to hear his report, he says: "Your home is dangerously toxic, and environmental law demands that it be vacated and destroyed." WHAT???!!! Imagine meeting with your physician, who begins with: "You have six months to a year to live." You would feel as if assaulted by blunt force. Later, you would feel angry at the blunt insensitivity of that assault.

Forecast Bad News Up Front

Professor Maynard suggests that forecasting bad news through behavior, tone, and language helps prepare a "social psychological environment" more conducive to the client's comprehension and acceptance of the news.[8] Thus, he recommends a "preannouncement" as a precursor to bad news.[9] Professor Linda Smith, Clinical Program Director at the University of Utah's College of Law, observes that medical counselling literature advises doctors giving bad news to begin with a "warning shot" . . . to prepare the patient and reduce the element of shock."[10] She recommends that lawyers also "open with a 'warning shot,' control the conversation and get to the point promptly."[11]

Thus, when you must convey bad news, *do* gently preface or provide warning of that bad news up front—*before* launching into the whys, hows, and therefores. This approach helps your client prepare emotionally for what is coming, and, if you communicate your unhappiness about his bad news, it helps maintain the client's feeling of connection. You might begin the conversation by saying:

> *I very much regret having to tell you of some recent developments that pose serious risks for your case. I am concerned about some legal hurdles that will make it difficult to achieve your goals through litigation, the way we thought the last time we met . . . .*

Where Appropriate, Consider Inquiry and Confirmation

Research from the medical context suggests that a doctor should begin by inquiring as to the patient's awareness of likely bad news. For example, the doctor might ask: "What do you feel these symptoms might mean?" If the patient indicates that he understands the symptoms to be troubling signs of a serious condition, or suspects the imminence of bad news, the doctor can then confirm the patient's intuition, and undoubtedly elaborate. Even if the patient doesn't fully recognize the extent of an illness, his suspicions begin the conversation, which the physician then moves to the more grave medical realities.[12] In some sense, the patient's bad news has come from within, which helps to prepare him emotionally for his physician's confirmation and elaboration.

The legal context sometimes presents opportunities for the lawyer to begin with an initial inquiry and then to confirm suspected bad news. For example, imagine that your defense client attended the deposition of her staff manager. She witnessed plaintiff's counsel's deliberate and prolonged questioning on the chain of decision-making with respect to the plaintiff's termination and sexual harassment claim. This deft questioning paid off; the lawyer was obviously satisfied—virtually triumphant in tone. When you meet with your defense client to break the bad news that summary judgment is just not going to happen (and may not be worth filing), you might begin by asking what her impressions were of the deposition. Perhaps she will comment: "I could see it didn't go well, because their lawyer was much too happy by the end. It made me wonder whether we will get rid of this case as quickly as I had hoped." You would then confirm your now entirely pessimistic estimate of the chances of avoiding trial in the case. Your inquiry and the client's response will have laid the foundation for bad news in a way that may be easier for her to recognize and accept.

After the Forecast, Be Direct; Don't Stall

Imagine that the expert you retained to assess environmental conditions at your home is a close friend as well as an accomplished chemist. He invites you to lunch to review his findings. While across the lunch table, he launches into a matter-of-fact, careful, logical description of spontaneous combustion, the circumstances in which it occurs, the chemistry it involves, and the fires it can create. He then informs you that he received a call from the fire department stating that your house and all your possessions went up in flames that morning due to spontaneous combustion.

Wouldn't it seem strange that your friend didn't mention your house fire until the end? If you thought about it (after that initial shock), wouldn't it seem odd—wouldn't it make you angry—that he was so calm and matter-of-fact, while knowing all along that, upon reaching the end of explaining spontaneous combustion, he was going to tell you the sad fate of your house? Obviously this friend doesn't care much about you. Your house fire did not affect him. It was just an opportunity for him to prove that he's a very articulate chemist.

Experience in hundreds of student-lawyer to actor-client counseling sessions supports this advice. When the actor-clients first learn of bad news only after their lawyers' matter-of-fact explanation of legal process and case law, they report feeling as if the lawyers had heartlessly walked them to the edge of a cliff and dropped them over the side. In contrast, they express appreciation for their lawyers' early and empathetic signal of bad news to come, followed by concise summary of that reality. Thus, we advise the lawyer first to say (in words or in substance):

> *I very much regret having to tell you of some recent developments that pose serious risks for your case. I am concerned about some legal hurdles that will make it difficult to achieve your goals through litigation, the way we thought the last time we met . . . .*

The lawyer should move to the real bad news, by saying:

> *I will explain these legal hurdles and issues and how and why they work, but you should know that, unfortunately, I am concerned because I think they create a strong risk that your case would be dismissed before we ever get to trial. I would of course fight that risk, for you and with you, but as your lawyer, I have to be straight with you about the chances of succeeding in litigation and why you might want to consider settling your case instead of continuing to litigate. After I've explained all of the risks, issues, and arguments, the direction we take will still be your choice.*

Explanation of legal process, issues and risks follow. The lawyer must explain summary judgment, how deposition testimony or documents discovered affect defenses and evidentiary burdens, how case law and precedent work, and all of the rest, whatever the realities in the particular case. But these must *follow* communication, in essence, that the news is bad. To do otherwise is to stall, which feels insensitive to the client, and renders it more difficult for the client to integrate and process information received along the way.

Don't Soften and Thus Distort Reality

When a lawyer "softens" bad news—*this* [nuclear bomb] *might be a little problem*—he obviously distorts reality.

"Softening" merits attention here because it is so terribly, understandably common. People much too often use euphemism, choose weaker adjectives, and insert hedge words when delivering bad news. I have seen lawyers who believe their clients' case is **highly likely to lose** at trial say, "Well, the trial might be a little bit risky." Might be a little bit? If and when the lawyer eventually communicates the harsher truth, after stalling and hedging, the client will be frustrated:

> *You said that the recent development could be "a little bit of a problem." Why didn't you TELL me that our motion is dead in the water?!*
> *You said the dollar offer was "a little bit low." Why didn't you TELL me it was less than a tenth of our bottom line?!*

As discussed in the next section, even without euphemism or inaccurate adjectives and adverbs, people often use vocal patterns that could be heard to convey (misplaced) optimism.[13] These too confuse and mislead—the client hearing upbeat vocal tones may make a different choice than he would have if the bad news been accurately communicated.

Why are stalling, euphemism, softening, and hedging so very common? The answer of course is that we wince at the thought of inflicting pain on another person and we fear their reaction. In a good lawyer-client relationship, we anticipate and seek to avoid our client's disappointment, anger, or despair. So, it's understandable. But it's no excuse. A lawyer should foreshadow, sensitively—"I wish I didn't have to give you this news, but there have been some developments that cause me great concern"—and then directly, accurately, carefully, and empathetically inform the client of the realities.

Voicing Bad News

In normal speech, when you refer to something negative— anticipated to have sad effect—your voice naturally lowers and slows. A lowered voice expresses seriousness, graveness, fore-boding, and warning of the ill to come.[14] Imagine talking about your neighbor's grave medical condition or destructive house fire in a high-pitched, perky voice. You wouldn't speak that way unless you were perversely happy at the news, as in "ding dong, the witch is dead." Generally, where a lawyer has a positive relationship with a client and is talking about a subject of grave concern to the client, his voice will not be breezy, light, or casual. People, including lawyers, of normal social intelligence and empathic capacity generally use appropriate vocal tones indicating concern.

In fact, adopting a vocal tone in complete contradiction to the meaning of your words is usually difficult. Imagine saying to a real client: "I regret to tell you of some serious concerns about your case. Based upon some very recent case law, I fear that the judge is likely to dismiss it." Just saying those words will impact your voice, lower-ing the tone and slowing you down. Thus, articulating the fact of bad news upfront also serves as a natural antidote for client discon-nection through vocal miscues of flat matter-of-factness or perverse perkiness.

Don't Let Your Voice Send False Signals

Even after prefacing in an appropriate tone, a lawyer should be mindful of vocal tone and speed when discussing bad news. Yet, as noted above, our voices normally reinforce our intended meaning. Then why worry about voice when discussing that bad news in more detail? Why wouldn't effective voice come naturally?

It happens that legal doctrine and process underlying "bad news" are often complex and unfamiliar to the client. As a lawyer labors to explain difficult concepts, the cerebral takes over. Enmeshed in the intellectual exercise of explaining what summary judgment is, or how jurisdictional challenges work, empathy fades to the back-ground. The brain is focused on black letter law, logical sequence, and decisions about how much technical description of legal process is necessary. While the words chosen may be clear, the voice used tends to reflect the intellectual task occupying the lawyer's brain.

I have observed many law students deliver perfectly accurate explanations of summary judgment to their actor-clients and then—without break in tone or speed—conclude with the bad news, stating, "That is why the other side is likely to win on summary judgment, and you will not recover anything." Our actor-clients note that the lawyer's matter-of-fact, even-keel voice pattern makes them feel as if the lawyer was just strolling along a logical road and is unaffected by its conclusion.

In addition to getting lost in logic, it can be natural for a lawyer to feel internal satisfaction at successfully conveying complex concepts, and for that to be reflected unintentionally in her voice. Some of us enjoy speaking of argument, counter-argument, and case analysis. Yet, if the lawyer's voice lightens or reverts to sing-song as she successfully walks through the legal analysis, the client may interpret the lighter tone to mean that circumstances are less dire, more optimistic. The client might begin to anticipate possible avenues of success. The lawyer's light vocal tone may unintentionally and subliminally reassure the client.

Perverse Habits of Nerves and Feelings

Ironically, not just logic but also the lawyer's emotions may generate vocal miscues. When a lawyer nervously and empathetically anticipates a client's reaction to bad news, he may nod, smile, and speak more quickly, in a higher pitch or with an up-tone at the end of a sentence—behaviors usually associated with positive emotions. The lawyer may understandably be uncomfortable, wishing he could make the news seem "not so bad." He may fear the client will blame the messenger. His nodding or smiling may reflect unconscious seeking of his client's approval, despite bad news. These signals may also diminish the client's recognition of the seriousness of the case development. Or, if the client does fully recognize the problem, he may again feel alienated by his lawyer's insensitivity.

When discussing bad news in full doctrinal and procedural detail, the lawyer should be mindful of slowing, deepening, and dipping his voice empathetically at appropriate junctures, to enhance connection as the client absorbs more fully the import of the bad news. If the news is really all bad, the lawyer's voice should reflect and reinforce that reality.

Confidence in Competence and Zealous Representation

Assume the client's feeling of connection with her lawyer remains intact despite the lawyer's having communicated the bad news that winning on a motion or at trial is unlikely. What if the client suspects the news is bad because her lawyer is less than effective in the litigation arena? The client might feel that the lawyer understands and cares about her, but conclude that he is not sufficiently forceful. Particularly where the bad news is predictive—a future defeat at trial or on a preliminary motion—how can the lawyer maintain client confidence in his analytical and persuasive competence and his willingness to advocate zealously on her behalf?

There is a bit of a paradox here, as some personal qualities of empathy and caring may be viewed as inconsistent with forcefulness. Excellent lawyers have both, but when the lawyer displays the "softer" characteristics, does he negatively impact the client's confidence in his ability to be aggressive? Some clients complain about the personal impact of a lawyer's insensitivity, but then seek the "tough mercenary" as best suited to wage war on their behalf.[15]

For a client to be fully informed, the lawyer must enable her to anticipate and understand legal arguments and counter-arguments, case or statutory analysis, process twists and turns, the magnitude of risks, and a range of possible negative and positive outcomes, including their costs. That means that, even if the news is not all bad, the lawyer must ensure that his client fully appreciates what is potentially bad, and why. Thus, lawyers need strategies for communicating the realities of risk and costly consequences to clients, while enhancing clients' confidence in their competent, forceful, and zealous representation. The balance of this chapter suggests such strategies, with full respect and appreciation for the difficulty of the lawyer's role and obligations.

Communicating the Force of the Other Side's Arguments (especially if you think they are likely to win)

The most challenging and important bad news for a lawyer to convey is a prediction that the other side's arguments or evidence are likely to prevail. Of course, lawyers sometimes must communicate a *fact* that is bad news—the court *did* grant the other side's motion for summary judgment—rather than a negative prediction. However, because negative predictions arise in contexts where the client is more likely to have choices and a decision to make, the lawyer's success in conveying them matters most. If the client understands and accepts the bad news prediction, he will carefully consider settlement options and, presumably, make a wise and informed decision.

So, what's the best strategy for ordering and structuring your presentation of your legal analysis and its conclusions—the negative prediction? Should you just state arguments that will be made by opposing counsel and explain that these were successful in too many similar cases? If you articulate the arguments for your client's position, will your client listen only to those and ignore or forget the opposition's strengths? Will your client then fail to accept your unwelcome conclusion that, despite valiant effort, her position is unlikely to succeed?

Unfortunately, many lawyers do just that: begin their explanation by presenting the other side's arguments. Fearing their clients will draw unwarranted optimism from review of their own arguments, the lawyers focus exclusively on the stronger arguments of the other side and their support in common law or statute. My experience suggests that the opposite strategy is far more effective.[16]

Start with Your Side, and Articulate Your Client's Arguments Forcefully Before Moving to the Other Side and a Full Analysis

Our actor-clients join me in recommending that your presentation to the client proceed in roughly the following order:

1) First, articulate the arguments you would make to the court or jury on your client's behalf;
2) then move on to articulate the opposition's arguments; and
3) finally, explain why you have concluded, in light of the applicable law, that the other side is more likely to succeed.

This order is more powerful—more likely to persuade the client while maintaining his confidence in your representation—than stating the opposition's arguments first, followed by a de-emphasized summary of your arguments.

Why? Imagine the conversation that starts with presentation of the opposition's arguments. As he listens, the client begins thinking: "Hey, wait a minute, that's not right! What about this fact and that circumstance? Did my lawyer forget that fact? We have something to counter that. . . ." The client isn't absorbing the strength of the opposition's arguments; he's pushing them away. He may become agitated and argue back, troubled or angry that his lawyer appears to be on the other side.

Now imagine that the lawyer *begins* by articulating the client's position first, saying, "Here is how I would argue on your behalf, in writing and before the court . . . " and then outlining all of the facts, circumstances, and legal points on the client's side. These are easy for the client to hear, and he listens. The lawyer should present them with echoes of the tone, manner, and polish she would use before the court. Impressed by his lawyer's command of the case and her forceful representation, the client hears her make all of the arguments supporting his position. He harbors no doubt about his lawyer's zealousness, loyalty, or advocacy skills.

Then, the lawyer can and should say: "It's important for you to understand the arguments of the other side and why I believe they are problematic." She should then proceed to articulate the other arguments with equal skill. While the client still may find this difficult to hear, he will not have the reaction described earlier—questioning whether the lawyer remembered that fact and this counter-argument. He is also less inclined to question his lawyer's forcefulness in making his arguments. He just heard her do so.

This order of presentation facilitates the client's acceptance of his lawyer's analysis. It is tremendously powerful for a client to see his loyal and forceful attorney hold all of his arguments in one hand, and then all of the other arguments in the other hand, and still, regrettably, reach an unfavorable or strongly pessimistic conclusion. That client is more likely to come to terms with the bad news, consider the consequences, and make a wise decision.

Reduce Resistance by Preserving Ego and Identity

A lawyer's choice of language, metaphor, elaboration, and inference in explaining a legal issue can greatly affect client response. Yes, the primary goals are clarity and accuracy. However, where a legal rule would suggest culpability on your client's part, clarity and accuracy are best achieved diplomatically, with attention to preserving ego.

Consider the plaintiff-client who slipped and fell on carrot juice spilled in a grocery store aisle. The defendant grocery store has filed a motion for summary judgment, under the "open and obvious" state law doctrine. Assume the lawyer has explained what summary judgment is and how the process works, and has signaled the bad news that the defense is likely to succeed on its motion. The lawyer now launches into a description of "open and obvious." He could say:

- *Applying the open and obvious doctrine, the court is likely to rule that the accident was more than 50 percent your fault because you could have and should have seen it and avoided the hazard.*
  Or
- *Under the open and obvious doctrine, the defense will argue that it was your responsibility to watch where you were going and the carrot juice on the white floor was so obvious that anyone who was paying attention would have seen it.*
  Or
- *Under the open and obvious doctrine, if a person is injured because of a dangerous condition that a reasonable person would have seen, the court holds them responsible. Here they are arguing that a reasonable person should have seen the carrot juice on the white floor.*

These characterizations of the open and obvious doctrine are all more or less accurate and clear. Your client would UNDERSTAND but would also resist, voicing a reaction, either internally or outwardly to the lawyer, such as this:

My fault?! My responsibility?! I didn't spill the carrot juice. How dare they?! I was paying attention, even if I wasn't staring at the floor while shopping for groceries. They weren't paying enough attention to clean up that spill. A REASONABLE person would have seen it?! I am a reasonable person, and I didn't see it. If I had seen it, I wouldn't have walked right into it, OBVIOUSLY!

Driving the resistance is personal identity/ego, making it difficult for the client to acknowledge that the court might indeed rule against him. If he acknowledges that risk, he must acknowledge himself to be a careless klutz, responsible for his consequent injuries and life upheaval.[17] That's painful, especially if it is inconsistent with his self-image (as it would be for most of us).

Avoid Blaming the Client

With the benefit of having observed hundreds of attempts at explaining the open and obvious doctrine, let me suggest this one instead to illustrate a different strategy of word choice:

> *If a hazard is out in the open, not covered or hidden, and there's an accident, and someone is injured by it, the law does not hold the property owner liable.*

Most clients will be more receptive to hearing that description and less inclined to fight it. What's different? This phrasing doesn't directly blame the client. It uses the neutral word "accident" and emphasizes the non-liability of the property owner. The reasonable person is absent because most clients bristle at any suggestion that they are not reasonable.

Of course, the phrasing *implies* most of what was troubling in the other explanations of the open and obvious doctrine. After all, the law doesn't impose liability on the store because the circumstances suggest the plaintiff's responsibility for this accident. Implication and inference are easier to let pass. This phrasing allows some time and some ego space for the client to listen, understand, and integrate his lawyer's conclusion about the risk posed by the open and obvious doctrine on summary judgment.

Remove the Safe Harbor of Unfair and Abstract

I have observed clients who, at some level, have come to understand the relevant law. However, because that law seems entirely and obviously unfair, they simply don't believe "deep down" that it would actually be applied against them. Lawyers and mediators become frustrated when clients hear patiently delivered, entirely clear explanations of the "open and obvious" doctrine, or "at-will-employment," or the "elements necessary to prove discrimination" and yet persist in certainty of victory, despite directly contrary case law or a lack of evidence. The lawyer has explained why the defense is *extremely* likely to prevail on summary judgment and why accepting a settlement offer makes sense. The client nevertheless looks forward to trial and requires infinitely more to settle. Is it about anger? Is the client saying he doesn't care about the risks? Maybe, but not necessarily. Sometimes, the client does *understand* the law, and *says* he accepts the lawyer's dire assessment, but he doesn't *really believe* it will come out that way.

Why doesn't he believe it could happen to him? Why can't he accept that his case will almost certainly end, before trial, without any recovery? Why isn't he worried that if he rejects settlement, he will come to regret it later? Has the client seen a dramatic film or read a novel on jury nullification of evil laws? Barring that theory, I suggest two reasons:

1) He can't imagine his case being dismissed. It doesn't seem real.
2) Losing would contradict his firm belief in the myth of our legal system as always just and fair, where the good guy always wins at the end.

Consider the strategies below when you sense your client understands your dire assessment but *can't imagine* or doesn't *believe* it.

Assist Imagination with Real Stories

Some clients are able to imagine the unimaginable upon learning of real people in similar circumstances for whom predicted bad news became reality. When lawyers refer to "comparable case law," we know that's what it means and, in the abstract, the client may also. Still, it is worth taking a moment to tell one of its stories:

> *In a recent Ohio case, a 32 year-old man broke his back when he slipped and fell, not in a grocery store but in a cafeteria, on some splattered tomatoes. The court applied the open and obvious doctrine and granted summary judgment, and he recovered nothing, even though he had severe injuries – $60,000 in medical bills and $50,000 in lost wages.*

The client can identify with another person who has a name, slipped and was injured, and perhaps faced a similar decision about whether to settle. Rather than just talk about it, make it tangible. Give your client a copy of the case decision (or two) to touch, read, and re-read.

Remember to Separate Liability from Harm

Well-educated and intelligent clients may simply assume that claims are won on proof of injury alone. When a lawyer notes the risk of losing at trial or on motions, the client may assume the reality of his injury is at issue. Thus, he may disregard any lawyerly concerns about risk because he *knows* the injury will be easily proven. The client may also feel insulted and reject the idea of risk because it suggests he is lying or exaggerating. Lawyers should anticipate this by clarifying up front:

> *There is no doubt that you were seriously injured and that you will be able to prove it to the jury. Even the defense recognizes and will certainly admit that you were injured in the accident. The problem is that we have to prove they were legally at fault and thus legally liable for the accident. Based on the witnesses*

*and other information gathered in discovery, I see a serious risk
of losing the liability question. If that were to happen, then even
though everyone can see you were injured, you would lose and
wouldn't recover anything.*

On Myth, Belief, and Reality

Sometimes, resistance arises from the direct conflict between the
lawyer's assessment and the client's strongly held myths about
the legal system, discussed more fully in chapter 3. In the slip
and fall example discussed above, the lawyer's conclusion that the
client is likely to lose on summary judgment conflicts directly with
the myth that the legal system is always fair and just and the good
guy always wins. To the client, this is not fair and he is the
good guy.

Banish the Fairness Myth

Too often, the lawyer's only choice is to expose and banish the myth
directly. You might say: "I know we are taught that our justice system
is perfect and fair, but it isn't, at least not all of the time." Reviewing
examples of dismissals or verdicts that seem obviously unfair is
important here, too. You can explain why and how, within our
system, this can and does happen.

Leaving aside the summary judgment example, imagine a case in
which you strongly predict your client will lose at trial, but the client
can ONLY believe the jury will see the truth, and that is, of course,
his truth. Address the myth of perfect truth head-on and note that
the jury wasn't present and has to rely on witnesses and expert
witnesses to try to reconstruct what happened. He may lose if there
are conflicting witnesses—even if he knows and testifies to what
happened.

Consider this example: your plaintiff-client maintains that his back injury was directly caused by the accident and the defense maintains he had a pre-existing condition in his back that was aggravated by lifting weights a few days before her fall. The experts disagree, of course. Your client knows his back was fine that day and he injured his back in the fall, and, because it is true and he is truthful (and good), the jury will recognize that. He doesn't really believe it could come out any other way.

The best advice for the lawyer is to acknowledge that perspective, first by articulating it directly:

> *I know it's difficult to imagine that the jury would find your back injury wasn't caused by the fall, because it's your back and you know that's what happened. You are an entirely truthful person. The problem is that the jury doesn't really know you – they don't have your back, and they can't feel it. Unfortunately, the system is not perfect. The jury has no crystal ball that enables them to recreate the truth.*

Or, Leave Myth Alone; Locate Reality Within It

Myths tend to maintain residence; we believe them despite banishment orders. After all, if we can no longer believe our laws are always fair, what other pillars must fall? However, if your client comes to see how a law might sometimes be viewed as fair, he will acknowledge its power and reality and, only then, its potential impact.

Assume you have explained the very high risk of the judge granting the defense motion for summary judgment, based upon the open and obvious doctrine explained earlier. The client says he understands, but he is determined to press on and asks what could happen at trial if he gets by the motion. You can tell your client is imagining himself testifying at trial, because he can't imagine that summary judgment will end it. When you raise the open and obvious problem again, the client responds: "The law isn't fair. It lets the grocery store get away with this. It helps the big corporation and not the little guy."

If possible, I recommend that you describe a hypothetical case in which that law would seem fair for your client. You might say:

> *Yes, the way the law applies here, it helps the store and not you. Of course, it could work the other way. Imagine that a storm blew a tree branch across the front walkway to your house. Your neighbor then came over to borrow the proverbial cup of sugar, tripped on the tree branch, and sustained real and costly injuries. She sued you, seeking payment. In that case,* **you** *would use the open and obvious doctrine to argue that the tree branch was out in the open and you shouldn't be liable to your neighbor. Of course, in your case, we will argue that the carrot juice was not as obvious as a tree branch and the defense will argue the opposite. As we discussed, I am concerned because I found a number of other cases in which judges applied the doctrine to some large spills and potholes. My point is that the open and obvious doctrine would protect you from your neighbor's suit, and you would find it fair. It does worry me here.*

While the client is asked to shift perspective in the example above, it is NOT for the purpose of generating empathy for his nemesis—the store. Rather, it is for the client to recognize that the law has a fairness rationale that he could accept in other circumstances. Not all "unfair" legal doctrines are so easily shifted for a client to see how he might seek their protection. However, it is well worth the effort to imagine and discuss such a circumstance, where your client is wrestling with a conflict between reality and the myth of fairness. Our actor-clients confirm that, when led to understand how the law *could* be fair, even to the "little guy"—and thus fit within the law's fairness myth—they will accept its reality.

Notes

1. "Gen. Colin Powell to speak at FGCU in March," *FGCU Vision*, Fall 2006, http://www.fgcu.edu/CRM/Files/Issue2-Volume6.pdf (accessed May 23, 2011).

2. William Shakespeare, *Henry IV*, part 2, act 1, sc. 1, http://www.opensourceshakespeare.org.

3. Douglas W. Maynard, *Bad News, Good News: Conversational Order in Everyday Talk and Clinical Settings* (Chicago: University of Chicago Press, 2003), 4.

4. Ibid. 12.

5. Ibid. 24 (emphasis in original).

6. E.g., Maynard, *Bad News, Good News*; Douglas W. Maynard, "On 'Realization' in Everyday Life: The Forecasting of Bad News as a Social Relation," *American Sociological Review* 61 (1996): 115; Linda F. Smith, "Medical Paradigms for Counseling: Giving Clients Bad News," *Clinical Law Review* 4 (1998): 391; Jeremy Freese and Douglas W. Maynard, "Prosodic Features of Bad News and Good News in Conversation," *Language in Society* 27, no. 2 (1998): 198. Maynard has been on the forefront of "bad news" research, and the discussion in this chapter draws primarily from his work, even as applied in legal settings. See Douglas W. Maynard, "Bad News and Good News: Losing vs. Finding the Phenomenon in Legal Settings," *Law & Social Inquiry* 31, no. 2 (2006): 477. Professor Linda Smith's discussion of delivering or receiving bad news in the legal context largely echoes Maynard's insight and advice.

7. Much of this specific advice can be found throughout Maynard, *Bad News, Good News*, and in Smith, "Medical Paradigms for Counseling."

8. Maynard, "On 'Realization' in Everyday Life," 110.

9. Maynard, *Bad News, Good News*, 38.

10. Smith, "Medical Paradigms for Counseling," 406.

11. Ibid. 411.

12. "Forecasting in the sense of preparation more effectively provides for recipients' realization because it enables recipients' own forecasting of the news in the second sense." Maynard, "On 'Realization' in Everyday Life," 110.

13. Increased speech rate and higher pitch indicate eagerness and excitement. Freese and Maynard, "Prosodic Features of Bad News and Good News in Conversation," 198.

14. Freese and Maynard, "Prosodic Features of Bad News and Good News in Conversation," 198.

15. A number of experiments report that an attorney's personality, expression of understanding (client orientation), and relationship skills were linked to greater client satisfaction. See Marcia Hillary and Joel Johnson, "Selection and Evaluation of Attorneys in Divorce Cases Involving Minor Children," Journal of Divorce 9, no.1 (1985): 93–104 and Stephen Feldman and Kent Wilson, "The Value of Interpersonal Skills in Lawyering," Law & Human Behavior 4 (1989): 311. In another experiment, clients tended to choose lawyers they perceived as competent but the clients were not skilled at perceiving competence. Surprisingly, in that experiment, lawyers scripted to use "sophisticated comforting skills" in a divorce case scenario were viewed as less competent by clients. The authors posit, however, that the personal nature of the case and "comforting" interventions at the beginning stages of an initial interview may have seemed inappropriately and uncomfortably intimate. I tend to agree, given the actual script used. David Dryden Henningsen and Iona Cionea, "The Role of Comforting Skill and Professional Competence in the Attorney-Client Relationship," Journal of Legal Education 57, no. 4 (2004): 530–538.

16. This approach draws upon insight into the "tension between empathy and assertiveness" described in the influential book written by Robert Mnookin, Scott Peppet, and Andrew Tulumello, Beyond Winning: Negotiating to Create Value in Deals and Disputes (Cambridge, MA: Belknap Press of Harvard University Press, 2000), 44–68.

17. Douglas Stone, Bruce Patton, and Sheila Heen, Difficult Conversations: How to Discuss What Matters Most (New York: Penguin Books, 1999), 111–116.

2

Translating the Terrain

"Translation is not a matter of words only: it is a matter of making intelligible a whole culture."

—ANTHONY BURGESS[1]

Linguistics professor Scott DeLancey writes: "In its communicative function, language is a set of tools with which we attempt to guide another mind to create within itself a mental representation that approximates the one we have."[2] Thus, by the end of a lawyer-client meeting, the fully-informed client's head should carry the same conceptual picture of the legal matter as that in her lawyer's head. But how well does the client "get the picture"? Consider the following two scenes set in lawyers' offices:

An esteemed plaintiffs' employment lawyer painstakingly reviews every twist and turn yet to come in the litigation process to his two clients laid off in a reduction in force (RIF) and claiming age discrimination against their former utility company employer. The lawyer completes this careful legal process explanation, pauses, and asks if they have any questions. One asks, "Could I have my job back before the holidays?"

The defense lawyer in a construction case explains the problem of parol evidence and the pre-trial *motion in limine* likely to be filed by plaintiff's counsel, seeking to prohibit introduction of testimony regarding alleged oral agreements to adjust the project price and materials. The lawyer cautions that the plaintiff's motion is likely to succeed, and that it will be damaging to their defense. The contractor client asks, "Well, don't you do something? Don't you have anything to say about that? Can't you write a motion, too? Don't I get to talk to the judge or the jury?"

It's a pattern. The lawyer explains. The client nods. The client asks a question that clearly establishes complete lack of comprehension. The lawyer is perplexed, astonished, annoyed, or just plain weary: "Wasn't this client listening to anything I said? Maybe he's ADHD, or not that bright, or willfully ignorant."

Listening, attention, and intelligence are not enough. No client can be fully informed in a language she doesn't understand.

Just as foreign languages arise in foreign cultures with shared norms, experience, and understandings, lawyers' "legalese" arises within their distinct legal culture. Lawyers learn the words, concepts, assumptions, and practices of the legal lexicon through immersion in law school and professional contexts. We speak legalese comfortably with law school classmates, law practice colleagues, and judges. We absorb legal process systems, norms, codes of behaviors, and ways of thinking that are unfamiliar to clients, particularly those who don't regularly travel across legal terrain.

Thus, lawyer-client communication may be understood as requiring an act of translation. Consider the many ways the following translations would NOT be effective:

- Corporate counsel meets with her client representative, a thirty-something creative marketing VP for hiking and cycling products at a high-end sports equipment manufacturing company. Counsel explains to the VP: *"The contractual language governing an earlier company division spin-off may give rise to a non-frivolous preliminary injunction motion to prohibit the newly designed 'frig pack' sales within the defined geographic area for the designated time period. Moreover, the parol evidence rule is likely to preclude testimony as to contemporaneous discussions regarding the parties' intent."* The VP rethinks: "But we can fight it, right?" "Yes," sighs corporate counsel, "we can."
- In a pre-mediation meeting, Plaintiff's counsel explains to his client who was injured by police officers' unwarranted use of

force: *"The city's potential immunity and legal limitations on damages for a municipality pose legal hurdles. These issues would be raised on motions to dismiss. Moreover, though the police offers may (or may not) be racists, their failure to use racial epithets against you means the city will move to dismiss the civil rights claim, which supports the damages multiplier and recovery of attorneys' fees. Though the individual defendants' liability is not limited, their assets may be limited, and the legal right to collect against those assets will depend on who holds legal title and state law on spousal property rights."*

Are these clients fully informed? No, not likely, if the lawyers used language such as that above to describe their legal circumstances.

The critical reader will no doubt observe that, as written, these descriptions of legal circumstances are overly cryptic and technical. Are these exaggerated and unrealistic renderings of what most lawyers would say? Perhaps. In practice, the lawyer might provide more detail, additional references to the underlying situation, dollar estimates of potential liability or recovery ranges, or an estimate of probabilities. Fair observations, all.

Okay then, I'll rephrase the question to allow some wiggle room: are these clients *on the way* to being fully informed about the choices they face? Would they understand the words the lawyer has chosen? Assume a dictionary at the ready, and time to look up unfamiliar words. Would they recognize what these words foretell about how their futures may unfold? Would they appreciate that now-abstract future choice and risk will feel real and difficult, with time? Will these clients see through the distortion of myth and false assumption to see exactly what the lawyer does? If the answer is no, then the paradigm of the "fully informed" client will prove elusive—yet again.

For a client to be "fully informed," the lawyer must become a master translator, adept at the art of translating from legal language, concept, and context to the client's. The client must understand her lawyer's words, recognize and come to terms with their practical meaning and impact, and accept their reality, at least to the degree asserted by the lawyer. (A client who understands fully but questions the lawyer's analysis is free to seek another's opinion.)

The fully informed client need not adopt her lawyer's advice. Client autonomy, ultimate authority to make decisions in her own interest, remains intact. The lawyer may recommend a decision, based on his analysis, as long as client feels free to reject that recommendation. After all, people with different risk profiles, identities, emotions, or personal and professional circumstances may fully accept the same information and analysis and yet quite reasonably make different decisions.

Fundamentally, the fully informed client makes decisions with her eyes wide open. This chapter is written for clients whose eyes remain "wide shut," who hear the lawyer's words but fail to fully understand them, or whose thinking is distorted by false belief, myth, and delusion. For these clients, lawyers are challenged to become more adept as translators from the realm of legal language, meaning, and process into the client's language, conceptual understanding, and social context.

Tracking Translation

If lawyers should be master translators, it makes sense to consult with translation theorists for insight and counsel. In *Meaning-Based Translation: A Guide to Cross-Language Equivalence*,[3] translation theorist Professor Mildred Larson writes: "Translation . . . consists of studying the lexicon, grammatical structure, communication situation, and cultural context of the source language text, analyzing it in order to determine its meaning, and then reconstructing this same meaning using the lexicon and grammatical structure which are appropriate in the RECEPTOR LANGUAGE and its cultural context." To explain this academic jargon (irony noted): when a translator listens to French and translates into English, French is the source language, and English the receptor language.

The most adept translators are equally comfortable in the source language as in the receptor language. Some theorists argue that the best translators are those whose mother tongue was the receptor language. If so, assuming lawyer and client are both fluent in English (or any other shared language), translating from legalese as source language to the lay person's receptor language would seem simple enough. After all, no lawyer's native language was legalese: we picked that up in law school.

Still, at least three types of problems arise for the lawyer-as-translator:[4]

(1) Words or phrases with "no meaning or uncertain meaning" to the client, absent definition

(2) Words or phrases with "non-synonymous" meanings—the client understands them to mean something different than their meaning in a legal context

(3) Words or phrases containing embedded, unrecognized concepts

Words of a Post-Deluvian Lawyer—After Law School's Flood

Most lawyers acknowledge the need to avoid legalese with clients or, at least, to define unavoidable legal language or terms of art. Unfortunately, the law school experience that so famously transforms thinking also seems to erase memories of what non-lawyers don't know and won't understand: "We will face a summary judgment motion. We'll have to prove *scienter*. The motion *in limine* is a threat. *Dictum* isn't dispositive but it is worrisome. Discovery is burdensome. Jury nullification isn't likely." It is quite astonishing to hear second-year law student efforts to describe legal concepts to a client. Phrases such as "material facts" and "dispositive motions" fill the air. Just one year after matriculation, they have lost awareness of the gaps in knowledge now separating them from lay clients. Paradoxically then, law school may graduate lawyers newly competent in law and newly incompetent at ensuring their clients are fully informed.

Perhaps because legalese and native or non-lawyer speech both occur within English, boundaries between the two are more difficult to remember and recognize. If I am translating between French and English, or English and German, I just don't confuse what are English words and what are German or French words. (Even though I am not fluent in either German or French, and may fail to retrieve the necessary words for translation, I do remember which is which.) In contrast, when lawyers or any professionals translate into lay language, they are apt to forget which words, phrases, and concepts were learned within their profession. So, computer programmers speak of java code, busses, and RAM; doctors speak of histamine reactions, pathologies, and REM; and lawyers speak of motion practice, SEC 10b-5, standing, and jurisdiction. They all seem perplexed by the others' confusion.

To translate effectively, the lawyer must remember or refresh his recollection of pre-law school language and thought. Be mindful of words you wouldn't have known. If you must use them—the client must be told "a summary judgment motion has been filed"—make sure you define and explain carefully.

Avoid Stylized Usage and Phrasing

Why does the lawyer's definition or explanation, aimed at client understanding, so often miss its mark? We fail to remember that the profession often uses non-legal words and phrases in highly stylized ways that clients find difficult to decode, at least at a fluent conversational pace.[5] For example, a plaintiff's lawyer explaining the defense's *motion in limine* might say, "The defense has filed a *preliminary motion* challenging the *admissibility* of this evidence." A lawyer might explain to a defense client, "If the plaintiff *survives* our motion to dismiss and then *prevails* on liability, the *court* will permit presentation of damages evidence." Few of these individual, italicized words would be impenetrable for a reasonably educated client, who will know common meanings of "preliminary," "prevail," and "court." But still, the overall meaning of these sentences might prove difficult. At the very least, the client would require a very long pause to parse words such as "prevail" and "survive" in context. The phrasing and usage are that of a lawyer, not of a client.

Most of us have had analogous experiences as patients with doctors who speak of "hematomas" instead of bruises, "morbidity" instead of disease, and "counter-indicated" instead of not recommended. As patients, we may successfully decode, and then feel mildly annoyed, recognizing that simpler words were possible. Or, we may be uncertain of our decoding, and hope clearer meaning will emerge from the sentences that follow. If we can't quite decode the words (or aren't sure), we may feel frustrated, lost, or perhaps embarrassed or diminished. The consequences for lawyers' clients are the same.

Non-Synonymous Meaning

The English word "full" translates to *pleine* in French. But the French word *pleine* also means pregnant. So, after a large meal, a French woman would *not* say: "Je suis pleine" ["I am pregnant"], unless she wished to announce an impending birth. The same word captures meanings in different ways, in different languages.

Certain words are used both in common parlance and in legalese, but carry somewhat different meanings in these contexts. The "reasonable person," "acting with knowledge," and "intentional tort" have discrete meanings in law. Clients who hear these terms will process their more colloquial meaning. Even relatively sophisticated defense clients sometimes express anger over the language in a complaint, language that any lawyer would recognize as chosen to meet the legal elements of the claim: "They accused us of *intentionally* setting up that terrible factory accident to injure them?!"; or "I didn't *intentionally* engage in a *pattern and practice* of discrimination!" For the lawyer, the client who expresses discomfort or confusion presents less of a problem. More challenging is the client who assumes the colloquial meaning and rejects it or seethes about it. Thus, when choosing words to describe legal issues, claims, and defenses, or reviewing words contained in the pleadings, lawyers are advised to consider how a lay reader might understand and respond to them.

Subtle Misleads

Some words are generally heard as positives or associated with positive news. When these words are used within a negative message, the listener may be subtly misled. For example, the word "good" "is usually heard as positive—good news. When we use a positive word to convey information that is fundamentally negative, we risk creating client confusion. The classic example, heard too often, is: "There's a good chance they'll win on the motion." By this, the lawyer means to say that his client faces a significant risk of losing and the other side will probably win. To the client processing the lawyer's sentence as phrased, it's momentarily confusing to hear "good" or "good chance" in connection with the other side's win— bad news.

The client who is listening attentively will adjust, and realize that the upshot of the latter end of the sentence is NOT good. The client who is not so attentive, or is psychologically inclined to listen selectively for the positive, may discount the seriousness of the risk. After all, her lawyer—her advocate—said "chances are good"—so it must somehow mean good. Our many actor-clients confirm this confusion and advise lawyers to be mindful of using words with positive emotional association when describing negative circumstances and *vice versa*. Where the other side has the stronger case, avoid positive words. Say instead: "Unfortunately, we face a strong risk of losing," or "Their argument presents a difficult legal hurdle." In short, be mindful of choosing words with consistent linguistic and emotional meaning.

Losing and Building Meaning in Foreign Lands

"To know another's language and not his culture is a very good way to make a fluent fool of yourself."

—WINSTON BREMBECK[6]

Missing Knowledge of Concepts Embedded in the Terrain

How is it that a lawyer may scrupulously avoid technical terms or stylized usage when describing legal concepts and *still* leave his client wandering between entirely lost and somewhat uncertain as to the intended message? Why might a lawyer's pretty-darned-clear explanation of a twist in litigation or legal impediment to a transaction still yield client puzzlement or incredulity?

Stepping back from words and phrases, lawyers must recognize that, outside of the legal practice, people lack shared knowledge about its workings. Thus, the lawyer translator must supply basic, missing knowledge of legal process, practice, and culture for her words to make sense. Without some of that knowledge, the lawyer's words lack meaning.

Consider this "parable" of two cooking translation challenges involving an accomplished caterer with a well-equipped kitchen and capable staff. He must prepare only authentic French menu items for two different dinner parties. (He cannot serve the same French meal twice.) Internet research yielded a plethora of recipes from famous French chefs. The recipes are cryptic—listing ingredients and sparse instructions—and entirely in French.

For the first dinner, the caterer forwards a large number of possible recipes to a French professor friend, who translates all of them into English and e-mails them back with the message "good luck." Does the caterer need luck? Not really. He will select wisely from among the many recipes, capably oversee cooking, baking, and timing challenges, and pull off a wonderful French meal. He knows the process.

For the second dinner, the caterer asks his French-speaking niece, who knows nothing about cooking, to first select one recipe for each course and then translate only these into English. How can the niece make wise selections? She can't tell which finished flavors work well together. She doesn't know the process of cooking or baking or time requirements for different preparations. Language alone is not enough. The caterer *will* need a lot of luck.

Moving from French cooking to the moral for lawyers and clients: to be informed enough to make wise choices, a client may need to understand the workings of law, the legal system, and legal process. Yet, many clients are unaware of basic legal impediments, such as motions to dismiss and for summary judgment, statutes of limitation, privileges, or evidentiary privileges and preclusions. They have little experience with the uncertainty of procedural twists or unanticipated legal tactics. They are shocked by the power of civil procedure's discovery phase to intrude on their lives and businesses, gaining access to files, financial records, medical records, and ancient email. They are dismayed at their inability to control the cost of reciprocal discovery obligations, the cost of counsel's time to respond to motions or prepare for depositions, or the cost of retaining an expert. They may be surprised to learn that one's own damaging information must be sought and then provided to the other side. They don't know how the system works.

Some Nitty Gritty: Missing Links and Legal Concepts

In less time than it takes to type the words, here is an entirely incomplete list of things lawyers know about litigation that most clients do not:

- To sue, you need to establish jurisdiction.
- Jurisdiction is. . . .
- Requirements of notice pleading are different than pleading with particularity.
- If you don't answer a complaint filed against you, a [default] judgment will eventually be entered.
- Cases can be dismissed by judges, without any jury involvement.
- A "motion to the court" can be made by either side. It is initiated by filing a written document and enables parties (through their lawyers) to ask the judge to take certain actions. When one side files a motion, the other side always has an opportunity to respond in opposition.
- Judges hear lawyers' arguments but clients cannot testify in most hearings on motions.
- A preliminary injunction can tie up your business for quite a while even though you haven't had a trial yet.
- Pre-trial discovery is expensive, long, and unavoidable.
- In discovery, the other side has a right to obtain your documents.
- In our system, the judges determine the law and juries decide facts, when the parties disagree about the facts. Unless you disagree about facts that are necessary to make a legal determination, there is no need for a jury.
- Law derives not only from what is legislated and "on the books", it is also found in judicial decisions recorded as case law.
- When deciding the law in a case, judges are bound to follow appropriate precedent—to be consistent with what other

courts have done in similar circumstances. Doctrine is a definitive rule derived from consistent reasoning and often named and articulated in judicial opinions.

- In most cases in the United States, the winner bears his own legal costs.
- Not every case can eventually go to the Supreme Court.
- *Scienter* means. . . Fraud means. . . . . Both can be challenging to prove.
- Anticipated lost profits from a deal may not be the measure of damages.
- Conflicts of law is a course unto itself.
- The same case can involve state and federal law; their application is not always obvious.
- An oral contract can be enforceable (absent statute of frauds protection).
- The statute of frauds makes it impossible to enforce many oral contracts.
- The judge can dismiss a case (on a j.n.o.v.) even if the jury found liability.
- Judges have the power to reduce a jury's damages award.
- Litigation is slow. The initial pleading and motion stage can take six months or much longer, completion of discovery and dispositive or pretrial motions another year to eighteen months (or more or less), and a first trial date a year (or more or less) after that. Courts often postpone trial dates.
- When you sue a company, no matter how much you win, you can only recover up to the value of its assets—after mortgages, etc.—even if the owner is rich. Piercing the corporate veil is not automatic.
- Appellate courts uphold lower courts' rulings in an overwhelming majority of cases.[7]
- After winning a verdict, collecting the award takes time, and it may require additional expense to acquire the assets.

Assume a lawyer trying to explain summary judgment risk to a client who knows none of the bullet point information listed above. He begins with the words: "The defense will file a motion for summary judgment with the court, arguing that there are no disputed issues of material fact and that we cannot prevail at trial." What meaning will that explanation have, and what questions will it raise?

First, the client doesn't know what a motion is, and he doesn't know what a "material fact" is. Assume he asks for definitions, and the lawyer translates those words within the sentence by saying: "The defense will file a document, a piece of paper with the court, called a motion for summary judgment, arguing that there are no disputed issues on any facts that are important, and saying that we cannot prevail—win—at trial, and so the court should prevent the case from going forward." Now, the client may understand that the defense will do something involving "arguing" to "the court" and that the other side wants to stop him from winning, of course. But when you take this sentence and overlay it on his incomplete knowledge, he still would not understand that:

- "To the court" means to a judge and not to a jury.
- You will of course be arguing against it.
- "Arguing" will also likely involve writing a lengthy document, and that will be expensive (unless this is a contingency fee case).
- He will not have the chance to get on a witness stand and tell his story unless his case survives the motion.
- If he loses on that motion there will be no trial and he will collect nothing (on the plaintiff's side), or he will be obligated to pay (on the defense side).
- Even though his physical or financial harms are undeniably real, a judge could indeed conclude his case is not winnable at trial.

Even a client who understands the words may not glean from them any sense of the steps that will have to be taken, the reasons why, or the potential impact. For the words to have meaning, the lawyer must supply information about the underlying layer of process, rules, legal reasoning, and convention, piece by piece.

Translating over Cultural Myths and Mistaken Assumptions

Beware the Under-Armor of False Belief

To complicate the translator's task, clients who inhabit our civic culture of high school government courses, television legal dramas, movies, and literary epics may share myths and false beliefs about the legal system. The lawyer's translation from the source language to the receptor language must anticipate and address those culturally-created myths and false beliefs.[8] Otherwise, whenever her lawyer's explanation and analysis contradict them, the client may have great difficulty understanding, accepting, or integrating what the lawyer has said. Here are some myths, common and often false beliefs:

- The legal system is always fair. Results are just.
- A trial reveals the REAL truth.
- In this country, we all have a right to our day in court and to be heard by a jury.
- Juries always vote for the honorable party. A jury decision is always fair and right.
- Because I have been sued, my name and honor have been damaged. My record is tarnished. The world will know. When I win, my name and honor will be restored.
- If I sue and win at trial, the other side's name and reputation will be ruined. The world will know. I have the power to injure!

- People can win millions of dollars in punitive damages whenever the other side deserves to be punished.
- No jury would award punitive damages against my company if we didn't intentionally do anything wrong.
- I can always appeal—all the way to the Supreme Court.

Unmindful of the client's under-armor of belief, the frustrated lawyer moans: "I've explained the realities to my client until I'm blue in the face. He just doesn't get the picture, or he doesn't want to get it. It's as if he doesn't care, or he's just oblivious!" The lawyer has indeed painstakingly, clearly, and carefully explained his analysis of the legal issues and the evidence. The client seems finally to understand the analysis, but it is without impact. The armor of myth and belief was neither addressed nor penetrated. "It's as if he's intent on walking off a cliff," laments the lawyer (or mediator), shaking his head.[9]

Beliefs Play Out in Practice

Imagine a 50-year-old business owner whose company is accused of gender discrimination in its initial demotion and then termination of a mid-level female manager named Sally. He was involved in the termination decision, based on the recommendation of the regional VP, a loyal member of his senior management team and his long-time golf buddy. The business owner's lawyer has explained that the patterns of hiring, firing, and promoting women in the region over the past 10 years, revealed in discovery, may appear not to favor women, and that his VP did acknowledge having made remarks such as "these gals just don't put out hard work like the guys do. They play too much with their kids." And: "Sally doesn't fit in with the team; she bitches and moans about nit-picky details, reminds me of my mother." The VP has steadfastly denied any biases and maintains that Sally really was a problem—all of the other (mostly male) members of the department will testify to that.

The business owner strongly believes that his VP is a decent, honorable man who had only the best interests of the business in mind. When his lawyer explains that on this evidence plus the testimony of the plaintiff and her witnesses, a jury might well find gender discrimination, the business owner may hear the words but flatly reject the idea of risk that any jury will doubt his VP's credibility. He has an abiding faith that the jury will find the real truth and vote for the good guys and he knows in his heart of hearts that he and his VP are the good guys. The jury will [magically] be able to separate fact from fiction and will therefore see that Sally really was incompetent and uncooperative and deserved to be terminated. The idea of punitive damages will not cause concern for a nano-second because, even if the statistics are awkward, his testimony will explain them. He would never have been intentionally unfair to any employee.

Myth or fantasy, plaintiffs who feel wronged by more powerful actors believe their lawsuit has the power to ruin the other side, or power to make them take notice and regret what they have done. Theoretically, if a large dollar verdict would bankrupt the other side, it might be true. But in a single plaintiff and corporate defendant context, the plaintiff sometimes envisions public damage—vindication of his public "record" and ruinous public image damage to the other. Indeed, that vision—mostly mirage—may be an important motivation for taking legal action. It is an attempt to equalize power imbalance, to become a threat, to let the world know of the wrongs committed. Some lawyers are faithful to these myths and see themselves as crusading warriors, and thus help to build the illusion that a public trial will topple the powerful and achieve heroic vindication. Yet this is the stuff of grand movies, and rarely, rarely of reality.

Grounded in experience and evidence, most lawyers become astonished or frustrated when their clients turn deaf ears to concerns about practical financial interests. As a mediator, I often witness a lawyer's incredulity and concern at her client's "irrational" rejection of a significant settlement in favor of waiting for trial and risking a low or zero-dollar verdict. That lawyer may have learned that the client deeply desires to resurrect his good name and ruin the other's. All too often, however, the lawyer fails to recognize the strength of the client's underlying belief that his legal action has the power to do so. Unless that belief is addressed and discussed, the client will cling to negotiating positions that cause his lawyer to shake her head in disbelief.

No Scripted Answers for Explanation

We accept that the lawyer's task is to translate language describing legal circumstances sufficiently to achieve the elusive "fully informed client." But, must all explanations of legal process include every possible twist, turn, and consequence, no matter how remote? How much information is too much? Completely eliminating the knowledge imbalance could take quite a while; law school was three long years. Must a lawyer anticipate, recite, and dispel every myth?

Is there a prescribed way for a lawyer to make these judgments? How could there be? Each client comes to the table with different capacities, engagement, and levels of curiosity.

Find the Foundation and Build There

It would be foolish for an architect to design living space without knowing whether the project is a renovation or new construction, or without having seen the foundation or the site. So, before explaining legal circumstances to a client, a lawyer is wise to learn something about that client's familiarity with law and the legal process terrain. As early as the initial client meeting or interview, do ask your client about any past experience with lawyers and the legal system. Both what that experience was and the way she speaks about it will provide insight into her facility with legal concepts and processes. If you didn't ask in earlier meetings, consider raising the question in a general, friendly way before focusing on explanation of legal circumstances in the client counseling session.

A word of caution: do not assume that college education, age, or general business experience give rise to a sophisticated client. Highly accomplished and intelligent people sometimes know astonishingly little about the legal system—astonishing to lawyers at least. Too often, when meeting with a professional client dressed in a suit and possessing an impressive title or resume, the lawyer assumes too much knowledge. It's natural. After all, the client looks and speaks much like the lawyer's colleagues: they appear to be from the same "speech community" (as that term is used at page 58). The opposite is also true: clients who do not appear highly educated or worldly may be quite aware of the way the legal system works. Some cab drivers study philosophy; a waitress may be an astronomy geek. Your grocery produce manager client may have helped his sister study for the bar. He may be an ardent environmentalist who follows Environmental Defense Fund litigation. You just never know.

Credit and Climb onto the Client's Understanding

Knowing a client's general experience with the legal terrain helps a lawyer make initial judgments about when translation is necessary, and what types of words to choose. To insure a fully informed client on legal circumstances and choices faced in *this* matter, there's no harm in the lawyer asking what the client has already gleaned. Imagine that depositions and other discovery are done. The lawyer sets up a meeting to discuss the status of the litigation and possible settlement. The lawyer might ask:

Could you tell me what you understand about where we are in the process? I don't want to take your time explaining what you already know.

One client might respond:

> *I think discovery is done because there's no one else to depose and everyone has everyone else's documents. Based upon the last time, I assume we'll file something to try to get rid of this case. If that doesn't work, trial is still a long time away. I also know there's a tactical question about whether we should look at settling now, or after we file that thing. And from the company's perspective, settling or not may have other repercussions.*

A different client might say:

> *I hope we're done with talking in conference rooms with stenographers, because I'm hoping you're going to tell me the trial will be soon and we have to get ready.*

Whichever client is yours that day, you will have gained valuable clues on where to and how to communicate effectively.

Fully Informed with a Little, a Lot, or Just Right?

Assume you are a master translator of legalese, deft at choosing language that communicates everything—every nuance of analysis, every argument, every possible process twist and turn—to all clients, whatever their level of intelligence or experience. Some clients are eager and curious to learn it all. Others are interested only in the bottom line: "What are the choices? What's the up side? What are the risks and consequences? Spare the details and how you got there."

Particularly where complete explanation of the legal circumstances would be intricate and lengthy,[10] I suggest offering your client an initial choice between detail and broad brush. You might say:

> *We face some large legal hurdles that will take some time and pose big risks for us. I can explain each of those in detail, and*

what the arguments and analysis are on both sides. You are more than entitled to know this. It's your case. Or, I can just give you my conclusions and we'll talk about some decisions you have to make. It's your choice. Of course, you can change your mind either way. I can start with the careful step by step and you can decide you want me to skip to the end. Or I can start with some conclusions and you can ask me to review the reasoning and analysis.

Offering this choice is an act of respect, providing the client some welcome control within the counseling session. It seems more likely to meet client needs than a prepared monologue at the level of detail the lawyer might want if he were a client.

Take Extra Care on Impact

Even where the client has expressed interest in the salient legal issues and analysis, your client's clear understanding of their impact is ultimately more important. When explaining summary judgment, it is not a terrible failure if your client misses the distinction between a material fact and a disputed fact. It is a failure if your client doesn't clearly understand the consequences of losing on that motion: there will be no trial; she will not get to testify; and she will get nothing. An appeal is unlikely to change that.

Ordering the Full Legal Plate

In some cases, communicating broad-brush conclusions just isn't sufficient, even if an individual client or corporate client representative might prefer it. In other words, given the possible consequences of the decision to be made, it's still your obligation to fully inform. You are committed to communicating all of the twists and turns that lie ahead, your analysis of the issues and arguments, your assessment of witnesses, risk, costs, damages, appellate questions, etc.

Is there a recommended order for serving up the full legal plate? Not really. The lawyer might start with a primer on the underlying structure and process of litigation first, and overlay an explanation of the law at issue, or she might interweave the two along the way.[11]

Once again, the lawyer could begin by asking the client's preference, saying, for example:

> *There has been a recent development in the case: the defense has filed something called a motion for summary judgment. In order to understand what that is and why it matters, you need to know something about the litigation process and the way courts work, as well as the law relating to this motion. I can give you an overview of the litigation and the court process first and then talk about this motion in your case, or I can explain process as we go through the law and this motion.*

Again, consider letting your client choose a path through the thicket.

Whatever the order, a word of caution from communication experts, discussed more fully in chapter 6, "Choices in Voice." Don't launch into a monologue. Deliver information in small bits, PAUSING—really PAUSING—between separate concepts and ideas. In other words, don't take the client's request for an initial overview of the litigation process as license to lecture without interruption on topics from dispositive motions to the possibility of j.n.o.v. and jury nullification. And don't just pause in passing. Come to a FULL STOP frequently along the way: see if the client has questions. Check comprehension: ask how the client understands the importance of the procedural move you just described. Discuss it together. Your client will appreciate a conversation far more than a lecture. And you will learn whether your translation is indeed creating an accurate picture in your client's mind.

Directional Prompts from Non-Legal Interest, Wide and Deep

The lawyer who is deeply familiar with a client's circumstances will be better able to judge what is most important for that client to understand. Thus, both lawyer and client are well served by early discussion of the client's business or professional context and, if relevant, personal or family situation, interests, goals, and constraints.

Watch for Intersections and Contact Points

Consider the small business owner who has ten employees and is facing college tuition expenses for his three children, one aged 17, and 16-year-old twins, beginning a year from now. He has sought a therapist's treatment since his former partner sued him personally for fraud and the company for "freezing him out." He claims rights under a stock buyout provision. The client owns a small downtown building he intended to develop into condominiums but he cannot obtain bank financing because of the fraud claim pending in this suit. He had invested much of his cash in the condominium property, anticipating that he would pay tuition with profits from unit sales. The client feels angry and trapped, and expresses dogged determination to punish his former partner and defend his own good name.

Assume the businessman's lawyer has analyzed the legal strengths and weaknesses of the legal claims and is prepared to explain them. Without knowing of the therapy, the unrelated condominium development, and the college tuition pressure, the lawyer might spend much of their meeting time reviewing relevant corporate and partnership law, explaining her concerns as well as real strengths of the case, based upon her initial interviews of other employees. She would provide a cogent (and, if appropriate, optimistic) assessment of the likelihood of a trial win, and an estimate of legal fees.

The lawyer who DOES know of these circumstances and maps them against missing legal process knowledge and "counter-factual" myths will see that timing is extraordinarily important for this client, as is stress reduction (affected by timing), and coming to terms with anger, hurt, and public insult. She should be prepared to walk the client through each step and its anticipated time frame within the litigation process. She should be clear about expenditures of time and money over which he will have control and which he will not. She should ask additional questions about the health of the business and its ability to fund litigation while maintaining salary. She should gently probe about the impact on his professional productivity and family. She should perhaps raise the myth about "public trials" and their effect on name and satisfaction.

With a different client, but the same claims and legal analysis, the lawyer's meeting agenda might be different. A different client might be loath to spend cash on settlement now, but anticipate strong revenues in the future from a new line of business he is building. Neither the lawsuit nor its fraud claims have had significant financial or emotional impact. His kids' college tuitions have already been set aside. Delays in the litigation would be welcome, and predictable attorney's fees are not problematic. His real concern is the possibility of a very large damages award and/or buyout obligation in the future, when the new project has borne fruit. The lawyer should focus on communicating analysis of liability and damages issues, using accessible language and addressing likely knowledge imbalance.

The fundamental point is that a lawyer's efficiency and effectiveness benefits from broad interest, curiosity, chit-chat, and of course, a client who values and trusts his counsel. In initial and subsequent client meetings, lawyers too often ask narrow questions relating to clients' legal claims but fail to learn about the broader context of their business priorities and projections, or the clients' professional or personal lives. Yet, a case always occurs within these contexts, which both impact and are impacted by the case process and its outcome. Lawyers are well advised to take time early on to learn the client context, and to inquire about changes along the way. When a client makes reference to a business wrinkle or a personal distraction, the lawyer should probe deeply, albeit gently, to learn more about underlying meaning, purpose, or concerns. Trusting his lawyer, the client will be free to discuss what matters most, enabling the lawyer to provide wiser counsel as the case unfolds.

Translation Theory to Speech Communities

As suggested by its title, this chapter has heretofore used the idea of translation as a framework for describing, critiquing, and prescribing how lawyers use language to explain clients' legal circumstances. When a lawyer-client conversation is focused solidly on legal terrain, the skilled lawyer might consciously consider himself a translator from legalese—that terrain's language and culture—to the client's language and culture. To do so, the lawyer must recall and take into account the "receptor language and culture" of one who has NOT gone to law school.

It seems irresponsible to close a chapter on communication through language without also speaking of "speech communities." Academics use "speech community" in service of the idea that common language is not necessarily sufficient for clear communication. Writing in the field of socio-linguistics, Professor John J. Gumperz[12] originally defined a speech community as a group of people who share a set of norms and rules for the use of language. If a lawyer and client come from very different speech communities, their communication may prove challenging outside any discussion of difficult-to-explain legal circumstances.

Socio-linguists are a technical bunch, and their discussions of speech communities are built upon observed differences in pronunciation, inflection, grammar, and usage. However, they ultimately observe that boundaries between speech communities are essentially social rather than linguistic. Thus, within a speech community, people communicate effectively because they share underlying grammar and rules for their use in socially appropriate circumstances.[13]

Speech communities are not geographically, but socially defined. An upper-class speaker in Manhattan may belong to the same speech community as an upper-class speaker in Boston. Their speech community is no doubt different from that in the South Bronx or in Dorchester. It may also differ from even upper-class communities in the deep South.

Stereotypes are often applied based upon difference in speech communities: President Jimmy Carter may have been viewed as less intelligent by some because of his distinctly Southern speech patterns. People from different speech communities may also interpret comments literally that were intended figuratively, leading to awkward interaction.

Lawyers should be aware that clients may belong to other speech communities. This means that certain phrasings or grammatical choices may be misunderstood or misjudged in both directions. Lawyers should be attentive to speech patterns—grammar and language choice. Be sensitive to areas of possible ambiguity and confusion. Be careful NOT to stereotype—to draw conclusions as to professional competence or intelligence—based upon speech patterns. And, note that your client may form impressions of you based upon your speech.

From the perspective of a socio-linguist, different competencies fall within the concept of speech communities. A computer service manager and a history teacher may be within the same socio-cultural speech community. Still, their distinct areas of competence may render the history teacher unable to understand the computer service manager's explanation of why the school's computer system has crashed. Coming full circle then, when lawyers DO explain legal circumstances to their clients, that may be understood as an act of translation across different competency-based speech communities.

Notes

1. "Found in Translation: To convey the writings or other languages is a noble and necessary art," *The Times*, January 11, 2010, http://www.timesonline.co.uk/tol/comment/leading_article/article6982969.ece (accessed May 24, 2011).

2. Professor Scott DeLancey, Department of Linguistics, University of Oregon, "Quotes about Language and Translation," The Language Realm, http://www.languagerealm.com/quotes/quotes.php. http://www.languagerealm.com/quotes/quotes.php (accessed May 19, 2011).

3. Mildred Larsen, *Meaning-Based Translation: A Guide to Cross-Language Equivalence* (Lanham, MD: University Press of America, Inc., 1984), 3.

4. See Robert W. Benson, "The End of Legalese: The Game is Over," *New York University Review of Law & Social Change* 13.3 (1985): 519–573. See also Peter Meijes Tiersma, *Legal Language* (Chicago: University of Chicago Press, 1999), chap. 12.

5. Anne Enquist and Laurel Oates label specialized use of common words and phrases as "argot" and include it under legalese. *Just Writing* (New York: Aspen Publishers, 2009), 132–133. The use of "argot" in the legal context can also be found in Lawrence M. Friedman, "Law and Its Language," *George Washington Law Review* 33 (1964–1965): 563. ("Legal style is characterized by its use of 'argot.'")

6. Patrick Schmidt, "Acquiring Culture," *The Vienna Review*, February 18, 2009, http://www.viennareview.net/node/1144 (accessed May 24, 2011).

7. "Appeals from General Civil Trials in 46 Large Counties, 2001–2005," Bureau of Justice Statistics, http://bjs.ojp.usdoj.gov/content/pub/pdf/agctlc05.pdf (last modified July 6, 2006); Donald R. Songer and Reginald S. Sheehan, "Who Wins on Appeal? Upperdogs and Underdogs in the United States Courts of Appeals," *American Journal of Political Science* 36, no. 1 (February 1992): 241–243.

8. "But of the 1,000 adults polled by telephone in August, 47 percent said they believed that the courts did not 'treat all ethnic and racial groups the same.' Thirty-nine percent said there was equitable treatment of minorities and 14 percent had no opinion. Also, 90 percent of

respondents said affluent people and corporations had an unfair advantage in court." Linda Greenhouse, "47% in Poll View Legal System as Unfair to Poor and Minorities," *New York Times,* February 24, 1999, http://www.nytimes.com/1999/02/24/us/47-in-poll-view-legal-system-as-unfair-to-poor-and-minorities.html (accessed May 24, 2011); "Public Understanding of Justice System," *American Bar Association*, http://www.abapubliceducation.org/publiced/resolution1.html (accessed May 19, 2011) (80 percent of respondents said the US justice system was the best in the world).

9. As discussed in the "Meaning Truths" chapter, myths often shape the way people understand the world and their own story with in it. Heroic myths are particularly strong and cross-cultural, including the notion of hero as warrior. See Joseph Campbell, *The Hero With a Thousand Faces*, 2nd ed. (Princeton, New Jersey: Princeton University Press, 1968), 334–341.

10. See chapter 4 on emotion and role.

11. See Stefan Krieger and Richard Neumann, *Essential Lawyering Skills* (New York: Aspen Publishers, 2003), chap. 21; Nancy Oppenheim, "Cognitive Bridges: Law Courses Structured for Application and Knowledge Transfer," *Journal of Legal Studies Education* 17, no. 1 (1999): 17–56. When conveying complex medical information, physicians are advised to weave together medical knowledge and their application, small bits at a time. Robert Buckman, M.D., and Yvonne Kason, M.D., *How to Break Bad News: A Guide for Health Care Professionals* (Baltimore: John Hopkins University Press, 1979).

12. J. J. Gumperz, "The Speech Community," in *International Encyclopedia of the Social Sciences* (London: Macmillan, 1968), 381–386.

13. Suzanne Romaine, "What is a Speech Community," in *Sociolinguistic Variations in Speech Communities* (London: E. Arnold, 1982), 14–24; and Suzanne Romaine, *Language in Society: An Introduction to Socio Linguistics*, 2nd ed. (New York: Oxford University Press, 2001), 23–25.

3

Meaning Truths

"These are my principles. If you don't like them, I have others."
—GROUCHO MARX[1]

"It's about principle," your client moans, predictably, "not about money." This client seems to mean it. "We didn't do anything wrong! I get all of your lawyerly logic, but giving up lets an extortionist win. I won't be a party to that. It's the principle!" shouts another client, slamming his hand on the table. The corporate whistleblower client stands up, calmly declaring: "I am honor bound to go after these greedy thieves to vanquish so many people's suffering. Their offer is dirty blood money." The small business owner asserts: "I must battle that man's lies about me and my company. The record must be set straight." The divorcing husband refuses to divide proceeds from the sale of the couple's lakeshore bungalow because "that would condone the adultery we now know she committed there for so many summers." Some obviously reasonable options are off the table because of what they mean.

Human beings seek and find meaning in life's major events and daily activities. Even those who understand meaning to be "socially constructed"[2] may care passionately about that meaning—the interpreted construal of what we do and say. At a minimum, our actions and words express our identities and reflect what we value.

When operating in relatively value-neutral contexts, decision-making is unencumbered by meaning or the search for it. Thus, if I am eating with my spouse at a Mediterranean restaurant, my choice among menu items carries no meaning beyond what I'd like to eat that evening, or perhaps a balancing of taste, calories, and cost among grape leaves, Greek salad, shish kebab, or filet. Yet, the same choice within a particular social context could generate meaning and reflect values. Imagine that I am in the same Mediterranean restaurant, hosting a meal for the first time with my son's future in-laws. Would ordering the most expensive menu items—delicacies for everyone—mean wealth, ostentation, or a celebratory spirit? If my spouse whispers to me behind the menus, suggesting the elaborate food order, I may be uncomfortable and shake my head. Because humility is important to me, I want to stick with grape leaves and shish kebab. To my spouse, a more elaborate food order may communicate generosity and hospitality, assuming it is understood the future in-laws will be our guests. That alternative meaning may not have occurred to me. Our identities—the way we view ourselves and represent ourselves to others—and the meaning we attribute to each choice—will determine our decision (and whether we will have to resolve conflict in the coat room).[3]

Surely, if meaning and identity can be found in the choice between shish kebab and filet, we will see them in more serious choices. Imagine that you've been invited to join the board of a local charitable organization. The board's function is largely to raise funds and advise the staff regarding policy and strategic issues. At the time of the invitation you are gainfully employed and have teenage children. Thus, while you have little leisure time, your life is under better control than when the children were younger. What does the invitation mean? Does it mean that your intelligence, middle-age, and wisdom are now recognized and you should take a place among community leaders? Does it mean that someone (whoever suggested your name) believes you to be financially well-connected, rightly or wrongly? If you turn down the invitation, does that mean you are selfish because you were unwilling to take on this responsibility and commitment to a worthy cause? Selfishness conflicts with your self-identity. Or, does turning down the board position mean you believe this charity's mission, while useful, does not address the more important, primary needs of the community? Perhaps turning down the charity could reflect your decision to prioritize—to reserve newly found and precious time for family and friends, rather than just saying "yes" to whatever comes along. Perhaps it reflects liberation from being reactive.

The board obligation to raise funds would most likely require you to solicit contributions from more affluent friends and colleagues. Are you someone who exploits relationships in that manner? Would your friends and colleagues view your solicitation as exploitative? Note that the word "exploit" is not neutral. Different meaning might be generated with a different word. Witness the source of ambivalence when we weigh competing choices: How do we define ourselves? What does each choice mean to us, and to others?

Client Meaning

Very often, clients view occurrences and choices in legal disputes and transactions as having profound and consequential meanings. A client is put in a bind when forced to choose between an action whose meaning conflicts with her identity or values and another that is "rationally" in her economic interest. If the client sees herself as a righteous, principled crusader and the other side as evil incarnate, then settling means "selling my soul to the devil." The meaning of the so-called "economically rational settlement" exacts too high a price. The lawyer's frustrated conclusion that the client is "irrational" ignores or misses that meaning and the conflict it creates. Self-interest may include economic interest, but the two are neither synonymous nor equally weighted. Your client might quote from the New Testament, Matthew 16:26: "For what if a man is profited, if he shall gain the whole world, and lose his own soul?"

Unlock the Meaning Trap

When one's soul is in conflict with material gain, the client may understandably choose to keep her soul. If the conflict is stark and irreversible and its meaning clear, then this is an admirable decision. However, if meaning is constructed and not intrinsic, then it may also be ambiguous, varied, variable, multi-dimensional, and changing through perspective and time. From a client counseling perspective, this is good because it permits meaning to be re-construed or generated anew.[4] The lawyer who offers an alternative meaning may release a client trapped between her values and identity and a choice that meets her other interests.

Find Meaning that Reinforces Values

Consider a proud personal injury client: the defense has just made a settlement offer somewhat higher than his lost wages and medical expenses. The settlement offer is lower than the likely trial award amount because of the high risk of dismissal on summary judgment or loss at trial under the state's "open and obvious" doctrine and contributory negligence standard. The lawyer has advised the client to settle at a dollar figure close to the settlement offer to avoid the risk of zero recovery. His recent divorce and financial needs are sad realities. The plaintiff fully understands the arguments and his lawyer's analysis of the strengths and (many) weaknesses in his case. Still he hesitates:

> I filed this lawsuit so the little person would be heard and not brushed off by the corporate giant. I was a loyal customer and they have treated me as if I were a pariah or a gold digger. I don't want them to get away with this. This money is a pittance for them. It won't make them change anything about the way they run their store or treat their customers.

If the lawyer listens to the client's expression of the meaning of the case and of the sum offered, she will recognize that taking legal action was her client's assertion of power, self-pride, and identity as one who takes action on behalf of others. The client interprets the settlement sum offered as a pittance, reflecting the store's rejection of him as well as the store's failure to take responsibility. The lawyer might respond:

> *I understand why it seems that way. However, there is another way to understand this offer. Perhaps it is the store's effort to take some responsibility by covering your economic losses—the costs of your injuries. It's a way of regretting the accident and acknowledging that your injuries are real. If the store thought you were lying or the store didn't feel some responsibility, it wouldn't be offering to cover these costs.*

Imbuing the monetary offer with this alternative meaning addresses at least part of the client's conflict between the "rational choice" and his identity and values.

Avoid Costly Negative Savings

It is important to highlight a particular negative application of law-yer-suggested meaning often observed in practice. Lawyers often characterize a settlement offer as reflecting the defense's desire to avoid litigation costs. This is a truth—one meaning of a defense offer—often articulated within an explanation of how the system works—but it is generally unhelpful. The client has no desire to generate a "savings" for the defendant store—quite the opposite. This meaning reinforces the client's interpretation of the offer as "brushing me away like an annoying fly." Thus, my advice is to avoid generating this explanation, unless pressed, and move to an alternative that is also true, but more palatable to the client.

Don't Seek to Dispel Illusions; Work with Illusions and Meaning

Mark Twain wrote, "Don't part with your illusions. When they are gone, you may still exist, but you will have ceased to live."[5] Your client's articulated illusions can be tools for your understanding and his realization. The whole of the client's lament reveals his illusion that the lawsuit gives him power against the corporation and power to change its practices to benefit others. That is why settlement means capitulation or selling out that power and abandonment of selfless motive. Illusions or not, asserting power and acting selflessly for others are components of the client's identity and self-pride.

Rather than diminish them, the lawyer might highlight the power and change achievable through settlement. She might observe that—even though the settlement seems small for a large corporation—just as all politics are local, so are grocery stores. The amount could be significant in comparison to the local store's net profits. The lawyer might observe that the lawsuit has already had its intended effect, as the client's deposition clearly shook up the store's manager and his staff. The lawyer may also suggest that the settlement amount is large enough to make the local store take better safety measures for its customers.

If the client re-interprets the lawsuit itself as an effective assertion of power and a deterrent to future accidents, the decision to settle is no longer in conflict with his identity. The lawyer might also contrast these new meanings of litigation and settlement to the meaning of continuing to litigate and losing on summary judgment. In that event, the store would pay nothing. The unintended and unpalatable meaning would be the store's triumphant conclusion that there are no consequences when a customer is injured in its aisles.

Address Public and Private Meanings of the Record

Clients sometimes value or fear the meaning of "public record," seeking to "clear my name on the record," or expose an evil-doer in public. Offering to settle may suggest lack of truthfulness and temerity, interpretable as fear of being revealed in public.

These concerns hearken back to the widely held myth that trials inevitably reveal truth[6] and what psychologists call the "spotlight effect"—our tendency to inflate our own significance in the narratives of others.[7] When completely absorbed in the details and drama of our own stories, we forget how little others know or care about them. Thus, the former employee is certain that the giant automobile manufacturer is concerned about exposure of the unfair promotion practices in its small Midwestern plant because of the publicity and public record. The client values having power—really an illusion of power—and would reject a beneficial settlement offer to keep it.

Here, it might be necessary and constructive to reveal that the power-of-public-record is but an illusion. The lawyer could enable his client to step back and see that many, many cases are won and lost without a line in the local newspaper (or on the internet), and that a trial in a small Midwestern courthouse will not shake up the company. While this diminishes the client's feeling of personal power to harm the company, it also diminishes the company's power to harm her. The client may see that it is not worth sacrificing—taking risk, going through trial, paying fees—for a power that is not real.

Reference Meaning in an Alternative, Less Abstract Place of Record

Where the client feels it important to clear her name "on the record," the lawyer might also help the client think through the social and professional contexts in which his name remains unblemished:

Who did you work with at the company? Where are they now? What did they think of your work quality? What did they think of your boss at the company? Did your termination change the way people you respected viewed you? Didn't it make your boss look like a fool? Among what group does your reputation matter the most? Isn't your name still good with them, without any trial? Aren't they the people who matter to you?

To diminish the force of a verdict as a public record, the lawyer might ask his client to name another employee who does excellent work. Then ask the client to consider whether her original view of that excellent work would be affected if that employee were terminated, filed suit for discrimination, and settled or lost at trial? Or, the lawyer might explore the opposite circumstance: an ineffective and unproductive employee who wins a wrongful termination suit due to jury manipulation—would that alter the client's view? In short, the lawyer and client are advised to consider carefully the meaning of "the record" and the client's name, to demonstrate that, whatever the verdict, a public trial may not operate in reality as it does in myth.

Move from Blame and Capitulation to Affirmation in Context

On the defense side, clients often equate settlement—or settlement beyond nuisance value—with acknowledgment of culpability to the plaintiff, professional colleagues, co-workers, industry competitors, or even "the world." This can be particularly difficult where the language of the claim suggests intent, at least to a lay person. Discrimination and intentional tort claims are perfect examples. In discrimination cases, "pattern and practice" evidence may lead to a plaintiff's victory, without proof of the defendant's conscious intent to discriminate on the basis of race, gender, disability, or age. In "intentional tort" cases, the standard is not actual intent to injure (as the title suggests), but rather "manifest or willful disregard for safety."[8]

Despite the lawyer's careful explanation of the legal standards, sophisticated business clients may resist offering substantial settlements in high exposure cases of this type because it "means" admission of deliberate wrongdoing. Resistance occurs even where the corporate decision-maker is not the individual accused of the wrongful decision (termination or demotion in employment, or failure to repair a dangerous condition). People in organizations tend to be loyal to one another and put faith in their colleagues' pure motivations. Even if the risk is inarguable and an economically rational settlement is achievable, the construed meaning of settlement can be a powerful impediment.

Consider how counsel might offer an alternative meaning, rather than simply repeating risk elaborations: she might ask the newish CEO to confirm that terminating the (older) public relations director was smart, as it generated immeasurable goodwill and measurable revenue gains. If so, then settling the consequent lawsuit might be viewed as the comparatively low cost of that sound business decision. Willingness to pay that cost means his original decision was "bold and brilliant"—a necessary and important judgment at the time.

While examples of meanings bound up in litigation and settlement are plentiful, they occur in a myriad of other contexts. Consider the businessperson loath to include a key term in a business transaction because it would be "caving in." An alternative meaning for allowing the term would be as a gracious accommodation for a less secure business counterpart. Perhaps such a gesture is the more powerful player's act of largesse. Unequal division of inheritance could mean unequal love by the deceased mother, or it could mean she worried about the other sibling's inability to accumulate any savings.

Narrative Emplotment[9]—Whole Story Alternatives

Beyond finding meaning in particular decisions, many understand their larger circumstances through narrative emplotment—story lines of cause and effect. Our culture provides archetypal romance stories of heroic triumph against all odds and tragedies in which destructive urges create victims of the once-mighty. The tragic hero

Hamlet comes to accept his fate, and the audience gains wisdom through his struggle. Disney, the Brothers Grim, and Hans Christian Anderson acculturate young minds with powerful narratives. The ugly duckling, Cinderella, Shrek, Bambi, and the Lion King suffer loss or adversity, but all is right by the end. Abe Lincoln and Daniel Boone both pursued unlikely paths to becoming historical and cultural icons.

When people seek meaning in challenges or adversity, in legal injuries and lawsuits, even in transactions critical to professional livelihood, they often locate themselves within an archetypal narrative. Those well-rehearsed story lines and roles as cast determine their choices and interpretations. While not always pernicious to make oneself the hero in a personal or professional story, it can be problematic if that story imbues other characters with pre-set meanings and intentions. It becomes a filtering, distorting lens through which elements of reality are ignored or magnified. In the story of victim and perpetrator, good vs. evil, the latter's intent is always malevolent. To negotiate with the evildoer is to become corrupt, and to listen to the evildoer's story is to risk being duped. *The Jungle Book*'s snake speaks with a forked tongue and sings hypnotically as his coils wrap slowly around his innocent prey.

Disney and Shakespeare aside, how do emplotment and narrative inform lawyering? Imagine that your client is the sole owner of a business with several fast food franchise locations. The business was under stress; he approached a specialty lender for financing absolutely necessary to renew his franchise terms, soon to expire. The lender provided a letter of intent and has been undertaking due diligence. As the letter of intent's deadline has approached, the lender demanded more and more documentation but refused to extend the deadline. The lender sent a letter re-asserting its right NOT to finance, based upon the letter of intent. The client company owner sees himself as the innocent victim and the lender's VP as evil and corrupt, purposely creating impossible hurdles. Predictably, the client notices ONLY the correspondence about "right to retract" and fails to see openings in the text for flexibility and dialogue. He certainly doesn't call the VP (or his staff) to meet and understand their concerns or resolve any conflicts. Because the VP is trying to "double cross" him, a meeting will be of no use. Instead, he demands that his lawyer immediately and forcefully threaten suit against the lender.

Of course, the lender's VP may see your client as desperate man seeking to obtain money by hiding information about his company's real (and precarious) financial circumstances and less-than-clean business practices. Every refusal to cooperate and every protest by your client increases her suspicions. A final "lawyer letter" threatening suit, rather than providing documents or explaining why he cannot, would confirm that the company owner is a snake, or a snake oil salesman.

Assume that threatening and then filing suit are likely to ruin the client's business. Without short term financing, the franchise contracts will expire. No other lenders are immediately available for this type of transaction. In this struggle between good and evil, the client has cast himself as tragic hero. The lawyer might intervene to suggest an alternative meaning, through different emplotment. Perhaps the client has the starring role in a story of a great statesman who puts aside the warrior's weapons and navigates the path to peace. Perhaps he is the long range hero who succeeds against the odds, through superior wit and will, and in so doing, wins over his former detractors. If the lawyer reinterprets the story and the client's role, he may be persuaded to negotiate rapprochement.

Of course, emplotment occurs for plaintiffs, too. A plaintiff client may recount the story of his fall while performing "heroic" work, venturing to a roof area that appeared inaccessible without different equipment, because the building owner begged him to finish the area that day. He fell, sustaining serious injuries. The building owner's initial low dollar settlement offer displays her evil selfishness. In settlement negotiations, it becomes clear that some legal hurdles coupled with your client's checkered past have led to a lower than anticipated "final offer." The client says: "Somebody has to stand up to greed.

They can't just use people and cast them aside. If I don't fight, who will? Sometimes you have to fight to be a man." He is locked into heroic narrative of fighting against the odds. Hearing this, a lawyer or mediator might evoke the alternative, culturally familiar narrative of the canny frontiersman who knows when to pick his battles and when to walk away. That man never hands the enemy a victory; he plays it smart and fights only where he will have an advantage.

Meaning to Reframe

Readers versed in negotiation and mediation literature may see the advice to offer alternative meanings by re-characterizing client choices or emplotment narratives simply as advice to reframe.[10] Good advice, but hardly original. Over the last decade or so, the concept of "reframing" has become ubiquitous. There are many reasons to "reframe" in dialogue: to de-escalate rhetoric and thus tension, to suggest a broader contextual perspective, to encourage empathy or, at least, recognition of the other side's circumstances and point of view.

Here, the recommendation to reframe focuses on a client's construed meaning. A lawyer should be attuned to a client's values, identity, illusions, or emplotted narrative, and how these may conflict with meanings found in the legal context. If, as Mark Twain said, "A man cannot be comfortable without his own approval,"[11] the lawyer should think to suggest alternative meanings—other truths—for client comfort and approval.

Curiosity as Best Counsel

Just ASK for Meaning!!!

When you wonder why your client can't get to a decision that makes logical sense: don't push; don't just repeat your reasoning. Wonder why.

Just ask your client, not with gritted teeth but with genuine curiosity and open gesture: "What does this case mean to you?" If your client is determined to pursue what seems to be a risky course of action, ask: "Why is that choice important? What does it mean for you?" Your client will appreciate the open question, which respects her autonomy and perspective (as suggested in chapter 4). The client may provide new information about business or personal context and interests that explain why the choice is important. It may meet her interests in intangible but nonetheless real objectives. And sometimes, you will learn of more than hidden interests—of deeper meaning, of how a choice echoes or diminishes your client's identity and values or fits within a greater narrative. Then, stand back and think from a different vantage point, informed by your client's meaning. From there, you may find and offer an array of alternative meanings and choices in harmony with your client's identity, values, and role.

On Truth and Manipulation

"It is the hallmark of any deep truth that its negation is also a deep truth."

—NIELS BOHR[12]

Truth is not always relative, nor is it always impossible to establish. Othello kills his wife in brutal jealousy. Your client was seriously injured when the railing collapsed. The defendant did deliberately steal customer lists and trade secrets. The statute of limitations does bar the claim.

No lawyer should deny the truth to his client in the act of counseling.[13] A lawyer's purposeful exaggeration of risk or legal opinion is manipulative, deceptive, and unethical. Thus, the lawyer should be admonished NOT to say, "There's just no chance of us getting past summary judgment, given the law and this judge" when he doesn't believe it—even if his goal is to convince the client to accept a settlement which would serve him well.

The lawyer's motive may be pure: worries about the client's precarious emotional health and ability to survive a zero-dollar recovery. But if there is real hope—in the form of some supporting case law and an assigned judge who may be receptive, it is unethical—deceptive and manipulative—to paint these out of the picture. A lawyer might try to rationalize exaggeration by noting that the client will no doubt discount a full description of the truth:

> When I say, "there is a small chance," my client seems to skip over "small" – and seizes on the idea of a chance, and starts to believe it's a good one. I am exaggerating because, given my client's misconceived optimism, it's the only way for him to get an accurate understanding.

Perhaps so. But in my view, this path is paved with deception and an unattractive paternalism (or maternalism). The lawyer violates fundamental contractual and ethical obligations to the client by deliberately distorting the legal analysis and predictions.

Yet, I strongly recommend that a lawyer provide alternative meanings—in effect—alternative truths for their clients. How is that different? Isn't it just as manipulative and paternalistic for a lawyer to suggest another meaning? No, as long as that meaning is *also* valid. The cross-examiner poses the question: "Isn't it true that, for the defendant corporation, this settlement saves costs, time and trouble and enables it to forget this plaintiff and avoid the light of trial?" The answer is yes. But is it *also* true that the corporation's lawyer has acknowledged the seriousness of the plaintiff's injuries, and that the dollar amount offered has been shaped by the client's out-of-pocket costs? Yes again. Upper management knows of the lawsuit, and the local grocery store manager is aware of the plaintiff and her injuries.

Often, we see only one truth—only one set of meanings—as if trapped in a small cubicle with them. We are unaware that this cubicle is but one of many, reflecting more complex realities, each with meaning, each true. When a lawyer suggests an alternative meaning, she opens a door to the larger atrium, filled with these cubicles, and invites the client to consider inhabiting another. More important than the particular alternative suggested is the invitation to select or construct one's own meaning. That is an act of respect. Untrapped, the client makes the choice.

Notes

1. Fred Shapiro, ed., *The Yale Book of Quotations* (New Haven, CT: Yale University Press, 2006), 498.

2. For an introduction to social constructionism, see Fiona J. Hibberd, *Unfolding Social Constructionism* (New York: Springer Science, 2005); or see Kenneth J. Gergen, *Title Realities and Relationships: Soundings in Social Construction* (Cambridge: Harvard University Press, 1994). Hibberd credits P. Berger and T. Luckmann with coining the term "social construction" in their text *The Social Construction of Reality* (London: Penguin, 1966). She credits Kenneth J. Gergen as the dominant theorist on the application of social constructionist theory in psychology. Several authors have discussed the social construction of reality in the lawyer-client counseling context. E.g., Clark D. Cunningham, "Legal Storytelling: A Tale of Two Clients: Thinking about Law as Language," *Michigan Law Review* 87 (1989): 2470.

3. Another way to talk about identity and meaning is within a "narrative framework." Shirli Kopelman, Lydia Chen, and Joseph Shoshana helpfully summarize narrative framework as one which views "stories as a critical means by which people make themselves intelligible within the social world. The narrative identity framework [citations omitted] conceptualizes identity as a story that is developed and refined, complete with settings, scenes, characters, plots and themes. . . ." "Renarrating Positive Relational Identities in Organizations: Self-Narration as a Mechanism for Strategic Emotion Management in Interpersonal Interactions," *Exploring Positive Identities and Organizations: Building a*

Theoretical and Research Foundation, ed. Laura Morgan Roberts and Jane E. Dutton (New York: Routledge/Psychology Press, 2009), 272.

4. This chapter's discussion of "making meaning" is consistent with insights from narrative therapy, a form of psychotherapy using narrative, primarily developed by Australian social worker and family therapist Michael White and New Zealand therapist David Epston in the 1970s and 1980s. Their seminal work was *Narrative Means to Therapeutic Ends* (New York: Norton, 1990). This chapter does not purport to describe or prescribe the methodology of the narrative therapist. For a comprehensive description of narrative therapy literature and related research, see Mary Etchison and David M. Kleist, "Review of Narrative Therapy: Research and Utility," *The Family Journal: Counseling and Therapy for Couples and Families* 8, no. 1 (January 2000): 61–66. Epston and White (and others) have authored numerous additional professional articles and books on the topic.

5. Mark Twain, *Following the Equator: A Journey Around the World* (Hartford, CT: The American Publishing Company, 1897), 275.

6. E.g., Ric Simmons, "Conquering the Province of the Jury: Expert Testimony and the Professionalization of Fact-Finding," *University of Cincinnati Law Review* 74 (2006): 1061 ("The central myth of the trial is that truth can be discovered in no better way, though it has long been argued that the drama really serves symbolic values more important than reliable factfinding."); see also Thane Rosenbaum, *The Myth of Moral Justice: Why Our Legal System Fails to Do What's Right* (HarperCollins: New York, 2004).

7. Thomas Gilovich, Kenneth Savitsky, and Victoria Husted Medvec, "The Spotlight Effect in Social Judgment: An Egocentric Bias in Estimates of the Salience of One's Own Actions and Appearance," *Journal of Personality and Social Psychology* 78, no. 2 (2000): 211–222.

8. The word "intent" is used throughout the Restatement regarding intentional torts to denote that the actor desires to cause consequences of his act, or that he believes that the consequences are substantially certain to result from it. Restatement (Second) of Torts § 8a (1965).

9. The term "emplotment" owes its current usage (outside of literary studies) to Hayden White's *Metahistory: The Historical Imagination in Nineteenth Century Europe* (Baltimore: John Hopkins, 1973), 7ff. Paul Ricoeur speaks of emplotment as selection and arrangements of elements in a narrative that transform it into a cogent story serving a

desired meaning. See Lewis Edin Hahn, *The Philosophy of Paul Ricoeur* (Chicago: Open Court, 1995), 84–85.

10. Erving Goffman must be credited with the concept of framing, writing that people frame their experiences by asking and answering for themselves the core question: "what is going on here now?" Framing is how we organize experiences and thus give them meaning. Erving Goffman, *Frame Analysis: An Essay on the Organization of Experience* (Cambridge, MA: Harvard University Press, 1974).

11. Mark Twain, *What is Man? And Other Philosophical Writings: Works of Mark Twain*, ed. Paul Baender (Berkeley: University of California Press, 1973), 138.

12. Quoted in Max Delbrück, *Mind from Matter: An Essay on Evolutionary Epistemology* (Palo Alto, CA: Blackwell Scientific Publications, 1986), 167.

13. "It is professional misconduct for a lawyer to . . . engage in conduct involving . . . deceit or misrepresentation." ABA Model Rules of Professional Conduct, Rule 8.4(c) (2002).

4

Emotional Effects and Affecting Emotions

"Emotions are celebrated and repressed, analyzed and medicated, adored and ignored – but rarely, if ever, are they honored."

—KARLA MCCLAREN[1]

Your shareholder client expresses disgust at his siblings' mismanagement of the family business and at his father's passive acceptance of their judgments. Another client sputters with anger when describing her former employer's humiliating comments at her failure to reach sales quotas. She expresses glee at her vision of publicly humiliating him at trial and vengefully imagines bankrupting the company with a punitive verdict.

A large consumer product company manager is frustrated and incredulous at your lawyerly conclusion that the non-compete in an earlier product spin-off transaction would rob him of the right to distribute a newly developed product.

Your divorce client insists that he will not pay any alimony beyond a year, because "that witch ruined year after year after year of my life." He is deaf to your advice that a judge's order will require more equitable allocation of marital assets, and thus, it would be wise to make a more generous offer to his wife.

Your business client speaks of the company's betrayal by its joint venture partner's "scheming, deceptive, and unfaithful transaction with our competitor."

If your clients were *Star Trek*'s android Data or Dr. Spock, you would give them logical advice: to make decisions only with reason, to put emotions aside. But, because we are human, that advice often proves impossible to follow.[2] Human emotions remain, visibly or invisibly directing our reactions and responses, our stated preferences, our capacity to analyze, and ultimately our decisions.

Emotion is not separable from human experience, whether that human experience is in the boardroom or the bedroom, the office or the playground. Clients and lawyers feel emotions when thinking about past facts, current circumstances, future choices, and legal analysis. We feel emotions as we think, and we often think about what we feel. Emotions create our fierce desire for legal analysis to support the decision or prediction that FEELS best. Emotions diminish our ability to grasp complexity or subtlety, execute strategy, and overcome obstacles.

Many logical lawyers say that they prefer reason to emotion and become frustrated when people react emotionally rather than logically to a reasoned argument. Ironically, lawyers tend to be passionate (thus, emotional) on this topic, as they believe strongly in the value of reason.

With deep appreciation for the wisdom of therapists, psychologists, physicians and other researchers into the human condition, I advise lawyers to abandon futile efforts to banish or ignore emotions.[3] These efforts render us blind to emotions' impact, or ill-equipped to respond when banishment fails and emotions re-enter, undeniably and inescapably. Thus, this chapter suggests ways to recognize, understand, observe, respond to, and influence emotion, focusing on common emotional states and emotional reactions within lawyer-client conversations. Without claims to exhaustiveness, it presents gleanings from research into the effect of emotion on decision-making, rapport, trust, and relationships. Meta-emotions—emotions about emotions—and self-identity's impact on emotional intensity are also discussed due to their particular salience for clients in legal disputes.

Finally, this chapter offers a practical approach to working with emotion in the lawyer-client context, applying the "core concerns" model developed by Professor Roger Fisher and Daniel Shapiro,

Ph.D., in their book, *Beyond Reason*.[4] The core concerns model was originally conceived as a "lens and a lever" for interactions at the classic negotiation table. However, my collaborative work with Dr. Shapiro confirms that the core concerns model provides insight for lawyers at two distinct levels: in the client's underlying legal dispute or problem, and in the lawyer-client counseling interaction.[5] The yield is practical advice for addressing the client's core emotional concerns at both levels. The result is more positive client emotion, better decision-making, and a stronger lawyer-client relationship.

First, we begin with some grounding in the literature and science of human emotion.

Emotional Grounding

The Oxford English Dictionary defines emotion as "[a]ny agitation or disturbance of mind, feeling, passion; any vehement or excited mental state."[6] Academics dispute whether the word "emotion" refers to our physical responses to an event, thought, or perception, our experience of physical responses, or the cognitive sparks generating those physical responses in the first place.

In his now famous book, *Emotional Intelligence: Why It Can Matter More than IQ*, Daniel Goleman acknowledges *The Oxford English Dictionary* definition and writes: "I take emotion to refer to a feeling and its distinctive thoughts, psychological and biological states, and range of propensities to act."[7] After recounting various anecdotes in which emotions propel people to heroic, tragic, or serendipitous ends, Goleman concludes: "All emotions are, in essence, impulses to act, the instant plans for handling life that evolution has instilled in us."[8]

Not surprisingly, scholar-researchers disagree about which emotions are most basic. Some posit a very few "primary" emotions from which all others are blended. Others name a wider array of elemental emotions. Goleman summarizes the "main candidates" and some of their families:

- *Anger*: fury, outrage, resentment, wrath, exasperation, indignation, vexation, acrimony, animosity, annoyance, irritability, hostility, and (perhaps at the extreme) pathological hatred and violence
- *Sadness*: grief, sorrow, cheerlessness, gloom, melancholy, self-pity, loneliness, dejection, despair, and (when pathological) severe depression
- *Fear*: anxiety, apprehension, nervousness, concern, consternation, misgiving, wariness, qualm, edginess, dread, fright, terror, and (as a psychopathology) phobia and panic
- *Enjoyment*: happiness, joy, relief, contentment, bliss, delight, amusement, pride, sensual pleasure, thrill, rapture, gratification, satisfaction, euphoria, whimsy, ecstasy, and (at the far edge) mania
- *Love*: acceptance, friendliness, trust, kindness, affinity, devotion, adoration, infatuation, and agape
- *Surprise*: shock, astonishment, amazement, and wonder
- *Disgust*: contempt, disdain, scorn, abhorrence, aversion, distaste, and revulsion
- *Shame*: guilt, embarrassment, chagrin, remorse, humiliation, regret, mortification, and contrition[9]

Beyond Control: Emotionality as Physicality

Nature has wired us with an emotional infrastructure. Charles Darwin first observed the universality of facial expressions as proof of evolution in the human nervous system.[10] More recent research confirms that facial expressions for fear, anger, sadness, and enjoyment, or their emotional families, are recognizable around the world, even in isolated tribes without exposure to media or mass entertainment.[11]

Whether defined as the physical state or its trigger, emotions are physically impossible to ignore or set neatly aside.[12] With anger, blood flows to the hands, heart rate increases, and adrenaline surges. With fear, blood travels to large skeletal muscles for the flight response. The body also freezes momentarily, and the brain's amygdala releases hormones. When we are happy, the brain fosters an increase in energy and dampens negative feelings and anxieties; the physiological response is quiet. Love and similar feelings generate a relaxation response of calm and contentment. Sadness is accompanied by a drop in energy and enthusiasm, and when one is depressed, a slower body metabolism. Surprise is seen in lifted eyebrows and wider open eyes. Disgust is seen as a curled upper lip to one side and sometimes a slight wrinkling of the nose.[13] Each emotional state is characterized by a different breathing pattern.[14]

The acting profession relies upon the fact of emotion as physically-generated. University of Cincinnati Professor of Drama Rocco Dal Vera[15] informs us that, to be convincing to an audience, actors are taught to generate *genuine* emotions in themselves by adopting the facial expressions, muscle tension, breathing, and vocal patterns of the desired emotional state. Soon, the actor who scowls and frowns begins to feel angry. The actor who adopts the facial expressions, posture, breathing, and voice of happiness will feel happy. In fact, maintaining an emotional state while adopting its opposite physical markers is difficult or impossible. Thus, one who wishes to shake anger or contempt would do well to "fake" contentment and respect.

Academic research confirms that adopting an emotion's facial expression will generate its physiology and thus its sensation. In one study, researchers asked a group of volunteers to remember and relive a stressful experience, while the researchers tracked the volunteers' autonomic nervous system responses—heart beat and body temperature. The researchers then taught a different group the facial expressions of anger, sadness, and fear; asked them to adopt those facial expressions; and tracked their autonomic nervous system responses. The facial expressions affected the subjects' autonomic nervous system as had the real experiences.[16] In another experiment, subjects who were asked to clench a pencil between their teeth, creating a forced smile, found a set of cartoons funnier than did volunteers holding a pen with their lips pursed around it, reading the same cartoons.[17] Facial expressions affect our own sensation and interpretation of emotion.

Emotion in Cognition and Judgment

"There is no instinct like that of the heart."

—LORD BYRON18

Inevitably, emotions affect our thinking, perceptions, memory, decisions, and relationships. Emotions have the power to disrupt rational thought, triggering intense and irrational behavior. We've all observed that emotion can escalate conflict, ruin relationships, and inspire bad decisions.

On the other hand, a growing body of research indicates that judgments based on emotion, or at least unarticulated intuition, sometimes lead to faster decisions that may be better. As reported in Malcolm Gladwell's popular book *Blink*,[19] a group of University of Iowa neuroscientists enrolled volunteers in a gambling game requiring them to choose cards from two red and two blue decks, in which the red cards are set to generate higher gains, but much higher losses, outweighing the gains. Long before the volunteers reported thinking something was wrong with the red cards, monitors on their hands registered emotional stress—sweaty palms—at taking red deck cards. At about the time their hands began sweating, they began switching from the red decks to the blue. In short, emotion pointed them to a decision before they became aware of its logic. In other experiments, neuroscientists found that people with brain lesions that diminish emotional responses also have diminished decision-making ability, taking excessive time to make a simple choice between appointment dates, and failing to select the cards needed to gain in a multi-choice, multi-phase game.[20] For better or for worse, for most of us, emotional response directs decision-making before intellectual cognizance—before we know it.

Flash of Client Emotion Offers a Flash of Insight

"Anger is a signal, and one worth listening to."
—HARRIET LERNER, *The Dance of Anger*[21]

Within the realm of conflict, emotional experience reveals morality and ideology. Our emotions reflect what we value, what we see as right and wrong. *Without* emotion, we are not interested or engaged and may not be capable of morality or ethics.[22]

Any strongly expressed or evident client emotion also provides clues to his past or his understanding of the present, as well as his values. For example, a client's sadness in response to a question about his initial meeting with the company president suggests that the meeting caused the client great discomfort. Did he feel intimidated and powerless at the meeting? What was the consequence? Were those emotions exploited in the deal they negotiated? The lawyer is wise to follow up with careful, gentle questions about the meeting and the president.

Imagine a different conversation between a lawyer and his client, a township council member, about the zoning of a parcel of land. When the lawyer raises the issue of how the zoning might affect the interests of the members of an adjacent golf club, the council member explodes: "***I DON'T GIVE TWO HOOTS ABOUT THEM! OUR TOWNSHIP HAS ITS OWN INTERESTS!***" The idea that the council member would be concerned about her township's interests is not surprising; the emotional explosion is. The lawyer's ear should be attuned and he should respectfully ask whether there is any history involving the golf club. It will not be surprising if the club previously rejected her (or a friend or family member's) application or if, when she was a member, the club failed to extend grace during a difficult financial period. Perhaps the club's chairman is a political party leader on the opposite side of the fence, as are many of its members . . . perhaps, perhaps . . . .

Don't just speculate or assume. Curiosity is well advised where emotions run hot and deep. Understanding their source will be necessary to resolving the current problem, or at least to help your client make wise decisions.

Authority of the Amygdala

The medically curious reader will be interested to know that our emotions are regulated by the amygdala, an almond-shaped organ in the medial temporal lobe of the brain, above the brainstem, near the internal ear structure. Considered part of the limbic system, it is responsible for the processing and memory of emotional reactions. When a patient's amygdala is severed from the brain, he loses most, if not all, of his ability to recognize his feelings. Assuming a normal brain connection, when the amygdala is stimulated into action by an emotion, it immediately triggers hormones that mobilize heartbeat, muscles, blood pressure, breathing, and concentration.[23]

The amygdala acts quickly. And, once in an amygdala-heightened state, we are literally incapable of processing complexity or subtlety. Thus, physiological responses we feel as emotions often explode before rational faculties can process and reason through information.[24]

Watch for Uncommon Floods

Lawyers are advised to be mindful that a client may experience "emotional flooding."[25] When in that state, one is overcome by a deluge of emotions and is incapable of real interaction. This should not be confused with just very strong emotion, expressed as an outburst. I might be very upset by a crank phone call, launch into a sputtering rant about political idiocy, or yell in high decibel, red-faced anger at a family member. But there I would be functioning and mostly coherent, even if emotionally charged. Emotional flooding is much rarer. It might be understood as an exponential escalation and intensification, rather than some degree stronger than the average emotional reaction. Experts suggest that a minimum of 20 minutes is required for anyone to recover from emotional flooding. There is no sense in seeking conversation or much interaction of any kind before then.[26]

About Anger

"Anger is a brief madness."

— HORACE, *Epistles (Book I)*[27]

"If a man be under the influence of anger, his conduct will not be correct."

— CONFUCIUS, *The Wisdom of Confucius*[28]

Lawyer-client counseling challenges are more often presented where your client is experiencing anger or other strong negative emotions[29]: his deposition was a disaster; the settlement offer is outrageously low; you've explained that the judge is likely to dismiss his case; the accusations in the complaint are insulting lies; the other party is insisting on an unpalatable contract, but he has no other alternative for saving his business. Your client must make a decision. As the lawyer, you must explain legal issues, choices, and trade-offs. Your client may feel anger, frustration, indignation, disgust, anxiety, shame, despair . . . name the negative. Here, the amygdala's capacity to shut down his cognitive abilities to think rationally and process complexity or subtlety is important, cruel, and ironic. Under the influence of that strong amygdala-generated negative emotion, his failure to grasp your explanation of complex concepts or nuanced reasoning is neither willful nor unintelligent. He is not being disingenuous when he fails to acknowledge his lawyer's point. He is not ignoring reason—he cannot process it.

At that point, where client emotions are strong, the lawyer must stop explaining, stop reasoning: stop talking like a lawyer. Instead, the lawyer must consider how to address and calm his client's emotion, or simply allow time for his client to regain balance. Later sections of this chapter provide some guidance for addressing and calming emotion triggered by the client's legal problem.

An Upside to Anger

Professors Jennifer Lerner and Larissa Tiedens of Stanford University have summarized research showing that while angry people may approach a problem with negative thoughts about others, their anger may also bolster their confidence and sense of control.[30] Consider how many times you have thought or said words to the effect: "*Dammit that makes me mad – they make me mad! Let's just go ahead and do it!*" (Whatever "it" is). Anger's value is in diminishing indecision, risk aversion, and avoidance by overanalysis. On the other hand, anger also makes us more susceptible to the psychological traps of overconfidence and foolish risk-taking, aggression and escalation (as discussed further in Chapter 5 on psychology).

Clusters and Meta-Emotions

When an event or interaction triggers a negative emotional state, more than one emotion is often in play. Assume my professional colleagues unanimously and unkindly reject my draft language and design for a marketing brochure, with little discussion of its merits. I might feel frustrated and angry, or disappointed, sad, and embarrassed. When something great happens, I might feel proud and joyful, or touched, wistful, and delighted—all at the same time. These emotions come in clusters.

We may see some order in that chaotic emotional cluster—a hierarchy that includes meta-emotions—emotions about underlying emotions.[31] I might feel angry and frustrated about rejection of my brochure, but also guilty, embarrassed, or a little silly at having taken the professional rejection so personally. If I feel a surge of pride and joy in my son's freshman year success, I may also feel embarrassment at being so invested in his performance. A parent might feel tremendous anger at his child's wrongdoing, and also experience the meta-emotion of guilt at his own anger. Once you start looking for it, a layer of meta-emotion is easy to recognize, in yourself or your client.

The Identity Kicker: Threats, Quakes, and Value Packages

When people experience very, very strong emotions, I propose an "identity kicker" as the likely suspect. I may feel frustrated if I am unable to learn to ice skate backwards, when others in the skating class are able to master it. But being athletically talented (at all), much less an ice skater, is not part of my identity. My frustration will not be strong and will dissipate quickly. But, if I learn that a book proposal has been rejected (albeit with a nice rejection letter) and being an author is part of my identity, I will feel VERY frustrated, angry, dejected, or despondent, and perhaps embarrassed by my response. After all, a professional should be able to take this in stride; she would maintain confidence in the merits of her book proposal. So, the rejection itself, and then my reaction, will trigger issues of identity, perhaps a full crisis in self-confidence or an "identity quake."[32] Maybe I should have gone to medical school instead!

Within a legal dispute, when your client is accused of gender discrimination by a terminated employee, he may be indignant, angry, fearful, or hurt: *How dare she or anyone else tell me who I can and cannot terminate? How dare she accuse me of such a twisted motive? How could she sue me for millions when she knows this could destroy everything I've built?* His meta-emotion may be guilt at his anger or embarrassment at his fear or hurt feelings. Often, that meta-emotion relates to identity. Your client may be angry with himself about feeling upset, thinking that a real executive would not let this get to him. If his identity is wrapped up in the persona of the impervious executive, this emotion will be strong.

The Value of Positive Emotions

Not all clients and lawyers can be happy, and no one can be happy all of the time. Yet, a lawyer will better serve her client when their interaction is as emotionally positive as possible. Why? Consider author Daniel Goleman's reflection on a body of research linking laughter with cognitive performance:

> Laughing, like elation, seems to help people think more broadly and associate more freely, noticing relationships that might have eluded them otherwise, a mental skill important not just in creativity but in recognizing complex relationships and foreseeing the consequences of a given decision. The intellectual benefits of a good laugh are most striking when it comes to solving a problem that demands a creative solution.[33]

Quite simply: positive emotions enhance cognitive skills, focus, patience, and creativity for clients and lawyers; negative emotions have the opposite effect.[34] The body of research establishing the power of positive emotion is growing, but here are some notable examples:

- People shown a short film of bloopers were over three times more likely to then solve a puzzle used to test creativity than were people shown a short math film. The researchers confirmed this result in a subsequent study where blooper-watchers were more than five times as likely to solve the puzzle as were math-watchers.[35]

- Internist participants were asked to diagnose a patient based solely on the patient's history and presenting symptoms. Some internists received a bag of candies as a token of appreciation before receiving the patient information. A control group did not receive candy. Those who received candy tended to be more flexible in their reasoning process and to more quickly diagnose the patient correctly than those who did not receive candy.[36]

- Participants shown *New Yorker* cartoons prior to a negotiation were less contentious in the negotiation, revealed more valuable information, and were more likely to achieve high outcomes.[37] Researchers theorize that "[w]hen negotiators display positive affect, they signal that they are trustworthy and are ready to cooperate—a signal that should lead other parties to trust them more. The increased trust should then trigger communication of interests and priorities, and to the discovery of compatible and tradable issues, giving negotiators more opportunities to expand the resource pie."[38]

- Researchers instructed some buyers in simulated interest-based negotiations to mimic sellers' mannerisms (face touching, foot tapping, etc.) on the theory that mimicry or mirroring creates feelings of social rapport and thus positive emotion. Buyers who mimicked were more likely to reach a mutually-beneficial deal than were members of the control group who did not mimic.[39] (See chapter 7 on the social power of mirroring.)

- Negative emotion has the opposite power to impair cognition. In a University of Michigan study, when a group of math test-takers were told that the test usually produces gender differences, women's test scores dropped (more than half) and men's increased by 33 percent.[40] When the test was administered without conveying this (false) information to test-takers, NO gender differences occurred in test results.[41] Another found that asking test-takers about their race before a test of verbal ability caused African-American students to perform 25 percent worse than when not asked.[42] And white students with high math proficiency performed worse on a math test when they were primed with a statement that Asian students consistently do better than white students on math tests and that their scores would be compared to Asian students' scores.[43] The reference to negative stereotypes may be understood to have negatively affected test-takers' emotions, and thus, performance.

The bottom line: a positive emotional state is important when clients will have to absorb complex information, consider their lawyer's advice, develop out-of-the-box options, or make difficult decisions.

From the Outside In

When affected by a dramatic negative event—loss of a job, death of a family member, failure on an important test—our negative emotions inevitably carry into our relationships and professional activities. Research indicates that even relatively trivial negative or positive experiences affect or "prime" our subsequent emotional states.

Thus, negative or positive emotions primed outside of a lawyer-client meeting affect the client's emotional state, as does the lawyer-client interaction at their meeting. A client may enter the lawyer's office feeling dejected and hopeless because her job search has been fruitless. Interaction with her lawyer may deepen those feelings, if the client feels frustrated and incompetent at her failure to grasp a legal concept. A different client may enter in a more neutral or positive state: company earnings are stable; his division is up; and his teenager's report card was good. Yet, the meeting itself may generate negative emotion if the lawyer seems arrogant and the client struggles to understand or make himself heard.

"Negative emotion" need not mean a strong or articulable negative state. According to Goleman, even mild mood changes can affect the way we think.[44] The impact may be more subtle: feeling vaguely uncomfortable, somewhat ill at ease, edgy. If I read of a recent tragedy and view the heart-wrenching picture, see disappointing program evaluations, or become involved in a minor conflict with my teenager, my emotion will be affected as I move to the next activity. If my supervisor initiates a telephone call while we are speaking—an act of disrespect—or her eyes wander off as I speak, I will experience negative emotion. Not tragic, not overwhelming, but negative. However, if I learn great news before entering or if, at the start of the meeting, my supervisor deliberately blocks incoming calls, listens attentively, and values my work, my emotional state will be more positive—even if the meeting was set to address a significant problem.

A lawyer should not aspire to turn a generally sad client into a generally happy one (except to the extent that transformation will occur by virtue of the lawyer's legal work). Nor should a lawyer decorate her office in balloons or start memorizing comedic one-liners. The latter portion of this chapter offers a strategy for lawyers seeking to generate more positive client emotions within lawyer-client conversations—by attending to the client's "core concerns." However, the research indicating that minor experiences can prime emotions in a measurable way underscores the importance of attending to small things, such as:

- Welcoming receptionist or administrative interaction
- Comfortable reception areas, with good magazines, music, etc.
- Other comforts: coffee, water, food (chocolate is good!)
- Validated parking or detailed advice if parking, directions, or traffic are likely to be tricky

Returns from an Unhappy Client?

"I've learned that people will forget what you said, people will forget what you did, but people will never forget how you made them feel."
—MAYA ANGELOU[45]

On a practical note for lawyers aspiring to repeat clients or referrals: it is reasonable to believe that, all things being equal, most people return to those toward whom they feel positively and avoid those toward whom they feel negatively.[46] Imagine that you are new to town and you ask your neighbor to recommend a pediatrician for your young children. She recommends a nearby pediatric group practice with a top reputation and admitting privileges to the best local hospital. Within a month, your son gets his first ear infection. You bring him in to the pediatric office for an appointment with anyone available. The doctor who sees you and your son is professional and thorough but he is also abrupt, uses medical jargon, and seems annoyed when you ask for translation. He asks exactly what time the fever started. You explain that you don't know; the child was with his grandparents over the weekend. He raises his eyebrows and asks, in a tone you interpret as disapproving: "How old are the grandparents and how long was your vacation?" Now here's an easy question: how likely are you to choose him as your child's regular pediatrician or refer him to your friends? Doesn't the same likelihood apply for a client who feels similarly after an interaction with his lawyer?

Toward Positive Without Punch Lines

"Empathy is full presence to what's alive in the other person at this moment."

—JOHN CUNNINGHAM[47]

By George, He's Got It!

Psychologists are trained to do it. Mediators are trained to do it. People in parenting classes are trained to do it. Counselors of all sorts (except perhaps lawyers) are trained to do it. What is it? Active listening and reflective dialogue: a continuum of ways to demonstrate and express attentiveness, understanding, and empathy.[48]

First, let's settle on what active listening and reflective dialogue look like and how they are practiced, even if a random group of mediators, psychologists, and counselors might not agree on precise definitions or descriptions. For the purposes of this book, I define active listening as "listening in a way that is fully attentive, fully present with the speaker, in a way that demonstrates that full attention."[49] Thus, at minimum, the active listener maintains eye contact, nods, and registers what is heard through her responsive facial expressions. The active listener may also paraphrase or concisely restate what she has heard.[50] Imagine that the speaker has described reaching a dead end on a project and a difficult but inescapable choice between options, driven by a deadline. When the speaker pauses, the active listener might restate or paraphrase by saying: "Sounds like you were forced to make a choice at that point."

Classic introductions to the active listener's restatement are: "So, I hear you saying that . . . "; "What I hear you saying is . . ."; and

"So, if I hear you correctly. . . ." After a time, these phrases can be as annoying as squeaky chalk on a black board and, in my view, are best omitted. However, the substance of the paraphrase seeks to clarify meaning and demonstrate attentiveness. If the speaker's intended message was not captured in the listener's paraphrase, the speaker can correct it. The effort demonstrates the listener's engagement and attentiveness to the speaker.

Empathetic listening may be thought of as similar to active listening, only more so—more attuned to and expressive of emotional content or meaning. Empathetic listening is characterized by reflective dialogue,[51] in which the listener-counselor goes beyond paraphrase to express the import, impact, or meaning behind the speaker's original statement. Where a client-speaker is highly emotional on recounting an event, evident from voice, tone, gesture, and language chosen, the lawyer-listener skilled at reflective dialogue would communicate that he "gets" that emotion. For example, a divorce client might say:

> Oh, I just don't know what I'm going to do. I know I can't make my soon-to-be ex give up this ridiculous new business idea. And I know that the judge isn't going to order him to pay all of his income to me and the kids, if he has any. But what am I going to do? I haven't worked in years. The mortgage is high. The kids are counting on me.

The lawyer skilled at reflective dialogue might say:

> That is scary. Your husband is going to take risk and leave you without a net. You can't stop him. You're very worried about your kids, and whether you'll be able to pay for what they need.

The lawyer's voice and tone might implicitly convey empathy, as he does indeed empathize with his client's fear and anxiety. Indeed, it would be difficult to say those words without feeling empathy.

But to expressly articulate empathy within the dialogue, the lawyer might also add:

> *I would be fearful too, and angry. It would make me want to shake him and say, "Wake up! This new plan of yours is a long shot and this is not the time. Your kids can't afford your mid-life crisis." And I understand why you'd have sleepless nights.*

"Getting It" Gets Emotionally Better

"Before you can inspire with emotion, you must be swamped with it yourself. Before you can move their tears, your own must flow. To convince them, you must yourself believe."

—WINSTON CHURCHILL[52]

"Anger as soon as fed is dead, 'tis starving makes it fat."

—EMILY DICKINSON[53]

Skeptical or not of the touchy-feely, a lawyer correctly disclaims any obligation, or any right, to become a client's therapist, psychologist, or guidance counselor. Yes, it's important to have enough "emotional synchrony" to establish rapport (see chapter 6), and to get the client's facts straight. Then why so much emphasis on listening, attentiveness, reflection, and empathy? Why do these fall within a chapter on emotion?

It's one thing to say that people cannot ignore or successfully suppress emotion. But surely, the lawyer is NOT wise to paraphrase, reflect, and empathize with an emotionally out-of-control client? Surely the lawyer's task is to move the client back to reason and reality. Assume, based upon earlier portions of this chapter, that the lawyer's task includes helping a client come to a more positive emotional state. Then, is it really wise to wallow in the client's negative emotional state—restating, reflecting, empathizing with the client's anger, fear, anxiety, disgust, embarrassment, etc.?

The answer is yes, the lawyer is well-advised to do so, just for a while. When we are highly emotionally charged, our emotions are calmed when someone gets what we are feeling, and why. Our listener doesn't necessarily have to share our circumstances, or even our world view, but he or she does have to register and accept what we feel as real and legitimate. After a number of years mediating gender discrimination and sexual harassment cases in a class action claims resolution process, a plaintiff's counsel explained to the mediator [in paraphrase]: "My clients like you because you get it. You don't always have to say they're going to win. But they know you get it. They feel that you understand what they went through and what it felt like. That really matters."[54]

Thus, the advice of mediators, psychologists, therapists, and all manner of other counselors is that we lawyers learn to use active listening and reflective dialogue and, where genuine, express empathetic understanding to our clients. It will help clients feel better and regain emotional balance, if not wander into positive emotional territory. And then, these clients should be better able to hear our reasoning.

Fundamental Strategic Advice

We'll next turn to the emotional core concerns model set forth by Professor Roger Fisher and Dr. Daniel Shapiro in *Beyond Reason*. The last portion of the chapter illustrates how each core concern might arise and be addressed in lawyer-client counseling.

A fundamental piece of advice informs all of it: *use the core concerns for targeted and strategic active listening, reflective dialogue, and empathetic expression.* In other words, when you see that a core concern is operative in the client's story, reflect *that* core concern when you restate, reflect, or empathize. This will immediately let the client feel that you *do* get it; you do understand why his emotions run strong and deep. You will not yet have solved the underlying problem, but you will have moved the client toward more positive emotions in your meeting.

The Core Concerns Model for Lawyer-Client Counseling

"Were we fully to understand the reasons for other people's behavior, it would all make sense."

—SIGMUND FREUD[55]

As a non-psychologist, without deep background on clients' emotional histories, what can a lawyer do to generate positive client emotions in the law office? When a lawyer meets with a client to review the status of his case, it is difficult enough to explain legal concepts. Must the lawyer also diagnose precisely when and whether a client is angry, depressed, frustrated, remorseful, hurt, upset, and which meta-emotions sit on top?

Moreover, emotions and emotional dynamics shift in the course of an interaction. What causes anger in one person might cause alienation in another and not much of a reaction in someone else. And different people express the same emotion in different ways.[56] Some people become quiet when angry, others explode. To accurately read emotional responses, the observer needs a baseline—familiarity with that person's responses in ordinary contexts. In practice, a lawyer is unlikely to be equipped to identify shifting emotions in real time or to measure them against a baseline.

The good news is that a lawyer can anticipate and influence his client's emotional state without micro-analysis of emotional shifts, personal history, or baseline effect. Fisher and Shapiro's "core concerns" model is directed toward recognizing and influencing emotion "as a lens and a lever" in negotiations. In the client-counseling context, their core concerns can also help lawyers see and influence the client's emotional map at two levels: in the client's underlying legal problem *and* in the lawyer-client interaction.[57] Before discussing their application to lawyer-client counseling, it's important to summarize the model.

The Five Core Concerns

Fisher and Shapiro posit that everyone has five core emotional needs or concerns. If these are not addressed, negative emotions will be triggered. However, affirmatively addressing these concerns will stimulate positive, helpful emotions. Fisher and Shapiro identify the five core concerns as:

1. Appreciation—One's experience of feeling heard, understood, and valued
2. Affiliation—One's sense of emotional or interpersonal connection with another
3. Autonomy—One's freedom to make decisions without imposition from others
4. Status—One's social or particular standing, often relative to another
5. Role—One's function or "job label"[58]

The text that follows offers somewhat more complete explanation and commentary on each of these core concerns, and some suggestions as to how a lawyer can address them in client counseling. Explanations are gratefully drawn from Fisher and Shapiro's work. The elaborations and examples are intended to place that work within lawyer-client counseling contexts.

Appreciation Calms the Conversation[59]

Appreciation—The experience of feeling heard, understood, and valued. Appreciation requires that you demonstrate respect for the speaker and his perspective by listening and then expressing your understanding and recognition of his point. You need not agree! However, dismissing or ignoring his perspective will not generate a feeling of appreciation. In this sense, when a listener "appreciates" a speaker, the synonym for appreciation is not gratitude for a gesture or gift, except perhaps gratitude for the speaker's act of communication.

A client may feel appreciated by his lawyer's simple, non-judgmental, active listening with a healthy dose of paraphrase. Fisher and Shapiro's advice for generating felt appreciation goes further, suggesting that you listen to understand the other's point of view, demonstrate your understanding, and find and articulate *some* merit in it. Again, you do NOT have to express agreement. You just have to express respect for it. Then, and not before then, you may express your own point of view.[60]

Imagine counseling a client regarding a tough negotiation stance on severance, or a possible legal action against his former employer. He says:

> *I had an opportunity to join an international consulting firm based in Tokyo two months before I was let go. If I had known that my company would be sold, and I would be let go, I would have bailed then, but I was too loyal. I think they should pay me for lost opportunity. This company's financial mess was their idiotic fault. The top brass could make risky decisions because their multi-millions were already in the bank.*

As the lawyer, assume that you know the client has little or no legal claim. The company hit hard financial times in the interim. The employee never told his superiors of the Tokyo opportunity and even if he had, it was his choice to take it or not. There is no indication of deception or reliance. Moreover, it's impossible to know how the "Tokyo opportunity" would have worked out. Nevertheless, you can express appreciation for his perspective by saying:

> It seems unfair that you were loyal to them, and they weren't equally loyal to you. Their financial decisions do appear to have been irresponsible. Sometimes it seems that people should be required to think and care about the fact that other people will suffer from their mistakes.

See if your client's shoulders don't relax a bit: you've got it!

Now, he will be more likely to listen when you explain that there is no such law and that he needs to focus on a decision that will best serve his interests.

Now, imagine a difficult conversation[61] with your client about payment of attorneys' fees. Your client has been offered $100,000 in settlement, which would entitle her to receive $66,666 under your contingency fee contract. After taxes, she would net approximately $45,000. Your client desperately needs $10,000 more than that to pay off outstanding debt. Still, you believe it would be better for your client to accept the offer than to take the risk of losing at trial. Imagine that your client (or a mediator) raises the possibility of your compromising the fee, given the efficiency of settling before trial. You and your law firm have expended enormous time on his case, fielding far too many phone calls, pouring effort into producing top quality briefs and preparing carefully for depositions. Even if you see it makes economic sense, you might *feel* angry or, at a minimum, "a bit ticked." Now imagine that your client says directly:

> I very much appreciate the top quality work and the quantity of time you and your associates poured into this case . . . and that these are what brought about this settlement offer.

You may or may not be willing to negotiate the fee, but you will likely *feel* better within the interaction.

Reversing roles in the same circumstance, you could "appreciate"—acknowledge and respect—your client's perspective by saying:

> *I understand that this is YOUR claim and your case, and you could have chosen any lawyer. I very much appreciate your selecting me to work with you. I also recognize that $33,000 seems like a large chunk, given that I didn't have to try the case to a jury.*

If you are watching, you will see your client visibly relax, perhaps nod her head. That may not change the fact that she would rather pay less than more, but you will have lightened the accompanying emotional response. She is more likely to listen now, when you explain the value of the time and risk you undertook.

A Look Underneath

Leaving aside lawyer-client interactions, it is worth considering how a perceived lack of appreciation has played a role in your client's underlying dispute. For example, in an employment context, employees laid off in a reduction-in-force, commonly known as an "RIF," are often angry because of their employer's failure to acknowledge their value to the company, and their continuing ability to contribute. Yes, people elect to sue, or at least seek legal advice, because they may genuinely believe their employer discriminated on the basis of gender, age or race in designating employee terminations in the RIF. It is also true that financial loss and insecurity following termination might be more than sufficient to inspire legal action. Emotions in such cases often run very, very high due to the employer's perceived lack of appreciation for the employee's work. This can cause deep feelings of anger, hurt, or humiliation—yielding a highly emotional, not entirely rational client.

Recognizing that lack of appreciation triggers negative emotional responses, the lawyer might defuse client emotion by acknowledging what the employer failed to acknowledge. Assume that in an initial interview, the client has told the lawyer of his selection for the RIF, the pink slip, and being sent to the HR office. The lawyer could articulate *her* recognition that the company violated her client's core concern for appreciation, by saying:

> *You clearly dedicated fifteen years of your time and talent to fulfilling the company's mission. They could at least have expressed appreciation for your work.*

Assuming the employee-client is rankled by the company's choice to retain a different employee in his department, the lawyer might acknowledge that by saying:

> *I see that with your demonstrated loyalty and knowledge of the history of the company, you were the keeper of the institutional memory of what had and hadn't worked over the years. I can see that, if they had kept you instead of the one with a more advanced engineering degree, you could have prevented them from going down blind alleys, making the same mistakes twice.*

The lawyer obviously cannot undo the termination, nor should the lawyer offer an apology for the other side. However, acknowledging and respecting a client's anger at lack of appreciation in the underlying dispute context may work to reduce the client's emotional temperature, as the lawyer reviews the status of the case and options going forward.

To enhance the likelihood of successful settlement negotiations, a lawyer for either side, or a mediator, could be similarly attuned to the appreciation issue. The lawyer or mediator might suggest an expression of appreciation for the strengths the employee brought to the organization, for his contribution to the corporate mission, and respect for his point of view on the termination question. Then, and only then, reasons for the RIF decisions may be proffered.

Autonomy

Autonomy is another of the core emotional concerns[62] and, I believe, is often the culprit in lawyer-client tensions. Fischer and Shapiro define autonomy as "the freedom to make decisions without imposition from others." As anyone dealing with a corporate executive (or a teenager) will readily testify, impinged autonomy can lead to strong resentment, anger, and frustration—negative emotions in one form or another. The degree and nature of the emotional response will inevitably vary by a person's expectations or normal degree of autonomy. A high-level corporate executive unaccustomed to constraints and more comfortable issuing orders than obeying them may have a strong emotional response to the threat of injunction—the legal system's removal of autonomy. A mid-level employee would of course recognize a threatened injunction as bad for business, but might be better able to rationally analyze its consequences and likelihood. Professional power is not the only predictor. Generally, adults expect and enjoy some level of autonomy and chafe at being "treated like a child," or deprived of autonomy. At the risk of venturing too deeply into pop psychology, it is not hard to see that as a teenager's identity is tied up in being recognized as adult, even minor challenges to his autonomy may evoke strong emotional responses.

Lawyers should be mindful that much about the legal system itself constrains client autonomy. Litigation presents a rigid set of rules and timetables to which the client must submit. Discretion in the operation of those rules and timetables rests with the court. Variance requires special request and is not always granted. The lawyer must convey the court's order to search through three years of documents, without regard for a business' low manpower and seasonal rush. The lawyer must counsel disclosure of corporate exposure in public filings, without regard for its impact on stock value and bonuses. The judge passes judgment on motions; the judge or the clerk determines placement on the docket. Viewed from this perspective, litigation is an exercise in the surrender of autonomy, even if your client initiated the suit. So much more so for the defendant, who did not choose litigation but is compelled to follow its rules.

The transactional arena presents its share of challenges to autonomy, too. Lawyers advise that certain contemplated terms violate anti-trust laws or public policy and cannot be included. One side to the transaction may enjoy greater power and demand certain provisions. The client must agree to the demand or step away from the transaction, an untenable choice for his business. Transactional free will often exists only in the abstract, not in reality.

Once again, the attuned lawyer is wise to scrutinize her interactions with the client and the underlying circumstance using the autonomy lens. To what extent have you laid down legal rules and requirements that conflict with the client's priorities? Have you presented legal constraints that the client would experience as impinging on his or her company's autonomy? Look back to the underlying dispute or transaction: to what extent did it present conflicts over autonomy? Imagine a family business dispute in which the older son challenged his father's decision not to invest in plant improvements, but rather to draw cash bonuses. Consider the employee instructed to leave her work team for an important R&D project to help with software troubleshooting. Try to identify with the developer working with a town committee insistent on drawing the boundary lines for green space, dwellings, and commercial structures before approving a zoning variance. Anticipate and understand that any of these challenges to autonomy will generate negative emotions for most. This will be true, apart from or layered over responses to the merits or consequences of the intended action.

We're back to the question: what's a lawyer to do? I suggest three strategies, each directed at the context in which client autonomy has been challenged. First, when listening to the client's narrative, you might choose to acknowledge explicitly that the client's autonomy was constrained, and that it was perhaps unusual and uncomfortable. You need not use these words. But do use the fundamental strategy of active listening and reflective dialogue *targeted to the autonomy concern.*

For example, when a client recounts his son's attempt to challenge his bonus vs. investment decision, the lawyer might say: "Hmm . . . . Had your son ever tried to reverse you before? Given that you own the company, his bucking your decision must have been hard to take." If autonomy is indeed the source of conflict (or one among many), he will agree that his son's second-guessing angered him. He may then elaborate in one emotional direction or another: on lack of appreciation for his prior sacrifice, on failure to respect his status, or on other ways the son has sought to challenge his authority. If you listen and express understanding over his response to these challenges, your client will trust that you "get it." Your reflective comments may calm him and encourage some self-reflection.

The lawyer should employ the same strategy regarding lawyer-to-client instruction or advice. Thus, when you must communicate regarding your client's legal obligation to produce documents or the need to adjust a deal structure, you could directly acknowledge the autonomy constraint. For example, imagine a court's order to search through and produce a large volume of documents and provide answers to interrogatories just before Christmas, the client's busiest season. A request for extension of time and reduction in scope has been denied. You might say to your client:

I understand that this is your business and that your good decisions about the product and the market have grown it to this point. It seems crazy that some judge can tell you what to do, forcing you to take key employees away from the phones to chase a bunch of documents. What chutzpah! It must make you mad to think the judge or the other side can order you around.

Once again, lawyers can't change the fact that compliance is necessary. But acknowledging the level and source of frustration can reduce the emotional heat.[63]

To address autonomy concerns in negotiation, Fisher and Shapiro dispense the classic advice: ACBD—Always Consult Before Deciding, while noting the risk that one may NGAD—Never Get Anything Done.[64] Model Rule of Professional Conduct 1.2(a)[65] codifies and strengthens ACBD, giving ultimate authority to the client for key decisions in a legal matter.

A third strategy for meeting the client's emotional autonomy concerns suggests ACBD regarding even minor decisions and interactions. In practice, lawyers sometimes make "inconsequential" or "normal" moves without client knowledge or permission. For example, a lawyer may casually raise the question of settlement with opposing counsel or agree to an extension of time for filing a brief as a professional courtesy. Where the core concern of autonomy is salient for a particular client, it's wise to err on the side of consulting with your client, even on the smallest of details, unless and until your client tells you it's unnecessary.

So, before you agree to opposing counsel's reasonable request for an extension of time, check with your client. Of course, you will explain that failure to agree will lead to a hearing and attendant costs, the judge's granting the request, and possibly the judge's negative impression of your uncooperativeness. Before you go to the deposition, explain to your client that it's not unusual to raise the possibility of settlement, particularly after the principal witnesses have been deposed. Ask if she would be comfortable with your exploring the other party's interest in settlement. Ask whether she would like you to raise it when you see opposing counsel in court, the next day by letter, or by e-mail today. Ask how she would like you to respond if opposing counsel raises the question with you.

If opposing counsel DID raise the idea of settlement (before you discussed this possibility), be sure to report to your client that "opposing counsel raised the idea of settlement and so I must discuss it with you," instead of saying "opposing counsel and I discussed settlement." Both reports are accurate, but the former makes clear that you did not broach the subject without authorization and emphasizes the client's authority.

You can also offer your client some autonomy at the micro-conversational level, in subtle ways, from the start of your next meeting. Consider a deliberate "agenda stage," after any chit-chat, when conversation turns to the subject at hand. In general, experience establishes that lawyers are wise to informally articulate a meeting agenda, as evidence of preparation and professionalism. (The agenda need not be written, if topics are simple and not too numerous.) Most clients happily interpret an articulated agenda to mean the lawyer views the meeting as important. However, for a client whose autonomy needs are high and who is chafed by legal process rules, you might opt to inject client autonomy at this stage. Thus, rather than leading with the agenda, you might say: "I've obviously come with several topics that we need to discuss, but it's important to hear what you have in mind, and then tackle them in the order you choose."

Ceding authority to determine the order is such a small move, but it fosters greater feelings of autonomy. The client is free to obtain information and advice from her lawyer in the order she chooses. Obviously, if one topic bears logically upon another, the lawyer might say:

> I'd be happy to proceed in the order you suggested, but I think that you'll want to know something about [issue B] before you make a decision on [issue A]. We could defer the decision on [A] until we reach [issue B]; what do you think?

You can also offer the client a choice in the level of detail you provide, by saying:

> This meeting could take 15 minutes or it could take much longer, depending on how much of my analysis you want to hear about

the issues on summary judgment. I'm happy to walk through
these issues with you with some care or just to give you my bot-
tom-line predictions and leave it at that. Or, I can give you the
shorthand version, and you ask me questions on particular con-
clusions you find troubling or annoying. How would you like to
proceed?

Your client will feel some autonomy by the invitation to direct your
discussion. There is no cure for the client's real lack of autonomy to
determine the litigation or transactional outcome. However, a high
measure of autonomy in the conversation may compensate, and
bring down the emotional temperature.

Affiliation

Fisher and Shapiro name affiliation—a feeling of interpersonal connection with another—as a core emotional concern, even at the professional level.[66] Imagine that you are talking with a colleague about
your tension and lack of sleep over an upcoming presentation. His
response is cold, unmoved, and unaffected. Or, you are representing
your company in joint venture negotiations. Your counterpart attorney is brusque and expressionless, even during meals and breaks.
He engages in no chatter, just looks away and consults e-mail whenever there is a down moment. You try to strike up a conversation.
He displays no interest. Your core concern for affiliation is unmet,
and you are likely to experience negative emotions as a result.

Fisher and Shapiro note that feelings of affiliation can be generated by structural connections: as classmates, clients, family members.[67] These connections provide sources of commonality and
familiarity, creating the basis for relationship. For some, finding
commonality is extremely important. I once witnessed a conversation between two scholars, one quite senior, and the other much
younger. While greatly respecting the senior scholar's contribution

to the field, the more junior had challenged some of his ideas. The senior scholar relished the intellectual engagement. Still, both men were observably guarded. When talk turned to personal histories, it was discovered that both had attended the same suburban high school, some 25 years apart. In an instant, this affiliation changed the entire chemistry of the discussion. The senior scholar was utterly delighted. In the language of this chapter, he clearly experienced an onslaught of positive emotions. The nature and depth of the conversation shifted as well, leading to a long friendship and years of candid, thoughtful, and enjoyable intellectual exchange.

At the risk of trivializing the work of the great philosopher Martin Buber, I suggest that his contrast between "I-Thou" and "I-It" explains the distance between affiliation and its lack.[68] In an I-Thou relationship, the other—thou—is understood, appreciated, and related to as a whole being, just as one's self. The relation is mutual. However, in an I-It relationship, I relate to the other—it—as an object, of concern only in its usefulness or difficulties for me. In the transactional context, the I-It negotiators regard each other solely as means to achieving a favorable deal. In the lawyer-client context, the I-It client is a source of revenue, or not. In litigation, the witness on deposition may be seen as the "it," who may or may not help your case. There is no mutual "whole being" relationship. We understandably experience negative emotions when we sense only objectification by another. In other words, we do not enjoy being used or exploited as a means to someone else's end.

Chit-Chat and Bric-A-Brac

Initiating chit-chat regarding areas of personal connection or commonality with your client is wise and easy. If you know of a common interest, highlight or ask about it. If a client came to you by way of recommendation from a law school classmate, ask how he knows him. If your classmate's and the client's sons play basketball together, you could ask about the team's season or mention your junior high

basketball travails. Or you might connect on the challenges of raising teenagers. In other words, spend a moment thinking about what
you and your client have in common. Are you both East Coast trans-
plants to the Midwest? You might reference that in conversation,
perhaps to explain why Midwest-based opposing counsel is reluc-
tant to risk an innovative or "new fangled" deal structure. When
a friend or colleague informs you of a client referral, it is worth
asking about the client's background, neighborhood, or role in the
community.

Of course, there's no harm in a quick Google search to obtain
information about favorite charities, political or religious activities,
sporting accomplishments, or other hobbies. The client may have
reached the quarterfinals in an amateur tennis league; she may have
contributed to NPR and the Nature Conservancy, or serve on the
Junior League and Children's Hospital Auction boards. If you are an
enthusiastic tennis player, or your daughter is an intern at Children's
Hospital, you have immediate areas of connection.

One natural way to find affiliation is to become a keen observer
of your client's belongings—briefcase, jewelry, picture frames. Take
note if your client comes in wearing a lapel pin or brooch that is
a cultural symbol. Watch for team sports insignias on canvas
briefcases and other bags; notice college rings, men's ties, women's
scarves. If you meet in your client's office, DO take the opportunity
to look for family pictures, trophies, photographs, or paintings
reflecting your client's hobbies and passions. You may see sheet
music on the side desk or an opera-themed poster on the wall;
perhaps you too sing, play, or enjoy classical music. Your interest
and expression of commonality will create natural feelings of
affiliation.

At this point, the skeptical reader might observe that such affilia-
tions are superficial. True, initially. But that little bit of found commonality or connection at the beginning makes us feel more
comfortable. That comfort facilitates greater ease in conversation,
creating rapport and, eventually, a stronger lawyer-client relationship.

It enables the client to trust that the lawyer's interest in providing assistance is genuine, not merely mercenary.

What if your client is a punk-rocker and you majored in classics? You can't imagine expressing admiration for her amazing (read frightening) tattoo with a straight face. It would be disingenuous, foolish, and undoubtedly unsuccessful to fabricate commonality. With or without any common background, most important is to cultivate and express *genuine* interest in your client's circumstance. You might ask how she first started in music or whether her band has a local gig.

Affiliation may be generated through your lawyer-client interaction. Observe and show concern for your client's reactions to the reality of uncertainties in litigation or negotiation. You might acknowledge the difficulty of making a decision when these uncertainties may determine the fate of his business. Commiserate: it's hard to make decisions when the future is unpredictable. When your client explains the way his co-venturer deceived him in the negotiations to structure the joint venture, you might note that you too were once deceived by a former partner (assuming it's true) and express empathy for that hollow feeling of betrayal.

Listen for Affiliation Breaches under All

Often, your client will feel strong emotion about her underlying legal problem or dispute because it involves lack or breach of affiliation. When a patient perceives her surgeon as cold and unfeeling, as having made no effort at a connected relationship or to express apology or regret, she is more likely to take legal action.[69] Family business disputes obviously involve breached affiliation, whether or not suit has been filed. In any employment termination or demotion case, emotions run high. But they run higher when the employee and the decision maker were "like family," sharing family cookouts, birthdays, and weddings before termination or demotion.

As you learn underlying facts, be mindful of where affiliation might have been expected and where it has been withheld or breached. If you think the core concern of affiliation is fueling your client's high emotions, be particularly attentive to affiliation within your interaction. In other words, spend a bit more effort on chit-chat and finding commonality than you might otherwise. And, when your client speaks of what happened, do articulate your understanding of your client's discomfort with the cold or severed relationship.

Status

Fisher and Shapiro write of generally recognized social status and particular status.[70] While some of us are more generally status-conscious than others, no one *enjoys* being made aware that he is viewed as lesser. One who has studied and worked to achieve particular status in a profession or vocation naturally chafes when status and expertise are ignored or dismissed.

Again, the strength of negative emotion from unmet status concerns depends upon expectations. An accomplished adult does not want to be spoken to like a first-grade child; a senator may not take kindly to a clerk's brusque manner in a department store; a socialite may bristle when her golf caddy is not deferential. Yet, the first-grade child, the frequent shopper, or the casual golfer is likely to be unfazed by similar treatment. People acquire social status expectations and experience negative emotions (typically anger) when they perceive treatment that is not up to par.

In General, Offer Equal and Higher Status

When someone of apparently lower general social status is treated with great respect by one of higher social status, powerful positive emotion and a lasting impression may be generated. Radio reporting on the passing of the late Senator Edward Kennedy was filled with story after story by grieving citizens testifying to his habit of manifesting respect and equality. They expressed love for the way the late senator spoke to them as equals, no matter how "lowly" the citizen's social station, education, income level, and speech pattern. In the lingo of this book, the senator's willingness to make people feel equal status inspired strong positive emotions and abiding loyalty.

Is it too obvious to suggest that a lawyer MUST accord ANY client respect in manner and tone at least consistent with equal status? To do otherwise will be to risk client anger, frustration, or alienation— all negative emotions. Some clients, perceiving their own social status as much lower than their lawyer's, will not expect this. Thus, a "street kid" or day laborer meeting with his lawyer may not be particularly angered or upset if the lawyer seems to be talking down. It was anticipated. However, these clients will feel so positively about the lawyer who elevates their status within the conversation.

Sometimes, the lawyer is the lowly one. Your client may be a corporate CEO, a university president, or other who perceives himself to be of higher status. In French, the verb *tutoyer* refers to using the less formal *tu* rather than more formal *vous* for the pronoun meaning "you." One does not *tutoyer* unless invited, particularly with one of higher social status. Translated to high-status English speaking clients, refrain from casual or familiar language or manner unless and until invited to do so by your client. Continue to address your client as Mr., Ms., Dr., or Professor, followed by a surname. While some chit-chat is still helpful to establish connection, be careful to stay within social boundaries.

This is not to say that a lawyer must be the obsequious servant to the high-social status client. After all, the client who seeks the lawyer's legal advice implicitly recognizes the lawyer's particular status—her legal expertise. However, when a client's higher social status is important to him, the lawyer is wise to recognize it. Predictably, failure to treat one with the deference he believes to be due will generate negative emotions. Bottom line: it's not worth fighting your client over general status issues.

Elevate Expertise and Experience as Status

My friend and neighbor is a physician. I am certain she does not consider her general social status to be higher than the rest of ours. However, imagine a neighborhood gathering at which the conversation turns to the season's flu virus, vaccination, contagion, prevention, and treatment issues. She would be understandably angered, indignant, or insulted if we did not seek her opinion and accord it some respect. She has particular medical expertise that merits recognition. In a legal context, your partner whose practice specializes in wage and hour law cases will experience negative emotions if you dismiss his opinion on such issues. Your electrician client will feel marginalized or angry (or both) if you dismiss his explanation of why the electrical system caught fire.

Highlighting *particular* status of experience or expertise can reduce or eliminate discomfort due to lower general status. Imagine that your client is that same electrician, with little formal education, unfamiliar with the legal system and apparently ill at ease in the formal law office setting. He seems painfully aware of lower social, education, or income status. The lawyer might ask the client about his work, about his progression from apprentice to master electrician. The lawyer might comment that he "could never get those electrical circuits to go in science class," or recount a mishap that proved "wiring is no job for an amateur." When the lawyer expresses admiration and respect for the difficulty of the client's particular expertise, the client's status is raised, generating more positive emotions.

Word to the Wise on Working with Work

To a mediator of innumerable employment cases, it's clear that clients who are "involuntarily unemployed," whether through termination or reduction in force, keenly experience lowered status. Employment is often an enormous part of our felt status. As the conversation inevitably focuses on the circumstances of the termination and difficulties in finding new employment, feelings of lower status deepen. The lawyer or mediator first met the client as someone who was terminated, not as a productive, competent, employed adult. Even if the lawyer or mediator would relate no differently to someone employed, the client may feel uncomfortable being known only as someone who was terminated. This engenders feelings of low status.

Given these endemic status concerns, lawyers working with an involuntarily unemployed or demoted client should initiate conversation about the client's positive work experience. When the client describes his education or training, followed by good work placements, or a period of success at the current job, the lawyer should express appropriate interest in and admiration for the challenges of that work. Be curious about the industry, about the client's role in the development of a product at a former job, even if irrelevant to the case at hand. As the client speaks of the substance of his earlier work, he re-inhabits that earlier, higher status self. Within the conversation, he becomes not just another "terminated unemployed person" but a normally productive and competent adult with a particular legal problem. He will feel higher status and more emotionally positive.

Check for Status Issues in the Underlying Case

Once again, the core concern of status may be salient in the underlying legal dispute or transaction at hand. The lawyer who understands this and communicates his understanding will strengthen the lawyer-client relationship. Imagine that your client is a university professor and department chair who recommended against tenure for a departmental faculty member. The department's vote on the tenure issue was close. Your client reviewed the faculty member's entire scholarship and laboratory work and found them lacking. Your client recounts how a tenured but junior faculty member sought a confidential meeting for reconsideration of the negative recommendation. This was against all protocol. Your client refused to meet. His recommendation went up. The provost asked your client for an additional written explanation. Ultimately, tenure was denied, and suit was filed, accusing your client and others on the committee of religious and gender discrimination.

As your client recounts the story, you might hear a status issue.

As department chair and senior faculty, his status was slighted by the junior faculty member's challenge. His particular status was also disregarded, as the research and scholarship were directly in his field. Strategic active listening is recommended here. The lawyer might comment:

> *What audacity for your junior to suggest you hadn't heavily weighed and considered all of the factors. Didn't they recognize that, as chair and senior member, you are well aware of your responsibilities? I can understand your being insulted.*

Or, as the client explains that his own chemistry research and the candidate's overlapped, the lawyer might say:

> *It must have been frustrating when the provost—who I assume has never gone near a chemistry lab—forced you to spend yet more of your time justifying your evaluation of the science.*

Hearing his lawyer articulate the status concern, the client feels that the lawyer really DOES understand the problem.

Role

The final core concern raised by Fisher and Shapiro in *Beyond Reason* is that of role.[71] One might think of role as a function label or associated set of activities. Not to be confused with general or particular status, role refers to the part one plays in an interaction, relationship, or context. Everyone wants to believe that she has a meaningful role in joint or collective tasks; no one wants to feel superfluous.

When a lawyer meets with his client to explain legal circumstances and discuss options and decisions, some clients are apt to feel lack of a meaningful role. Even if the client technically makes the ultimate decision, she may feel powerless or passive as the lawyer reviews the legal issues. The more passive, the less of a role, and perhaps the more withdrawn, unengaged, and negative.

One way to address the role concern is to emphasize the client's power at the beginning of the session, and to offer input or control regarding certain aspects of the discussion addressed. The lawyer might ask the client to raise details about the personalities and work habits of potential witnesses whom she knows best. In short, before meeting with your client, consider ways to enhance her role within the interaction. It is particularly important where your client felt lack of meaningful role in the circumstances that brought her to your office.

Core Concerns and the Identity Kicker

As suggested earlier, very strong emotions arise with an "identity kicker."[72] Applying the core concerns model: when one's identity is highly linked to a particular core concern that is unmet or violated, anticipate a STRONG emotional reaction. For example, if being "the [autonomous] boss" is an important part of your client's identity, her anger at challenge to autonomy will likely be stronger than that of someone who doesn't see herself that way. If your guidance counselor client identifies himself as someone who forges strong interpersonal relationships, a perceived attack on affiliation will lead to high emotion.

When working with clients, the good news is that everyone has multiple self-identities or value-packages. A corporate CEO may resist compliance with a demand that seems to challenge a core autonomy concern—linked to his identity as boss. If so, his lawyer is advised to reframe compliance by raising a different identity or value set. The lawyer might suggest: "I know you are someone who would never cheat, who plays by the rules." Or the lawyer might raise the salience of status by suggesting:

> While the demand does seem unnecessary or petty, surely a company of the stature of yours wouldn't want to be seen fighting about this. Saying yes might just give you the upper hand, or at least the moral high ground.

Summary

Emotions matter. They affect interactions, relationships, cognitive processing, creativity, energy, patience, and decision-making. Human beings cannot just turn their emotions off or set them aside. As lawyers, ignoring or denying emotions in ourselves or our clients is unwise. Generally, more positive emotional states lead to better decision-making, through enhanced cognition, creativity, energy, and patience. Positive emotions—the client's good feelings when speaking with her lawyer—also foster trust, rapport, and loyalty.

Fisher and Shapiro's core concerns model offers a practical heuristic, a lens for scanning the emotional map of the client's underlying legal problem as well as the lawyer-client interaction itself. The core concerns facilitate insight into what might cause a client's high emotions. If the dispute in a client's family business is likely to challenge autonomy and status concerns, the lawyer should attend to these. When actively listening to that client speak, the lawyer should demonstrate understanding of what makes him angry. The lawyer can also find ways to offer "micro" autonomy—suggesting that the client set the initial agenda. The lawyer can acknowledge the client's status by noting the success of his business venture, congratulating him on election to the presidency of his professional organization, or conversing about his particular technical expertise. Of course, recognizing the core concerns enables the lawyer not only to compensate for the negative, but also to generate positive emotion when interacting with any client.

Lawyers cannot cure all of their clients' worries or ills. But lawyers can seek to foster positive emotions in lawyer-client meetings, and thereby build rapport, communicate complexity, and facilitate wise client decisions.

Notes

1. "Karla McLaren Quote" Wisdom Quotes, http://www.wisdom-quotes.com/quote/karla-mclaren.html (accessed May 26, 2011).

2. For a discussion of the privileged status of analytical intelligence in law study and practice and an argument that this privileging is appropriate, see Marjorie Silver, "Emotional Intelligence and Legal Education," *Psychology, Public Policy & Law* 5, no. 4 (1999): 1173–1203.

3. Roger Fisher and Daniel Shapiro were among the first in popular negotiation literature to strongly assert that, even in a professional context, one must work with emotions (rather than attempt to blot them out), in their book *Beyond Reason: Using Emotions as You Negotiate* (New York: Viking, 2005).

For those interested in further reading on emotion, the "Works Consulted" section at pages 213–230 of *Beyond Reason* contains terrifically helpful, accessible, and erudite descriptions of books and articles focused on emotion-related topics.

4. Fisher and Shapiro, *Beyond Reason: Using Emotions as You Negotiate*.

5. I am indebted to Dr. Shapiro for his collaboration on the program "Counseling and Convincing Difficult and Emotional Clients," which was offered as Continuing Legal Education through the University of Cincinnati College of Law's Center for Practice in Negotiation and Problem Solving in 2004–2005.

6. *Oxford English Dictionary*, 3rd ed., s.v. "emotion."

7. Daniel Goleman, *Emotional Intelligence: Why It Can Matter More than IQ.* (New York: Bantam Books, 1995), 289.

8. Ibid., 6.

9. Ibid., 289–291.

10. Goleman gets credit for this link to Darwin. Ibid., at 7.

11. Paul Ekman, "Expression and the Nature of Emotion," in *Approaches to Emotion*, ed. Klaus R. Scherer and Paul Ekman (Hillsdale, NJ: Lawrence Ehrlbaum Associates, 1984): 319–343. For a summary of this evidence, see Hillary Anger Elfenbein and Nalini Ambady, "On the Universality and Cultural Specificity of Emotion Recognition: A Meta-Analysis," *Psychological Bulletin* 128, no. 2 (2002): 203–235. Further evidence for the universality of emotional expression comes from David Matsumoto and Bob Willingham's study finding no significant differences between the facial expressions of sighted, congenitally blind, and noncongenitally blind Olympic and Paraolympic medal-winners. "Spontaneous Facial Expressions of Emotion of Congenitally and Noncongenitally Blind Individuals," *Journal of Personality and Social Psychology* 96, no. 1 (2009): 1–10. However, Matsumoto and Willingham, and many other researchers who favor an evolutionary explanation, also note the influence of cultural "dialects" on expression and interpretation of emotional expression. Ibid., 9; Hillary Anger Elfenbein, Martin Beaupré, Manon Lévesque, and Ursula Hess, "Toward a Dialect Theory: Cultural Differences in the Expression and Recognition of Posed Facial Expressions," *Emotion* 7, no. 1 (2007): 131–146.

12. James J. Gross, Jane M. Richards, and Oliver P. John describe research showing that efforts to suppress emotion impair cognitive processing. The authors theorize that suppression uses cognitive resources that could be used more productively. "Emotion Regulation in Everyday Life," in *Emotion Regulation in Families: Pathways to Dysfunction and Health*, ed. D. K. Snyder, J. A. Simpson, and J. N. Hughes (Washington, D.C.: American Psychological Association, 2006), http://www-psych.stanford.edu/~psyphy/pdfs/everyday.pdf (accessed March 26, 2010).

13. This is a summary and sometimes a paraphrase of Goleman's descriptions in *Emotional Intelligence*. Goleman acknowledges having drawn from various sources, including Robert W. Levenson, Paul Ekman, and Wallace V. Friesen, "Voluntary Facial Action Generates

Emotion-Specific Autonomic Nervous System Activity," *Psychophysiology* 27, no. 4 (1990): 363–384.

14. Rocco Dal Vera, "The Voice in Heightened Affective States," in *The Voice in Violence and Other Contemporary Issues in Professional Voice and Speech Training*, ed. Rocco Dal Vera (New York: Applause Books, 2001), 54.

15. This advice was also conveyed by Professor Dal Vera while teaching lawyers and law students in "Actor's Directions for Winning Trial Performance," offered through the University of Cincinnati College of Law's Center for Practice in 2009, 2010 and 2011.

16. Levenson, Ekman, and Friesen, "Voluntary Facial Action," 376. Another discussion of this experiment is found in Paul Ekman, "Expression and the Nature of Emotion," in *Approaches to Emotion*, 324–327.

17. Fritz Strack, Leonard L. Martin, and Sabine Stepper, "Inhibiting and Facilitating Conditions of the Human Smile: A Nonobtrusive Test of the Facial Feedback Hypothesis," *Journal of Personality and Social Psychology* 54, no. 5 (1988): 768.

18. "Lord Byron Quotes," ThinkExist, http://thinkexist.com/quotation/there_is_no_instinct_like_that_of_the_heart/146410.html (accessed May 26, 2011).

19. Malcolm Gladwell, *Blink: The Power of Thinking Without Thinking* (New York: Back Bay Books, 2005), 59–61. The original experiment is found in Antoine Bechara, Hanna Damasio, Daniel Tranel, and Antonio R. Damasio, "Deciding Advantageously Before Knowing the Advantageous Strategy," *Science* 275, no. 5304 (1997): 1293–1295.

20. Antoine Bechara, Daniel Tranel, and Hanna Damasio, "Characterization of the Decision-Making Deficit of Patients with Ventromedial Prefrontal Cortex Lesions," *Brain* 123, no. 11 (2000): 2189.

21. "Quote Details: Harriet Lerner," The Quotations Page, http://www.quotationspage.com/quote/1839.html (accessed June 3, 2011).

22. Sidney Callhan argues that "[e]motions energize the ethical quest. A person must be emotionally interested enough and care enough about discerning the truth to persevere despite distractions. Even more, a person who wrestles with moral questions is usually emotionally committed to doing good and avoiding evil. A good case can be made that what is specifically moral about moral thinking, what gives it its

imperative "oughtness," is personal emotional investment. When emotion infuses an evaluative judgment, it is transformed into a prescriptive moral judgment of what ought to be done." "The Role of Emotion in Ethical Decisionmaking," *The Hastings Center Report* 18, no. 3 (1988): 9.

23. Graham V. Goddard, "Functions of the Amygdala," Psychological Bulletin 62, no. 2 (1964). A comprehensive collection of articles regarding the amygdala is found in Paul J. Whalen and Elizabeth A. Phelps, eds., *The Human Amygdala* (New York: Guilford Press, 2009).

24. Robert S. Adler, Benson Rosen, and Elliot M. Silverstein, "Emotions in Negotiation: How to Manage Fear and Anger," *Negotiation Journal* 14 (1998): 161.

25. Goleman, *Emotional Intelligence*, 139.

26. Andrea Bodtker and Tricia Jones, "Mediating with Heart in Mind: Addressing Emotion in Mediation Practice," *Negotiation Journal* 17 (2001): 217; for further discussion of flooding, see Goleman, *Emotional Intelligence*, 138–141.

27. Horace, *Epistles (First Book of Letters)*, epistle 2, line 62.

28. "Confucius Quotes," Notable Quotes, http://www.notable-quotes.com/c/confucius_quotes.html (accessed May 25, 2011).

29. However, difficult decisions are less likely to be required when your client processes jubilation upon receipt of great news—*the judge ruled in your favor and this case is a slam-dunk winner.*

30. Jennifer S. Lerner and Larissa Z. Tiedens, "Portrait of the Angry Decision Maker: How Appraisal Tendencies Shape Anger's Influence on Cognition," *Journal of Behavioral Decision Making* 19, no. 2 (2006): 132 (Angry people "approach a situation with the tendency to feel confident, in control, and thinking the worse of others.").

31. Horst Mitmansgruber, et. al., "When you don't like what you feel: Experiential avoidance, mindfulness, and meta-emotion in emotional regulation," *Personality and Individual Differences* 46 (2009): 448–453; John M. Gottman, Lynn F. Katz, and Carole Hooven, *Meta-Emotions: How Families Communicate Emotionally* (Mahwah, NJ: Lawrence Erlbaum Associates, Inc., 1997).

32. Authors Stone, Patton, and Heen discuss the "Identity Conversation" and under the header "An Identity Quake Can Knock Us Off Balance," observe that sometimes a conversation seems to be saying something "about us that rips the ground from beneath our feet . . . . Getting

knocked off balance can even cause you to react physically. Images of yourself or of the future are hard wired to your adrenal response, and shaking them up can cause an unmanageable rush of anxiety or anger, or an intense desire to get away." Douglas Stone, Bruce M. Patton, and Sheila Heen, *Difficult Conversations: How to Discuss What Matters Most* (New York: Penguin Books, 1999), 113.

33. Goleman, *Emotional Intelligence*, 85.

34. At least one physiological cause is that positive emotions trigger the neurochemical dopamine which improves cognitive ability and creativity. This and related research is synthesized by Daniel Shapiro in "Emotion in Negotiation: Peril or Promise?" *Marquette Law Review* 87 (2004): 737.

35. Alice M. Isen, Kimberly A. Daubman, and Gary P. Nowicki, "Positive Affect Facilitates Creative Problem Solving," *Journal of Personality and Social Psychology* 52, no. 6 (1987): 1122–1131.

36. Carlos A. Estrada, Alice M. Isen, and Mark J. Young, "Positive Affect Facilitates Integration of Information and Decreases Anchoring in Reasoning among Physicians," *Organizational Behavior and Human Decision Processes* 72, no. 1 (1997): 117–135.

37. Peter J. D. Carnevale and Alice M. Isen, "The Influence of Positive Affect and Visual Access on the Discovery of Integrative Solutions in Bilateral Negotiation," *Organizational Behavior and Human Decision Processes* 37 (1986): 1–13. See also, e.g., Joseph P. Forgas, "On Feeling Good and Getting Your Way: Mood Effects on Negotiator Cognition and Bargaining Strategies," *Journal of Personality and Social Psychology* 74, no. 3 (1998): 565–577 ("The main consequence of good mood seems to be a marked inclination to be more cooperative and less competitive.").

38. Cameron Anderson and Leigh L. Thompson, "Affect from the Top Down: How Powerful Individuals' Positive Affect Shapes Negotiations,"*Organizational Behavior and Human Decision Processes* 95 (2004): 126.

39. William W. Maddux, Elizabeth Mullen, and Adam D. Galinsky, "Chameleons Bake Bigger Pies and Take Bigger Pieces: Strategic Behavioral Mimicry Facilitates Negotiation Outcomes," *Journal of Experimental Social Psychology* 44 (2008): 461–468.

40. Steven J. Spencer, Claude M. Steele, and Diane M. Quinn, "Stereotype Threat and Women's Math Performance," *Journal of*

Experimental Social Psychology 35 (1999): 13; see also Catherine Good, Joshua Aronson, and Jayne Ann Harder, "Problems in the Pipeline: Stereotype Threat and Women's Achievement in High-Level Math Courses," *Journal of Applied Developmental Psychology* 29, no. 1 (2008): 17–28.

41. Spencer, Steele, and Quinn, "Stereotype Threat and Women's Math Performance," 13.

42. Claude M. Steele and Joshua Aronson, "Stereotype Threat and the Intellectual Test Performance of African Americans," *Journal of Personality and Social Psychology* 69, no. 5 (1995): 797–811.

43. Joshua Aronson, et al., "When White Men Can't Do Math: Necessary and Sufficient Factors in Stereotype Threat," *Journal of Experimental Social Psychology* 35 (1999): 29–46. It is noteworthy that white students with only moderate math proficiency performed better when primed with the same statement, suggesting that the impact of stereotype threat depends in part on one's degree of emotional investment.

44. Ibid.

45. "Don't Break the Elastic-Maya Angelou," The Leadership Hub, http://www.theleadershiphub.com/blogs/don039t-break-elastic-maya-angelou (accessed May 25, 2011).

46. For example, Stephen Feldman and Kent Wilson had student participants watch videotapes of lawyers in mock initial client interviews. The students then rated the lawyers in terms of expertise, attractiveness, trustworthiness, likelihood of satisfying the client, and probability of being referred and returned to. On all measures except expertise, students rated lawyers with low competence but high relational skill higher than lawyers with low relational skill but high competence. "The Value of Interpersonal Skills in Lawyering," *Law and Human Behavior* 5, no. 4 (1981): 311–324.

47. "John Cunningham Quote," Wisdom Quotes, http://www.wisdom-quotes.com/quote/john-cunningham.html (accessed May 25, 2011).

48. For further description of active listening, see Bernard Moss, *Communication Skills for Health and Social Care* (London: SAGE Publications, 2008), 14; Kathryn Robertson, "Active Listening: More Than Just Paying Attention," *Australian Family Physician* 34, no. 12 (2005): 1053–1055.

49. For thorough discussion of collected descriptions of active listening, see Dana Heller Levitt, "Active Listening and Counselor Self-Efficacy: Emphasis on Microskill in Beginning Counselor Training," *The Clinical Supervisor* 20, no. 2 (2002): 101–115 (internal citations omitted).

50. Moss, *Communication Skills for Health and Social Care*, 18.

51. Arthur J. Clark describes a method of "empathic understanding" (which I call reflective dialogue) in which a counselor "attempts to sense the feelings and personal meanings that a client experiences on a moment-by-moment basis in the therapy process. This awareness is then communicated verbally and nonverbally to the client in the immediacy of a human encounter." *Empathy in Counseling and Psychotherapy: Perspectives and Practices* (Mahwah, NJ: Lawrence Erlbaum Associates, 2007), 22–23 (internal citations omitted); Clark, *Empathy in Counseling and Psychotherapy*, 28 (describing research); Sandra C. Paivio and Christine Laurent, "Empathy and Emotion Regulation: Reprocessing Memories of Childhood Abuse," *Psychotherapy in Practice* 57, no. 2 (2001): 218 ("Empathic responses can reduce arousal by providing understanding, acceptance, and support.").

52. Winston S. Churchill, "The Scaffolding of Rhetoric," in Randolph S. Churchill, companion volume, pt. 2, to *Youth: 1874–1900*, vol. 1 of Winston S. Churchill (London: Heinemann, 1967), 816–821.

53. "Emily Dickinson: Complete Poems," Bartleby, http://www.bartleby.com/113/1068.html (accessed May 25, 2011).

54. Linda D. Friedman, Esq. (plaintiff's class action attorney at Stowell & Friedman, LLC, in Chicago), in a conversation with the author, approximately 2003, paraphrased from the author's memory.

55. "Sigmund Freud Quote," Wisdom Quotes, http://www.wisdomquotes.com/quote/sigmund-freud-7.html (accessed May 25, 2011).

56. For a review of research on individual variation in facial expression, see Dacher Kelter and Paul Ekman, "Facial Expression of Emotion," in *Handbook of Emotions*, ed. Michael Lewis and Jeannette M. Haviland-Jones, 2nd ed. (New York: Guilford Publications, 2000), 236–249.

57. Author's discussion and preparation with Daniel Shapiro for Continuing Legal Education program, *Dealing With Difficult and Emotional Clients*, first presented by the Center for Practice, University of Cincinnati College of Law, 2007.

58. Fisher and Shapiro, *Beyond Reason*, 15–21.

59. Ibid., 25–31.

60. Ibid., 37.

61. This phrasing is deliberate and made with grateful reference to the book by that name, *Difficult Conversations: How to Discuss What Matters Most*, by the author's former colleagues at Harvard's Program on Negotiation, Douglas Stone, Bruce Patton, Sheila Heen, and Roger Fisher. The advice contained in this chapter, and indeed in this book, should be read as consistent with that in *Difficult Conversations*. I am indebted to these former colleagues and their insightful work.

62. Fisher and Shapiro, *Beyond Reason*, 72–93. Fisher and Shapiro list autonomy third in their order. They do not purport to list the concerns in their order of importance. However, lest the reader tire, I have taken the liberty of discussing it second because of its importance in the client counseling context.

63. As a mediator, your author is sorely tempted to suggest a next move to reframe by noting that the quarterback always plays by the rules to win, even when the rules are tough or the ref seems unfair. However, to move to discussion of reframing here would be to digress.

64. Fisher and Shapiro, *Beyond Reason,* 84.

65. Generally, "a lawyer shall abide by a client's decisions concerning the objectives of representation and, as required by Rule 1.4, shall consult with the client as to the means by which they are to be pursued. A lawyer may take such action on behalf of the client as is impliedly authorized to carry out the representation. A lawyer shall abide by a client's decision whether to settle a matter. In a criminal case, the lawyer shall abide by the client's decision, after consultation with the lawyer, as to a plea to be entered, whether to waive jury trial and whether the client will testify." ABA Model Rule of Professional Conduct, 1.2(a).

66. Fisher and Shapiro, *Beyond Reason*, 52–71.

67. Ibid., 54–59.

68. Martin Buber, *I and Thou*, trans. Ronald Gregor Smith (New York: Scribner, 2000).

69. Philip J. Moore, Nancy E. Adler, and Patricia A. Robertson, "Medical Malpractice: The Effect of Doctor-Patient Relations on Medical Patient

Perceptions and Malpractice Intentions," *Western Journal of Medicine* 173, no. 4 (2000): 244–250.

70. Fisher and Shapiro, *Beyond Reason*, 94–114.

71. Ibid., 115–140

72. Stone, Patton, and Heen, *Difficult Conversations*, 113.

5

Predictable and Potent Psychology

"The purpose of psychology is to give us a completely different idea of the things we know best."

—PAUL VALERY[1]

"I don't believe in psychology. I believe in good moves."

—BOBBY FISCHER[2]

Star Date Logs, Telepaths, Crystal Balls, and Odds-Makers

In the world of *Star Trek*, if a question arises as to what happened, when, and to whom, the captain need only ask the computer to project the video log of occurrences on board the Starship Enterprise.[3] Viewers are able to see and judge the characters' words, voices, facial expressions and actions, exactly as they occurred. If necessary, the Betazoid "empath" Counselor Troi opines regarding a character's sincerity and motivation.

Leaving aside the occasional time travel episode, neither the captain, nor the android Data, nor any Starship personnel know the future. They can provide copious information on the characteristics of solar systems, star fields, and alien civilizations. They crunch information and statistics to calculate the probability of success for weapon strikes and engineering repair efforts. Still the unexpected sometimes happens, especially with time left in the episode. There is no galactic crystal ball.

A crystal ball is exactly what we want when making a decision with significant consequences that rest on future uncertainties. The lawyer who advises and the client who decides to accept a real estate deal despite the seller's refusal to indemnify for future environmental liabilities want to know if he will rue that decision or enjoy uninterrupted productivity on the property. The plaintiff and his lawyer faced with a lower-than-generous but sizeable settlement offer want a crystal ball to view the summary judgment outcome. The corporate defendant and his lawyer want a crystal ball for reassurance that fraud and punitive damages claims will not bankrupt the company.

Recognizing the absence of crystal ball technology, most lawyers discuss the *chances* that various versions of the future will occur. Lawyers (if not clients, initially) understand that variation among jurors, judges, or arbitrators and uncertainty about opposition strategies, witnesses, and other uncontrollable factors make many imaginable endings possible. Thus, most lawyers analyze and describe future possibilities as "long shots," "slam dunks," "highly likely," or carrying "significant risks." They recommend adjusting settlement offers or demands or transactional terms to reflect degrees of uncertainty and exposure. Some lawyers use the more explicitly numerical approach of formal risk analysis,[4] assigning estimated probabilities to each major uncertainty. To assign percentages and dollar values, we must ask: If this motion were heard or this case were tried 100 times, what results would I predict? Would there be a plaintiff's verdict 40 percent of the time, 50 percent of the time, or more? Of all juries that find liability, what percent would find fraud and award punitive damages?

With or without formal risk analysis, most lawyers and many clients analyze legal issues, case precedents, and witness performances at depositions in an effort to predict the future. They consider: what are the *chances* of summary judgment, of critical evidence being admitted, of the jury finding the client credible and his nemesis reprehensible? Will the fraud claims succeed? Is the counterclaim based on strong or weak arguments? What are the highest and lowest amounts the jury could award (without judicial correction)? What's your best estimate as to the likely damages if the jury finds for the plaintiff? In classic negotiation theory, and in practice, this analysis is critical, for it becomes the "BATNA"—Best Alternative to a Negotiated Agreement[5]—the measure against which decisions to settle or to walk away from the negotiation table are often made.

To the extent humans can emulate Star Trek's computer or the android Data, lawyers are obligated to analyze legal and factual circumstances and arrive at objective, intelligent assessments and predictions. Lawyers are further obligated to communicate these clearly to their clients. The lawyer fails only if his analysis is weak or distorted, his predictions ill-founded, or his client doesn't understand what he communicated.

A lawyer does not fail every time her client rejects her advice. Still, the lawyer who clearly communicates thorough analysis, well-founded prediction, and sound advice may feel frustrated, worried, and uncomfortable when her client makes a contrary decision. This chapter posits that, were a cognitive psychologist in the room, he would recognize the influence of various biases or traps common in human decision-making. Thus, a lawyer who understands the psychology of decision-making—how cognitive patterns often trap the human decision-maker—will become a more skilled client counselor.

This chapter may be read as lawyers' "Cliff Notes" on cognitive psychology, encouraging more robust analysis and more accurate predictions, and enabling lawyers to recognize and work more effectively with known perceptual and decision-making traps. We look to psychologists' research and insights that illuminate common flaws in the way all of us—lawyers and clients—perceive, analyze, predict, and decide.[6] Thorough review of cognitive psychology literature is not possible here. Our focus is upon gleanings most salient for clients' and lawyers' perceptions, predictions, and decisions.

On Structure

The first goal is awareness of psychological traps and tendencies that lead to regrettable decisions. As a lawyer who strives for accurate assessments and wise advice, when you recognize (or suspect) these patterns in your own or your client's thinking, you are bound to examine conclusions more critically.[7] Moreover, awareness that these thinking patterns are common, indeed normal, make us more PATIENT. And patience can be essential to maintaining a strong lawyer-client relationship.

Important concepts in cognitive psychology for client counseling are presented in four layers: perception, memory, prediction, and decision frames. Perceptions of the present, memories of the past, predictions of the future, and framing current choices all impact lawyers' advice and clients' decisions about legal problems. Consider what a typical employment dispute might be built upon: a client's perception of her boss as threatening or mocking, her description of earlier office meetings to her lawyer, their conclusions about key players' character and motivations, the lawyer's assessment of evidence and predictions of the negotiation or litigation outcomes, the client's acceptance of the lawyer's analysis, predictions, and advice. All rest upon multiple, layered, and progressive perceptions, memories, predictions, and decision-making.

A note to skeptics and enthusiasts concerning the research findings: no psychology researcher claims that *everyone* inevitably shares observed psychological tendencies. Research describes behavior patterns "in the aggregate and on the average." For example, while the research establishes that people are often overly confident or optimistic about their own abilities, a minority tends toward pessimism. Many people fall prey to the "fundamental attribution error" discussed below, but not everyone. Thus, the field of psychology describes patterns in human perception, memory, attribution, analysis, prediction, and decision-making. It cannot determine what any individual will do.

Deconstructing the Psychology of Perception and Memory

Perception may be your client's reality, but it is NOT necessarily the only perceived reality with claim to truth, and your client's memory of past perceptions may be far from accurate. If only we could retrieve that Starship log video recording. When interviewing your client, considering what questions to ask, conducting follow-up investigation, or reviewing negotiation options to pursue, it's helpful to know how people's perceptions routinely color their accounts of events, circumstances, and characters that brought them to their lawyer's office. Thus, the following portions of this chapter describe common patterns in perception and memory, and suggest how effective lawyering should integrate awareness of these patterns.

Naïve Realism Gets Around

Naïve realism is the "feeling that [one's] own take on the world enjoys particular authenticity, and that other actors will, or at least should, share that take, if they are attentive, rational, and objective perceivers of reality and open minded seekers of truth."[8] As author Kathryn Schulz wryly observes in her terrific book *Being Wrong: Adventures in the Margin of Error*: "Naïve realism is an automatic tendency, not an intentional philosophical position."[9]

The notion of naiveté arises from developmental psychology's finding that young children falsely believe the world is simply and exactly as they see it and thus believe it to be. The original false belief experiment which gave rise to the label "naïve realism" established that children under the age of four who witness an object being hidden in a room will assume that people later entering the room "just know" the object is there. They "seem to think the mind contains a *replica* of reality: the world as rendered by Xerox."[10] After toddlerhood, we come to recognize that our beliefs and experiences are not straightforward reflections of a one-dimensional world.

In adults, naïve realism comes about when "we all too easily lapse back into the condition of toddlers, serenely convinced that our own beliefs are simply, necessarily true."[11]

Before heaving a self-congratulatory sigh of relief that we lawyers are too sophisticated for naïve realism, consider the following accounts of reality:

- Your law office colleague says that he attended the toughest law school in the region. The competition was cut-throat; most of his classmates were unfriendly, driven, and paranoid. The first-year professors were uncaring and delighted to humiliate students whenever possible. This is just true: all students could see it. He was amazed by a recent encounter with a first-year section classmate who described their law school as having a relaxed academic culture, open to intellectual exchange, with a collegial atmosphere and caring professors. "That's just not the way it was," he exclaimed. "Clearly the sugar-coating of time has warped her memory."

- Last summer, you attended a production of *Hamlet* performed by a famous Shakespeare stage company. The production was atrocious: the character played Hamlet as manic at all moments, relentlessly yelling his way through the script. He spoke at such a high-speed, vociferous monotone that it was often impossible to make out the words (despite prime seats and perfect hearing). Though Hamlet was worst, many other actors' spoke in invariant rants as well. ANYONE watching and listening to the play could observe what you did. If not, then they obviously don't know what theater (not to mention Shakespeare) is supposed to be. You could show a videotape to 100 professional actors or directors, and you know all 100 would agree with you.

- Your law firm partner's son just entered a large public high school. Over morning coffee, she described her dismay at the recent parents' night. It was disorganized and unprofessional.

The school principal first addressed the parents in the auditorium. Despite his offensive arrogance, the principal's speech was uninspiring, poorly structured, and memorable only for its preposterous threats regarding students who fail to attend to every rule. After the assembly, your colleague attended each ten-minute "bell" session with his son's teachers. With one or two exceptions, she was dismayed to see that these teachers were primarily disciplinarians. "They evidenced no intelligence, no talent for teaching, and no interest in deep student learning," she tells you. "Despite this high school's vaunted reputation, the 'emperor has no clothes.' If other parents can't see this, they are plain ignorant or willfully blind."

- Your client's company owns and operates a dozen fast food franchises in the region. Declining sales prompted your client to try to sell a few restaurants in tougher areas and invest in renovations for restaurants in better locations. It was (and still is) imperative that your client keep up licensing and supply payments to the franchisors and receive good ratings from the franchisor auditors. Your client applied for a large loan from a specialty financing company, which issued a letter of intent. Your client maintains that, as soon as the letter of intent was signed (and he ceased pursuing other lenders), the specialty lender began deliberately dragging its feet. Delays created the need for franchisor payment extensions for several restaurants. This morning, your client walked into your office, yelling about the lender's new request for "extensive, ridiculous, and unnecessary" financial paperwork from 10 separate locations, threatening not to provide the promised financing unless documents were delivered within 5 days. "That is simply not possible, and they know it!" your client yells. "They are making up excuses to wiggle their way out of this loan commitment. That's the only possible reason! They are out to ruin my business!"

- Due to a reduction-in-force at a large pharmaceutical company, your client was laid off from her position as a technical

compliance manager. Under company rules, long-time employees laid off without cause are entitled to consideration for
open positions. A posting came open for a training staff
position, working with company sales people and customers
on proper use of medical devices. In early discovery, the
HR manager reported that your client lacked the required
educational background for the position but was granted
an interview "as a courtesy." She maintains that, in the interview, your client acknowledged "not having much strength in
a lot of talking and being diplomatic." Your client denies
ever having uttered such a thing in the interview. The HR
manager is adamant and seems sincere in her account of the
interview.

If any of these scenarios sound plausible or familiar, particularly
expressions of certainty about an inarguable truth, then "naïve realism" is alive and well for us, our friends, colleagues, and clients. The
naïve realist does tend to over-estimate "the degree to which others
share their perspective."[12] Because the naïve realist has fervent faith in
the accuracy of his own observations and conclusions, he is confident
in his ability to persuade others. Anyone who disagrees and cannot be
persuaded is viewed as unreasonable, irrational, unintelligent, or
biased.[13]

Just like four year-olds, we think or unwittingly assume that
other people know more about our circumstances than they do, and
that others share our interpretive frames. Thus, the franchise company owner assumes that the financer knows and considered how
precarious his relationship is with the franchisor (and thus intends
to further injure it). Your client at the pharmaceutical company
assumes the HR manager knew she had done sales presentations a
decade earlier, and so "it was a deliberate lie to say she thought
I wasn't articulate enough for the job."

How do we know "naïve realism" is real? Implicit in the concept
are two assertions: that we exalt our perceived reality above all

others, and yet our reality is often either wrong, incomplete, and unknowable by others, or far different from others' legitimate perceptions of the same circumstances.

First, let us agree that people witnessing or participating in the same event or environment often report seeing it entirely differently. A room of people watching the same video recording will report different observations and reactions. Give a class of students the same written role information and they will interpret and respond to it differently. When a witness testifies before a room of senators, congressmen, or arbitrators, some will judge him credible, intelligent, and trustworthy, and others will perceive the opposite. The range of human responses, our variation in sensitivities, taste, and observation, should not surprise us.

Yet, our degree of certainty is striking. We believe that our own observations are accurate and true and those of others are not. In the rather famous "f" exercise, run by Professor Roger Fisher and his colleagues at the Program on Negotiation at Harvard Law School (and now by many negotiation professors), a roomful of people are shown a sentence projected onto a screen and asked to count the number of "f's" and silently record their count. When asked, most affirm that they are quite confident in the accuracy of their count. The presenter next asks how many people recorded 8, 9, 10, 11 or more f's. Clusters of people in the room raise their hands for each number. Before the correct answer is revealed, the professor asks how many remain confident of their original answer. Inevitably, the majority remains confident, DESPITE learning that many others observing the same sentence counted a different number of f's.

In short, when people learn that someone else witnessed the same circumstances but perceived them differently, most retain unshaken faith in their own perceptions. Interestingly, those in more powerful roles may tend to be most confident, and thus most susceptible to naïve realism. The powerful are less likely to consider another's perspective and less likely to remember that others lack their privileged knowledge. They are also less accurate in identifying emotions in others.[14]

Many people resist accepting even objective facts that contradict their perceptions. Consider the 1977 experiment by psychologists Richard Nisbett and Timothy Wilson, in which people in a Michigan department store were asked to compare four samples of (allegedly different) pantyhose. In fact, the samples were identical. Nevertheless, most people did select a favorite and described what they perceived as differences between the samples. The experiment is of interest for several reasons: it confirms how vulnerable perception is to suggestion. For the purpose of naïve realism—or stubborn faith in our own perceptions—it is telling, and troubling, that when the experimenters revealed the truth, many people simply refused to believe the pantyhose samples were identical, arguing that they could detect differences and sticking with their reported preferences.[15]

No adult is an intentional "naïve realist." Nevertheless, we insist on our own beliefs because our perceptions are real.[16] To your colleague, his law school was cut-throat; you saw that the *Hamlet* production was an abomination; your friend knows the high school's vaunted reputation to be a sham; your client is certain the human resources manager deliberately cut her out of a job with a false interview report; and the finance company was deceitfully looking for a way to escape the letter of intent. No other explanations could be true! But, of course, that's false.

Cognitive Egocentric Biases Distort, Mislead, and Deceive

Naïve realism explains why we FEEL so right. And it explains why we insist that other, right-thinking people must agree. But why are our perceptions or beliefs so often incomplete, hyperbolic, or entirely and objectively wrong? Cognitive psychology names multiple egocentric biases as likely culprits.

Unduly Inflated, Optimistic, Positive Self-Assessment

One of the most robust findings in psychology is that people tend to have inflated and optimistic views of their own abilities and performance. Perhaps we have a common ancestor from Lake Wobegone, because we are all "above average."[17] Most of us believe ourselves to be of high intelligence, and to be better-than-average drivers and employees. Professionals rank themselves highly among their peers.[18] We rate ourselves more likeable, friendly, socially intelligent, and likely to succeed than others. Though generally aware of rates of divorce and small business failure, we predict high likelihood of success in marriage and start-up businesses.[19] We are confident that our better-than-average intelligence, social skills, and professional expertise will enable us to beat the odds.

The late Princeton University Sociology Professor Marvin Bressler observed, in these words: "No truly great man ever had a perfect sense of his own proportions."[20] In order to achieve mightily, to take on the risks of marriage, business, and other challenges, optimism is healthy and helpful. Nothing ventured IS nothing gained. We might never venture if fully cognizant of our no-better-than-average capabilities.

Unfounded optimism, a large gap between self-assessment and reality, and unshakeable faith in one's abilities and judgments lay the foundation for being woefully wrong much of the time. It makes a fool of the client who is entirely confident NO judge or jury would ever doubt his judgment, competence, or sincerity. Lawyers too must beware of this natural psychological tendency. Lawyers' overly optimistic assessments of their skills at drafting, negotiation, oral argument, or trial presentation may lead them to neglect self-critical review and ignore others' input.

Schemas, Scripts, Inattentional Blindness, and Amnesia

People perceive the world through basic knowledge structures or "schemas"[21] that help us visually and cognitively interpret what we see, hear, and understand. We anticipate that a lawyer or a client will act and speak in certain ways, following common scripts. In a business dispute, your client's expectations, based on roles, stereotypes, or earlier judgments, will have shaped his observations and conclusions regarding central characters. These schemas will affect what your client remembers and what he focuses upon in describing what has occurred. They may also affect the lawyer's observations, focus, and recall from discussions with his client, and his review of documents and other evidence.

People can be astonishingly blind to that which doesn't fit within an expected framework, task, or schema. Researchers Arien Mack and Irwin Rock first coined the term "inattentional blindness" to describe people's failure to see unexpected objects.[22] Consider these astonishing and amusing experiments demonstrating inattentional blindness:

- Professors Christopher Chabris and Daniel Simons conducted the now famous "invisible gorilla experiment" in which subjects were asked to watch a video of a group playing a fast-paced basketball game and count how many times the ball was passed back and forth. During the video, a person in a gorilla costume walks into the middle of the group of players, beats its chest and wanders off. Approximately half (56 percent) of the viewers failed to see the gorilla[23] as they focused on counting passes.
- In a study by Professors Daniel Simons and Daniel Levin, an experimenter stopped people on a college campus to ask for directions. During their conversation, a visual obstacle (two men carrying a large board) passed between them, and the first experimenter was replaced by another. Though the two experimenters looked nothing alike, many people failed to notice the switch. This experiment established "change blindness,"[24] an aspect of inattentional blindness.
- In a tragic and very real example of inattentional blindness, in 1972, an Eastern Airlines Flight crashed in the Florida

Everglades. The cockpit voice recorder revealed that the cockpit crewmembers were focused upon solving the problem of a failed light on a control panel and failed to notice the plane's continuing descent on auto-pilot.[25]

Additional research establishes a related tendency: "inattentional amnesia."[26] When people initially perceive a full set of welcome and unwelcome details, their memories later edit out or "delete" items that are inconsistent with expectations and biases. Your defense witness may have seen the clutter in the grocery store aisle or another dangerous condition but fail to remember it because it runs counter to his view of the store manager's fastidiousness. Your disabled client may have been aware of her supervisor's acts of kindness or accommodation at the time and yet sincerely forget them after her termination. We simply fail to perceive or remember what we do not expect. Whether past memory or current awareness, our "schemas" and biases influence what we perceive, what we remember, and what we think we know.

Bias As an Old Case of First Impression

As inattentional blindness stories vividly demonstrate, human beings perceive selectively. Often, that selection reflects our established beliefs or expectations. Perhaps you have heard an elementary school student complain, in effect: "Ever since I threw that paper airplane and went to detention, my teacher HATES me, but I haven't done ANYTHING wrong since then. It's not fair; the teacher likes Joey and Jane. They pass notes and make noise too! But she still blames me for everything."

The student may be right. Well-established research supports the power of reputation and first impressions. When primed to view students as difficult, teachers will observe and count their troublemaking.[27]

Positive biases work the same way. When particular students are represented to teachers as talented, the teachers are likely to see only (or mostly) demonstrations of that talent. Have you ever heard a parent explode about his son's basketball coach: "I don't know why the coach won't let Mike have more playing time. He played great and got two baskets the last time he was in the game!" While no doubt a great kid, Mike also dropped seven passes, was tagged for traveling, etc. Yet, his father sincerely thinks Mike's play surpassed that of his teammates on the bench. His evaluation of what he saw might also be due to "biased assimilation of information," the common tendency to absorb and value information supporting one's views and discount or ignore countervailing evidence.

Such biases in perception, memory, and evaluation are readily observed and confirmed by a plethora of research. For example, in one well-known experiment, college students assigned to watch video footage of a football game counted more referee error or "unfairness" toward their favored teams.[28] Similar results were famously obtained from voters supporting Nixon or Kennedy and viewing their first televised debates. Not only did the voter groups evaluate the performances differently, they also failed to observe or were unable to recall mistakes made by their favored candidate.[29] In yet another classic experiment, students at Stanford business school[30] were assigned the role of buyers or sellers of a company and provided information about the company's business history, plans, revenues, expenses, and projections. To no one's surprise, sellers valued the business more highly than buyers, because sellers selectively focused on the positives, and buyers focused on the negatives in the information provided.

"Professionally Objective" Lawyers and Judges Have Biases Too

Not surprisingly, selective perception and biased assimilation of information are alive and well among lawyers, clients, judges, and juries. For example, one study found that socio-political attitudes biased the way state court judges and law students evaluated research on capital punishment. In numerous experiments,[31] lawyers or law students assigned to represent a client on one side of a simulated fact pattern evaluated their assigned client's case more favorably than the other side's, downplaying the importance of potentially harmful evidence and over-weighing favorable evidence. Thus, in the author's law school class' negotiation of a business fraud case one year, students acting as plaintiff's counsel estimated the likelihood of a liability finding at an average of 80 percent and students acting as defense counsel estimated it at an average of 40 percent, on the same basic facts.

Partisan perception bias runs strong in our affirmatively partisan legal context. Blind to other than a schema in which the client was wronged and the other side incompetent, irrational, or a culpable evil-doer, both lawyer and client will cling to confirming tidbits and minimize or miss countervailing evidence in plain view. Selective, partisan perception leads to over-confidence in ill-founded and inaccurate predictions . . . and predictable, unwelcome surprises.

A Word to the Smug—Watch for Bias Blind Spot

While many people recognize that biases are common and normal, they tend to believe their own judgments are less susceptible to bias than others.[32] Given the strength and prevalence of optimistic and egocentric biases, this "bias blind spot" is no surprise. After all, people tend to believe that they are more objective, less self-interested, and more moral than others.[33] This is consistent with seeing ourselves as "above average." It is also consistent with naïve realism, people's tendency to believe their own understanding of the world as simply accurate and thus conclude that others' different views stem from bias or ignorance.

Unfortunately, immunity to the bias blind spot is not achieved through education alone. Research indicates that even if people are sufficiently educated to acknowledge that their judgments may sometimes be biased, they are still unlikely to concede that bias

caused a particular judgment. So, your defense client in an employment discrimination case will assert: "Well, yes, sometimes I might
not be impartial. But this time, I KNOW I was being objective when
I reviewed all employees' performance before the lay-off decisions. I
also know that the other side isn't looking objectively at records of
our employment decisions."

Why? And is your client's assertion reliable? When asking ourselves whether bias influenced a particular conclusion, we engage in
introspection. We look inward to think about whether our thought
process was biased—as if bias left a mark. As psychologists Ehlinger,
Gilovich, and Ross note: "Introspection will more often than not
yield a verdict of not guilty. . . . One's conscious efforts to have
avoided bias, in fact to have 'bent over backwards' to do so, are likely
to be highly salient, and forces of self-interest or pre-existing attitudes are likely to be ignored. Thus, introspection more often leads
to (mistaken) absolution for ourselves. Because we cannot intro-
spect for another, we are happy to conclude that they have fallen
prey to the usual biases and wishful thinking."[34]

Fundamental Attribution Error

When a client presents a transactional problem or ongoing dispute,
she often describes other relevant actors in negative and blameworthy terms, guilty of some form of deceit or incompetence. The client
might say:

- *I am worried about this provision in my will because my
  daughter-in-law is greedy and shady. I want to keep my money
  from her.*
- *I want to revise our partnership agreement because I don't like the
  way my partner squanders our business reserves. He spent thousands on some technical do-hickey to increase efficiency that never
  worked. He's so dumb that he—and our partnership—are at the
  mercy of every snake oil salesman who comes along.*

- *The CEO of this finance company just wants to pull the plug; he would love to see my business go down the drain. There's no negotiating with him. I want to get an injunction to force him to live up to his commitment letter.*

Perhaps these perceptions are entirely accurate: the referenced actors on the other side may indeed be greedy, stupid, lazy, reckless, or downright evil. Yet, quite likely, a microphone planted in their lawyers' offices would record them attributing the same or equally negative characteristics to your client. They too may be entirely right, wrong, or influenced by selective perception and premature, hyperbolic judgment.

A psychologist listening to these descriptions of the other side would observe that the "Fundamental Attribution Error" is in full operation. So familiar as to be known by its acronym, FAE describes people's natural tendency to ascribe the causes of a negative human event to the other actor's character and ill motives. Yet, when we cause a negative event, we ascribe it to context and circumstance. In the simplest terms, if opposing counsel is very late to a scheduled meeting, I might conclude: "He is just plain disorganized, scattered, and unprofessional"; or "this was an intentional power play to keep me waiting." If I am equally late, I name the causes as "horrendous traffic and unexpected trouble finding a parking space."

Often, long before your client's arrival in your office, her FAE was operating in collaboration with egocentric biases and selective perception. Your client sees only the ways her supervisor is deliberately plotting to get rid of her because of a disability. Every meeting that occurs without her proves his deliberate campaign to exclude her from the loop. Never mind that the supervisor took pains to write up and e-mail meeting notes to her immediately. Irrelevant that the meeting was an emergency to solve a technical glitch before a holiday weekend. He has become Darth Vader. No accommodation to her disability could possibly work if she's under his evil command. She must transfer to another department, or be paid a large severance.

In an important study of attorney-client discussions, Professors Austin Sarat and William Felsteiner found "motive mongering," along with FAE, to be prevalent among lawyers. Motive mongering occurs when "construction of vocabularies of motives in lawyer's offices connects ideas, beliefs, experiences and interests."[35] They observed that lawyers and clients together use the character flaws and motives attributed to players on the other side to construct a narrative around otherwise ambiguous facts and actions, in effect writing a morality play.[36]

"Motive mongering" or the process of "naming, blaming, and claiming" in the lawyer's office may greatly affect client decisions.[37] People are more likely to file a lawsuit "if blame can be placed upon another, particularly when the responsible agent can be seen as intentionally causing or aggravating the problem."[38] Lawyer-client conversations may shift the presumed cause of the dispute from unintended mistake to malice, bad faith, or willful disregard. This fuels client anger, emotion, and desire for retribution through legal action. Consistent with textbook FAE, in the Sarat-Felsteiner study, clients explained their own undesirable behaviors as caused by circumstances—provocation or duress. Unfortunately, many lawyers accepted these explanations without challenge, and solidified narratives of the other as evil and blameworthy, and the client as blameless victim.[39]

If the attributions are correct, and the other side *is* evil incarnate, forswearing settlement in favor of vindication may be the better choice. However, if the attributions are in error or highly exaggerated, they needlessly prevent us from attempting constructive ways to handle real problems. Perhaps a reasonable accommodation WOULD have been possible, and the supervisor WOULD have honored your client's need for information and participation. Perhaps the finance company's CEO WOULD have agreed to provide some of the loan money, if additional information were conveyed on a reasonable schedule. Perhaps he would have persuaded the franchisor to maintain your client's licenses. Perhaps your client's son-in-law would welcome a separate vehicle for his wife's inherited share of the family business, protecting it from his creditors. As long as they are irrevocably viewed as evil-doers, opportunities are lost and potentially optimal solutions ruled out.

Viewed from a litigator's perspective, FAE may lead to blindsiding in deposition, document discovery, or adjudication. Though your client pictures his nemesis as Darth Vader, to the trier of fact, he may look harmless and credible. Your client's supervisor's explanations of emergency meetings and his efforts to convey information may be heard as reasonable and sincere. The finance company's explanation for requesting additional documents before the scheduled closing may make sense. The neutral trier-of-fact may not adopt your client's convictions as to good and evil and may not employ the schema of his morality play when evaluating the evidence.[40]

Notes on Memory, Reconstruction, and Source Confusion

Seeking yet more evidence that it is naïve to be certain of our own, our clients', or the witnesses' perceptions, recorded and recounted as memory? Even if these perceptions were accurate in that moment, human memory is astonishingly *unreliable*.

Vivid Does Not Mean Accurate

Memory deteriorates over time, and what is remembered is often quite different from that which occurred. Most important and surprising, memories regarding unusually shocking events—memories we experience as vivid—are just about as likely to erode over time. In 1986, psychology professor Ulric Neisser surveyed his students the day after the space shuttle Challenger's tragic explosion, and then again three years later. He found that "less than 7 percent of the subjects' second reports matched the initial reports, 50 percent were wrong in two-thirds of their assertions, and 25 percent were wrong in every major detail. Although the memories seem vivid, research indicates that their accuracy erodes over time at the same rate as our every day recollections."[41] Similar research carried out in the wake of the September 2001 World Trade Center disaster confirmed these results.[42]

Memories Change in Storage and Retrieval

When seeking to retrieve a memory, we lack the Starship Enterprise's authoritative and singular recording system. Extensive research indicates that we construct, or reconstruct, memory from multiple sources, conversations, others' descriptions, emotions, and construed meanings. We often prove unable to distinguish between perceptions at the time and these other sources. When retrieving memory, people draw upon "their own 'internal mental representation of the event,' other basic information they have about how the world works, their schemas of how events such as this one typically happen, what they have been told by others about what happened, their experiences in other similar situations, stereotypes, what they imagined doing, and so on."[43]

Counsel John Dean's testimony in the Watergate Hearings strikingly illustrates the way our thoughts, inner dialogues, emotions, and self-concepts enter into memory. Dean testified cogently and thoroughly about a meeting with then President Nixon. He provided clear and confident details about what he told the president and the president's response. It made perfect sense. However, later transcripts from recordings in the Oval Office revealed a conversation quite different. Assuming his sincerity, Dean's testimony reflected some combination of what was said, what he may have been thinking, and how he viewed his own role.[44]

Moving back to our common experience: When we recall a painful argument, do we remember the precise words hurled at us, or what we understood the words to mean? Do we remember the words we said, or what we were thinking and feeling at the time? Can we distinguish between what was said explicitly, and what was shared knowledge? After rehearsing the conversation with family and friends, how can we distinguish their input and interpretation from the original, for which there is no recording?

Source Confusion and Suggestibility Impact Honest Intent

Far too much frightening research has been done on the topic of eyewitness credibility or, more precisely, lack of credibility, for summary here.[45] With a focus on lawyer-client counseling, it bears highlighting the extent to which suggestions and even questions influence memory. In one experiment, participants were shown a videotape of an automobile accident and then asked a question about the speed of the car as it passed a barn. A week later, when asked questions about the video, 17 percent reported having seen a barn, though there was no barn in the video.[46] In a similar study, participants were asked about a car accident observed on video, including questions about the speed of the car "when it ran the stop sign" or "when it turned right." Though there was no stop sign, its mention increased the percentage who reported having seen one.[47] Further studies indicate that subtle shifts in the way questions are worded can influence witness memory.[48]

Our feelings about people and events also affect our memories. Consider a study in which people were asked to remember a video recording they had seen of a customer leaving a restaurant without paying. Those given a reason for the customer's leaving that would make him less culpable remembered the price of the meal as having been lower. However, participants given negative information about the customer "remembered the prices of the meal as higher, were more likely to overestimate the price of the meal, and were more likely to incorrectly report that the customer had also failed to pay for a pre-dinner drink."[49] Thus, your client's feelings about key players and events in his case may affect her interview responses and eventual testimony.

Could We Have Confidence in Confidence?

What if your client tells you he is completely confident of his memory as to a certain event? Should you worry less about the accuracy of that memory? Maybe not. In general, research indicates that people's level of confidence is not correlated with the accuracy of their memories. However, different confidence levels reported by a particular person may be significant and helpful. If your client's confident recollection has proven accurate as to certain details, verified by documents, physical evidence or other witness accounts, then his level of confidence as to a different episode should be taken seriously.

From Psychology of Memory to Remembering Lawyers

The wise lawyer will consider the uncertainty of memory when preparing and evaluating any case that relies heavily upon eyewitness testimony. Clearly, lawyers interviewing clients regarding important events should beware of the way they ask questions and avoid suggesting information. Lawyers should recognize that their clients' memories may have been influenced by a variety of suggestions, conversations, subsequent occurrences, and emotions. The suggestibility, plasticity, deterioration, and construction of memory also bear upon how best to counsel clients. Before formal discovery, the lawyer should prepare his client for conflicting accounts by apparently sincere witnesses. The lawyer should advise his client that the other side's witness may not be a scoundrel and a liar when he testifies to his different memory of an event.

Uncertainty, Prediction, and Psychology

"To be uncertain is to be uncomfortable, but to be certain is to be ridiculous."

—CHINESE PROVERB[50]

"Unpredictability, too, can become monotonous."

—ERIC HOFFER[51]

Most legal problems involve ambiguity played out on uncertain ground. Unequivocal answers, black and white standards, and clear facts are the exceptions.[52] If only the license to practice endowed lawyers with the power to predict with perfect accuracy and confidence! If not perfect, lawyers might, at the very least, be given the power of unbiased, objective prediction! But, alas, that power is not included in the law school graduation package.

Reality Check on Assumptions About Lawyers' Analysis and Advice

Most of this book assumes the lawyer's analysis and advice are sound, and it has addressed the challenges of understanding, acceptance, and coming to terms with difficult choices. However, given that a lawyer's advice often rests upon prediction of the likely outcome of motions, trial, or regulatory action, this assumption bears scrutiny. Thus, the next few pages present a dose of reality regarding lawyers' ability to predict legal outcomes. After establishing the dimensions of the prediction problem, we'll return to psychology's insights into why and what a lawyer might do.

Neutral Anecdotes and Observations on Lawyers' Predictions

Mediators of legal disputes are often heard commiserating or chuckling about cases in which the two lawyers' cumulative estimates of success add up to more than 150 percent. Sometimes, one lawyer seems to have a more balanced view—cognizant of risk and downside as well as strengths. The mediator shares frustration at the impossibility of reaching settlement with a plaintiff's lawyer "on Mars." On other days, the defense lawyer predicts that the jury will "see through that sleazy plaintiff" when, to the mediator, the plaintiff presents as wholesome and sincere as a first grade teacher. Mediators hear sophisticated lawyers assert confidently that the jury will favor their corporate VP who was "shafted" by the devious sellers of a hometown family business. Inconsistent technical evidence or callously worded memoranda found in discovery are breezily disregarded as inconsequential or inadmissible. Sometimes, counsel is spinning the mediator. Too often, counsel's (and client's) optimism is sincere but entirely unjustified.

Yes, We Have a Prediction Problem!

Unsurprisingly, experimental and empirical evidence confirms mediators' anecdotes: neither law school training nor considerable lawyering experience make most lawyers competent at prediction about how a neutral decision-maker—judge, jury, or arbitrator—will rule.[53] In their landmark study comparing trial attorneys' predictions and later reported trial results, University of California, Irvine, Professor Elizabeth Loftus and Leiden University Professor Willem Wagenaar found great divergence between prediction and results. As a whole, attorneys were over-confident and inaccurate predictors. The more highly confident lawyers did not prove more accurate, just more over-confident.[54] In fact, civil attorneys' confidence levels in their cases had little relationship to their actual results. A later unpublished study by Professor Loftus and others confirmed that lawyers' predictions about whether their clients would win or lose were barely more accurate than chance.[55][56]

These findings support much earlier experimental research by Brigham Young University Law School Professor Gerald Williams, who gave the same case facts to 40 practicing lawyers in Des Moines, Iowa, with 20 assigned to the defense and 20 to the plaintiff's side. Presumably based both on differences in negotiation style and case assessment (jury prediction), the plaintiffs' attorneys began nego-tiations by demanding between $32,000 and $675,000, and the defendant's attorneys initial offers ranged from $3,000 to $50,000, with ultimate settlements ranging from $15,000 to $95,000. This wide range of results—and variation in assessments among coun-sel, even those on the same side of a case—is replicated every semes-ter in my law school negotiation classes and, I suspect, those of all law school negotiation professors.[57]

A Word to the Wise on Dollars and Underestimation

Research suggests that a defense lawyer's (and most likely defense client's) blind spot causes her to underestimate dollar amounts of damages exposure, at least in the personal injury arena. In one experiment, plaintiff's and defense lawyers, judges, and jurors were presented with descriptions of personal injury cases and asked to rate the severity of the injury and an appropriate level of award (lia-bility was not at issue). The results: considerable consistency in the way respondents analyzed injury severity and thought about awards where they had no partisan stake in the outcome. However, the larg-est deviation was found between defense lawyers and all other par-ticipants. Defense lawyers tended to rate described injuries as less severe, resulting in lower awards. Researchers concluded that defense lawyers' assessments may be "less responsive to case details" and "more mechanical."[58]

In his recent book, *Beyond Right and Wrong: The Power of Effective Decision-Making for Attorneys and Clients,* author Randall Kiser offers more recent evidence that defense lawyers (or their clients) fail to adequately assess the risk and dollar value of high plaintiffs' ver-dicts. The book reviews a comprehensive, empirical 2008 study con-ducted by Kiser and colleagues, comparing final settlement offers and demands and trial results in 5,653 civil cases from four data sets in California and New York, involving 11,306 attorneys and their clients, evenly divided between plaintiffs and defendants.[59]

One significant finding was that, while plaintiffs were somewhat more often mistaken about winning on liability, the mean *cost* of defendants' "decision error" (defined as the difference between the last offer and the ultimate award) was 17 to 19 times higher than that of plaintiffs.[60]

This author cannot resist noting that unpublished results from data in her annual law school negotiation course suggest that defense tendencies to under-estimate damages exposure begin early. As reported earlier, when law students and their business school clients estimate the likelihood of a plaintiff's verdict in a case of alleged breach of contract and business fraud, both sides display typical partisan perception bias. More striking is that defense-side estimates of damages in the event of plaintiff's verdict have averaged between 10 percent and 25 percent of the plaintiff side estimates—4 to 10 times lower—based upon the SAME spreadsheet information of business revenues and projections, etc.

This leads to some important and uncomfortable advice to defense counsel (and clients): don't conflate the likelihood of a defense verdict and the measure of its consequences. Remember that your hundredth personal injury claim will be the jury's first. What might the award be if the jury or the arbitrator rules against your client? One mediator (not to mention the defense) still ruminates on the $40 million-dollar jury award in the case where, in caucus, the possibility of damages beyond a few million was waved away as silly by confident, analytical lawyers (and the mediator). Don't fail to consider the worst-case scenario.

Maybe Lawyers Can't Predict Because It's Just Plain Unpredictable? No Such Luck!

Perhaps juries (if not judges and arbitrators) are just plain unpredictable—to anyone! In theory, that would let lawyers off the hook for bias, while undercutting our claim to expertise.

Fortunately, research debunks this theory. In fact, law school graduates who are *neutral* decision-makers tend to agree on winners and numbers. In the influential 1993 book, *The American Jury*, author-professors Harry Kalven and Hans Zeisel reported on their study in which more than 500 judges in 400 civil jury trials recorded their opinions of the cases' difficulty and how they should be decided, before learning the jury verdicts. The results: judges agreed with the jury's verdict 78 percent of the time.[61] When they disagreed, judges would have ruled for the plaintiff 10 percent of the time and for the defense 12 percent of the time—a statistically even balance. Many other studies have yielded consistent or even more striking findings of judge and jury agreement, including a 1995 Chicago Jury Project Study in which judges disagreed with the jury's liability decision in only 1 percent of the cases.[62]Finally, contrary to popular wisdom, a series of empirical studies establish that juries are *not* more likely to award punitive damages or higher punitive damages amounts than judges would.[63]

Summarizing forty years of studies on judges, juries, and attorney decision-making, in *Beyond Right and Wrong*, Kiser makes the point that "studies consistently demonstrate that jurors understand trial evidence and the applicable law, and judges agree with their verdicts in the large majority of cases."[64] It makes sense then, that Kiser's study found lawyers with training as neutral mediators tended toward lower decision error rates. It's not law school that diminishes prediction capacity; it's the partisan role.

Experience is No Antidote

Practice experience may worsen the problem, as lawyers become entrenched on one side. A study by Jane Goodman-Delahunty found lower calibration between prediction and results among lawyers in practice for more than 30 years.[65] Similarly, in Kiser's study, attorneys practicing between 30 and 40 years had increased decision error rates. Decision error rates tended to be lower than average for relatively inexperienced defense counsel, and higher than average for inexperienced plaintiffs' counsel. These reached an average plateau somewhere between 6 and 10 years of practice, through 30 years.[66] Various explanations have been suggested: perhaps more experienced counsel are handling more difficult cases; perhaps with experience comes greater over-confidence. To all lawyer-readers over 50, please read this paragraph as a peer's respectful word to the wise.

Anecdotal and empirical evidence agree then. Lawyers acting as partisan advocates often fail to predict how a neutral decision-maker will rule in their clients' cases. Why? It appears that lawyers are people too and thus unable to remain objective. Lawyers fall prey to the same psychological tendencies as clients: egocentric and partisan perception bias, built upon selective perception, biased assimilation of information, fundamental attribution error, and many elements of naïve realism. To this list of psychological tendencies impinging upon lawyer-client counseling and decision-making, a few more must be added.

Judgmental Overconfidence

Judgmental overconfidence may be thought of as corollary to or enhancement of partisan perception bias. Assume a lawyer calmly predicts that his client will win the case. If I ask him how confident he is about that prediction, and he says, "Ninety percent," I'd say he is manifesting "judgmental overconfidence." In other words, he made a predictive judgment (likely an optimistic one), and he is also *confident* of that judgment.

Not surprisingly, social science research establishes that judgmental overconfidence is entirely normal, and widespread. Research examining attorneys' trial predictions in terms of confidence levels confirms that we tend to be overconfident concerning our often inaccurate predictions.

Beware of Commitment and Hindsight Bias

Lawyers beware, because overconfidence tends to increase as we commit to a course of action. A classic 1968[67] experiment at a Vancouver racetrack makes the point. Experimenters asked prospective bettors before a racetrack window how confident they were that their horse would win. After placing their bets, they were greeted by different experimenters asking the same question. Lo and behold, having put their money down, the bettors became confident—even though their horses had not gotten any faster! In the legal context, after rejecting early settlement and moving to discovery and then motions, do lawyers and clients become more confident, whether or not the facts improve? Most likely yes, as research indicates that once people envision an event, they expect that it can occur.[68]

Of course, when unexpected and devastating new evidence emerges in discovery, and a judge denies pretrial evidentiary motions, most lawyers undoubtedly reassess and adjust predictions. We are not fools. The problem, however, is that these adjustments are often insufficient, due to the power of perception biases, relative overconfidence, and all the rest.[69]

A phenomenon called "hindsight bias" may also play a role here. Once we arrive at the future, we experience it as having been inevitable in hindsight. We see only the factors that pointed in that direction and ignore or forget all counter-indicators. Hindsight bias occurs for decisions, not just future events. Decisions to pursue an acquisition or take a litigation route seem so clearly right in hindsight. We forget or ignore risks or counter-arguments once recognized as making the decision difficult. Thus, the decisions are never re-examined, leading again to overconfidence.

Antidotes, Anyone? The Jury Is Out on Self-Administered Efforts

A legitimate question follows: how can a lawyer free himself and his client from the traps of partisan perception bias and judgmental overconfidence? The best advice is to seek independent, objective views, and listen to them.[70] Experience and some recent research suggest that adopting the other side's perspective—looking at facts and arguments as they might—is one way to more accurately perceive their weight. The exercise cannot be passive or casual. It is NOT enough to think (or say), "Well, the other side is emphasizing the credentials of its expert witness and, if he is as smart as they say, that might hurt us." Instead, it is important to articulate, in your own words, EXACTLY what the other side's evidence and counter-arguments are. Take on the role of opposing counsel, scour discovered documents and depositions as if representing the other side. Discuss this with your client. Encourage your client to articulate what this story might look like to the other side. At the very least, articulating the other side's view forces recognition that there IS another side, mitigating client perception that "this is entirely frivolous and they're just maintaining this suit as pure extortion [etc.]." It is not necessary that your client *agree* with the other side. But recognizing that their position is not wildly frivolous or purely spiteful can make your client more open to negotiation and compromise.[71]

Note that asking your client to consider the opposite view is not panacea. Research suggests that even actively taking the opposing view is less effective when that view challenges strongly held personal values or identity.[72] Still, at least the lawyer should gain insight from the exercise. After all, lawyers must and do maintain some professional distance. Their personal identities should be more easily extricated from particular cases and clients. Thus, lawyers should be able to weigh the strength of opposing arguments, even if clients who self-identify with their own case cannot.

Availability, Salience, and the Vividness Effect

Assume you are an experienced lawyer who tends *not* to fall into the traps of perception biases or overconfidence. Your assessments of risk and consequences in transactions or at trial generally prove to be accurate. When in doubt, you consult others for more neutral perspectives. The problem is persuading your client. Sometimes, your client says he understands and accepts your assessment of the summary judgment risk or the (un)likelihood of his prevailing at trial. But still, the client is determined to reject a significant settlement offer. Why?[73]

Somehow, there is a difference between intellectual understanding of a prediction and belief in its reality. People more easily accept a future as real, and act to avoid or to reach it, when they are able to imagine it—to see it—and then to feel what it will feel like. Events or circumstances we can vividly imagine become salient and powerful.

Psychologists refer to these as "availability," "vividness," and "salience" effects. People tend to count upon or be excessively concerned about the events easily available for recall—they are "salient" in our awareness, thinking, and decision-making. Thus, we worry about being murdered, readily recalling news stories and gruesome movies, but we don't worry much about under-reported causes of death known to be more frequent. We read of rare multi-million dollar jury verdicts, or see them on a television courtroom drama series, and easily imagine that happening in our cases. Even when made aware of the frequency of case dismissals, defense victories, or more modest dollar awards, people cannot easily imagine them.

Vividness is closely related to salience. A vividly described event is easier to recall and thus remains salient. So, numerical tallies of murders, military deaths, or of juries' findings may have less impact than a particular, detailed, and colorful story. This is why the movie *Schindler's List*, with its vivid personal stories of people trapped in the Holocaust, seems more powerful than Holocaust statistics.

In a client-counseling context, lawyers are well advised to assist their clients to imagine possible consequences. For example, suppose your analysis of relevant case law strongly suggests that your client's case is likely to be dismissed on summary judgment.

To explain this, you might relate the story underlying one or more of the cases on point, saying:

This Mrs. Jane Smith case is an example of several cases that are cause for concern. Mrs. Smith, a widowed woman just a year or two older than you, suffered terrible injuries in a fall when her second story balcony railing collapsed. She had a broken collar bone, fractured hip [and so on], three surgeries, and was unable to work full time after the accident. It said in the case description that she was unable to lift her young children [and so on]. Still, because of the same legal issue raised by the defense in our case, the court granted summary judgment, dismissing her case, and she recovered nothing for her injuries.

Hearing these vivid details enables your client to imagine it happening, if to the woman in the case, then possibly to her. Research regarding the impact of vividness supports this advice, as do the many actor-clients with whom the author has worked. These actor-clients note that it is easy to lose sight of the fact that case law is built upon the cases of real people faced with similar decisions. Learning their stories helps the plaintiffs understand that "what might happen," in the abstract will be quite real if it does happen.

Salience and vividness also operate as vehicles for defendants' engaged consideration of reality. A defense client or client representative is sometimes faced with future risk of enormous exposure under various measures of damages. Before making a decision, he would be wise to imagine what would happen if his business were to face a judgment in the "x million dollar range," or an injunction that would prevent sales for some period or some product line. Unless he has imagined the consequences, he cannot and will not appropriately factor this risk into his decision. Thus, the lawyer is advised to gently ask questions, enabling the client to envision it. Without any hint of threat or coercion, do elicit your client's full understanding of real impacts of possible legal outcomes. For example, if your client were faced with a non-frivolous fraud claim giving rise to punitive damages, you might say:

> *I agree we will put in strong evidence of our good faith efforts to make the product safe. As you know, I am concerned about some of those memoranda written by the company's engineers that will also come into evidence. So, it is important for us to consider all of the possible ways this could turn out: the good, the bad, and the very ugly. Well, what if punitive damages were awarded, as in [Such-and-Such case]? We know that punitive damages in cases like these typically range from $[x] to $[y]. It's worth thinking about what that would do to your company's cash position, and whether some of it could be covered on your line of credit, and if so, how that would affect your business.*

Or, in the event of a possible injunctive prohibition:

> *It is worth thinking about what would happen if your company was enjoined from distributing this product. What percentage of current revenues and expenses are from this product? How many employees would it impact? Could the company absorb them into other divisions? Do its sales representatives typically sell a line of related products? How would an injunction affect these other product sales?*

As your client imagines the consequences of a possible but unwelcome outcome, he comes to terms with the idea that it could become real. It will then be vivid and appropriately salient when he weighs his decision.

Leaving aside litigation risk, imagining "what if" may also yield strategic moves to lessen negative impact. You might ask whether your client's company can undertake a strategy now to unbundle these products, just in case. If so, your client's "BATNA" will improve.

Not coincidentally, this will also improve your client's negotiating position, and may eventually drive more favorable settlement terms.

Psychology of Presentation, Frame, and Decision

Anchoring

Much like its anchor on the ocean floor pulls a boat against the tides, initial numbers and positions tend to pull us their way in any negotiation. Anchoring competes for the prize for the most robust, consistently demonstrated phenomenon in research on psychology and decision-making. (As discussed in chapter 8, anchoring in communication and theater seem to be related.) When lawyers and clients consider negotiation strategy and response, they should be aware of the power of anchoring. Leaving aside the question of whether lawyer-client counseling constitutes a negotiation, intentionally or inadvertently placed anchors can strongly affect your client's decisions. Thus, lawyers should anchor only intentionally, and be prepared to advise a client when any anchor is working to undermine his interests.

The most famous early experiment demonstrating the psychological force of anchors was performed by Professors Amos Tversky and Daniel Kahneman. Business student participants were presented with a "wheel of fortune"-type roulette wheel secretly preset to the number 10 or 65. They were also asked to estimate the percentage of African countries in the United Nation. For classes in which the roulette wheel had spun to 10, the average estimate was 25 percent and for classes in which the wheel spun to 65, the average estimate was 45 percent.[74] Clearly the preset wheel numbers served as tremendously powerful anchors: not even business students would think the roulette wheel was related to the United Nations or Africa.

Many, many subsequent experiments have shown that starting numbers greatly impact people's thinking. For example, real estate brokers who expressed certainty that an asking price would *not* influence their independent assessments of a property's value were given identical property descriptions and information, with different asking prices. In fact, asking prices did have a strong anchoring effect: the brokers' average estimates were higher for the same property when labeled with a higher price tag.[75]

Anchoring affects judges and jurors as well. In a study by Professors Guthrie and Rachlinski and Judge Wistrich, 167 federal magistrate judges were given the same case descriptions, but with different dollar demands, and were asked to estimate an appropriate damages award. To no psychologist's surprise, the judges reported much higher damages awards when the demand numbers were much higher.[76] A great quantity of jury research establishes that counsel's higher damages demands at trial yield higher awards.[77]

In the negotiation arena, extensive experimental research establishes a strong correlation between initial offers or demands and the final resolution point.[78] While high-ball or low-ball numbers are common and sometimes maddening, they may be understood as attempts to anchor the negotiations. In a study by law professors Russell Korobkin and Chris Guthrie, subjects were given identical information about a legal case and offered the opportunity to settle it for $12,000. Students told the defendant's initial offer had been $2,000 were far more likely to report that they would "definitely" or "likely" accept a final $12,000 settlement than students told the defendant's initial offer had been $10,000. The $2,000 low-ball offer anchored the negotiation, making the final $12,000 seem more generous and acceptable.[79]

Lawyers and clients must consider numbers in so many arenas: settlement offers or demands, purchase or sales prices, lease terms, licensing or royalty proposals, sales territory restrictions, and plea agreements, to name a few. Initial anchors—set by you, your client, or someone else—can have unintended influence. Assume that when your client discussed the circumstances of his age discrimination case he pressed you to name how much he could possibly receive at trial. You finally said: "If everything breaks your way, you might recover a top sum of $750,000 at trial." You took great pains to emphasize that this was a high trial estimate. You explained that no estimate would be meaningful until after discovery, and then risk and settlement value should also be assessed. Perhaps you mentioned your firm's recent $800,000 jury award in an age discrimination case. Or, perhaps you never mentioned a number, but your client's brother-in-law told him about that $800,000 case. Any or all of these numbers can become anchors in your client's mind. Much later, an objectively reasonable $100,000 defense offer pales in comparison.

Anchoring works in the opposite direction, too. You may have a defense client being sued for age discrimination who says: "Remember that last case you managed to have dismissed on summary judgment. That only cost me $5,000. Will it cost me more than that for summary judgment here?" The answer, of course, is that drafting a motion might cost more or less, but discovery may be more complex and yield more problematic, disputed, and ambiguous facts. Unfortunately, your client is anchored at $5,000.

Anchors don't end the discussion. They do impact the starting point and thus how far your client has to travel. As you and your defense or plaintiff client review the contexts and the facts and move through either informal or formal discovery or discussions with opposing counsel, the other side's settlement positions will shift. When you inform your plaintiff client of the strong risk of losing his age discrimination case on summary judgment, uncertainties at trial, and low chances of front pay or emotional distress damages, he will stop counting upon an $800,000 bank deposit. The defense client, faced with mounting deposition and other discovery costs, will recognize that this case may cost more. People adjust down or up from anchors. But we move only slowly, grudgingly, and often insufficiently from where the anchor has set in our emotional, psychological mud.[80] Our anchors define our initial hopes, if not our expectations. Much lower than $800,000 or much higher than $5,000 feels like losing. "Realistic" numbers are difficult to accept.

Hence, some practical advice:

- AVOID creating client expectations and PARTICULARLY avoid mentioning numbers at the outset. No matter how many times you say "only if," "assuming everything breaks our way," or "in the best case scenario," your client will remember the number and forget the caveats and contingencies. Despite your outstanding representation in a difficult legal case, the client is more likely to feel disappointed.

- After assessing facts and legal issues, do provide your client with descriptions of what might happen in the legal process. Those descriptions should include numerical dollar estimates, assuming dollars are at issue. To avoid anchoring, be careful to provide numbers at *both* ends of the range, as well as intermediate, predictable outcomes. Do articulate the steps in the process at which your client might recover $0, as well as the legal theories and findings leading to high, reduced, mid-range, or low damages, and why. For example, in a plaintiff's suit for back and knee injuries, where the defense alleges a pre-existing condition and contributory negligence, you would articulate the numerical ranges of awards if the jury finds causation for the back and the knee, or for the knee only. And do estimate dollar recovery after possible reductions for comparative negligence.

- Defense counsel faces the parallel task. For example, in an employment discrimination case, do balance estimates of more modest "back pay only" awards with calculation of different front pay ranges, emotional distress, and compensatory damages claims. A wave of the hand—"of course there could be BIG emotional and compensatory damages"—will not counter the effect of more optimistic numerical anchors. Instead, you should calculate and present all of the numbers, including all damages categories.

· Consult and quote comparable jury verdict or settlement data. When your client first invokes his brother-in-law's cousin's neighbor's $800,000 case, it's wise to mitigate that anchor's force with numerical counter-anchors from other cases—best gleaned from available databases, not simply your own experience. For example, the lawyer might immediately note that, while that was a terrific verdict, in a study of employment discrimination cases filed in federal court from 1988 to 2003, 19 percent are dismissed, and of the 6 percent of total filings that make it to trial, only 33 percent win.[81] The lawyer might also be prepared to provide data on average local verdicts (perhaps as a multiple of lost wages).

· Early in a lawyer-client relationship, quoting pessimistic data is admittedly tricky, as a client may feel that the lawyer doesn't believe in her, or doesn't believe her case is different from any of the others. No one enjoys feeling like a statistic. As discussed earlier, client feelings about your interaction are important and may determine whether he becomes or remains your client. Thus, do express concern for your client's individual circumstances. You need not force statistics on every client at first meeting. However, if and when you sense that an extreme outside anchor—that multi-million dollar case on the news—is exerting great influence, presenting additional data is important.

· People want to feel that their compromises are justified, not just a sign of capitulation, and that they are being treated fairly, at least in relative terms. Data from other case verdicts as well as information regarding other settlements can be extremely helpful for this reason as well. Assume your client learns that cases of his type win at trial 49 percent of the time, and that the damages ranges average 3 times the lost wages amount. If it's true, explain that reported employment case resolution data indicate that settlements are rarely more than 1 year of lost wages, plus some additional allowance for attorneys' fees. Now, you have created different anchors. Weighed against these anchors, the defense offer totaling 2 years of lost wages may feel more reasonable and fair, less like a weak-kneed drop to the floor.

Status Quo Bias and Endowment Effect

Psychologists tell us, and experience confirms, that people are prey to the "endowment effect"—over-valuing what they have—as well as "status quo bias"—reluctance to depart from current circumstances. These two tendencies are linked and sometimes interact in frustrating ways in the client-counseling context.

First, the customary serving of the classic research: Psychology professors worked with unsuspecting Cornell University undergraduate students in the first well-known experiment demonstrating the endowment effect.[82] In one group, all students were given a mug and asked to record how much they would sell it for. In a second group, all students were given money, shown the mugs, and asked how much they would pay to purchase the mugs. In a third group, students were given nothing, but asked to choose between receiving money and a mug. Astonishingly, students who had been given the mugs valued them at a median price of $7.12. For students spending money to purchase mugs, it was $2.87. And for students permitted to choose between money and mugs the median value was $3.12. Felt "endowment" led to highest valuation, yet THE MUGS WERE ALL THE SAME!

You'll recognize the endowment effect in many arenas. Have you ever tried to purchase a home from its original owner? The house might seem comparable to many other houses for sale in the area, but the proud owner believes his is far more valuable. Business purchasers will tell you that acquiring a business from its founder is much more difficult than from a subsequent corporate owner. The endowment effect is strong and broad. We feel endowment not just in property but also our ideas and our proposals. What's ours seems better, because it's ours.

Thus, your client asserts: "my claim is stronger," "my customer lists are more valuable," "my idea for solving the indemnification problem is more efficient," or "my proposed structure for the lease term is better." The client's claims, customer lists, ideas, and proposals may indeed be quite valuable. But to the extent that the endowment effect inflates their perceived value, it may cause him to dig in and reject others' worthy proposals.

Status quo bias may encompass the endowment effect.[83] It suggests that we tend to overvalue our current known state, as soon as someone suggests changing it. Consider parents who regularly complain about shortcomings in their current school system and neighborhood. As soon as comparable jobs become available in another region of the country, the positive aspects of their current circumstances, to be lost in the move, will begin to loom large. Of course, if the status quo is terrible and everything about the new placement is much better, status quo bias is silenced. But, decisions are rarely so clear. Trade-offs and ambiguity are the norm. Status quo bias suggests that we tend to over-weight the positives of what we have and fear their loss, just as we discount the positives associated with the change and disregard their loss. After all, we haven't owned them yet.

It sounds odd, but for some clients, "in litigation" becomes the status quo. It defines their relationship to the dispute, to their adversaries, and their current state of being. An article titled "Death of a Claim," by authors Dwight and Helaine Golann posits that litigant emotions may parallel the states of a grieving process.[84] Add the claim's endowed value, and we understand some clients' reluctance to shift away from being in litigation.

For clients on the precipice of a new transaction—perhaps a joint venture or merger agreement—status quo bias and endowment may work against closing the deal. Despite objective recognition of the joint venture's synergies and the need for additional revenue, the status quo feels more desirable once it is threatened. And the endowed value of your client company's contribution seems greater than the other side's.

This is not to say that every transaction should reach closure. Indeed, business clients are wise to weigh risks, to avoid blind enthusiasm for every proposed deal. Psychological phenomena of status quo bias and the endowment effect are referenced here as reasons your client, after hard-boiled analysis and negotiation, might inexplicably dig in or retrench over minutia. Again, counselor, patience is key. Consider taking a deep breath and then asking your client about the downsides of the status quo or his vision and valuation of the transaction's consequences.

Risk, Loss, Gain, and Framing

Imagine that you have objectively analyzed your client's case: all psychological biases have been exorcised. You have communicated the legal issues, procedural twists and turns, risks, and possible outcomes to your client, who seems to understand it all. Your client relationship is strong. You set about discussing your client's choices under the circumstances. In fact, the way you frame those choices—your phrasing—could dramatically affect his decision. Frame it one way, and he is more likely to choose a risky alternative. Frame it another way, and he is more likely to choose a certain offer.

The idea that client choice could be significantly impacted by a lawyer's random, unintentional choices in framing is antithetical to well-informed and purposeful lawyer-client counseling. That is why this last segment on psychological tendencies focuses on what is known about people's responses to risk, gain, and loss, and how that should inform the way lawyers frame choices when speaking with their clients.

Professors Tversky and Kahneman originally articulated the now widely accepted tenets of "Prospect Theory,"[85] including at least four important findings about the way most people respond to risk, gain, and loss:

1. **People tend to be risk-averse as to gain. Once we have gained something we are loath to give it up in favor of a relatively strong chance of getting more.** Preference for the "bird in the hand" over the "bird in the bush" is the operative aphorism. This is true even when the "rational" choice—in terms of mathematically discounted value—is to take the risk. Thus, most people prefer a sure gain of $240 over a 25 percent chance of winning $1,000.[86] Different people's breakpoints will be different. I might settle for $175, or even $150 (or less). Others might take no less than $200, and be comfortable with rolling the dice. But few of us will insist upon every penny of $250, the mathematically discounted value.

2. **People tend to be risk-seeking as to significant loss.** We hate to pay up and declare defeat right now. When people are given a choice between a 75 percent chance of LOSING $1,000 or just paying $750 (or, I suspect, $740 or even $700), most will choose to roll the weighted dice. We would rather not choose loss, particularly current loss, if it can be delayed.[87]

Lawyers who have worked with corporate defendants facing a significant chance of monetary loss have no doubt witnessed this tendency in action. In an employment discrimination case, the defendant's VP seems to understand and even agree with counsel's estimate of 50 percent or a far greater chance of a plaintiff's award. He recognizes that damages will likely range from a low of $140,000 (one year's back pay plus benefits, plus statutorily mandated attorneys fees) to $320,000 (adding the average front pay award of 2 years), plus a non-trivial emotional distress amount, plus etc., etc. Yet, he refuses to offer more than $60,000 to settle the case.

What makes no sense to an economist is entirely understandable to a psychologist.[88, 89]

At the risk of distraction from these two well-accepted findings, Kahneman and Tversky's research also found that the tables were turned for insignificant gains and losses. When offers are low, and there are small chances of large gains, people tend to be risk-seeking. On the other side, people would rather pay a bit more than discounted value to avoid the small chance of enormous loss.

For the legal community, the research of Professor Christopher Guthrie (now dean at Vanderbilt University Law School) proved the point in simulated settlement negotiations.[90] This research as well as practice experience suggest that plaintiffs who recognize they have but a small chance of winning a *very* large amount at trial will prefer gambling to taking a pittance, even if that pittance is the discounted value. This is true even if the plaintiff *really does* accept and understand the chances of winning are indeed very, very, slim. So, she might acknowledge a mere 5 percent chance of winning $200,000, and yet turn down a $10,000 offer. Why? Well, perhaps the $10,000 won't dramatically affect her fate. It won't enable her to retire or pay her kids' college tuition. She may not be overly concerned about experiencing great regret over the loss. And, much like buying a lottery ticket, she may enjoy holding onto the possibility of the unlikely jackpot. (Of course, any or all of the other factors discussed in this book may also be at work.)

On the other side, the defense client faced with a 5 percent chance of that same $200,000 loss may be willing to pay more than the economically rational $10,000. Why? People are sometimes willing to pay a premium for certainty—peace of mind. And we are motivated to avoid regret.[91] To the defendant, over-paying a little bit enables him to avoid entirely the fear of having to pay $200,000, particularly if that would severely impact his business or corporate career.

3. *People tend to prefer positively framed choices—certain gains from a reference point—over choices involving risk.*

4. *People tend to prefer choices involving risk over negatively framed alternatives—certain losses from a reference point.*

If we accept that people are risk-averse as to gain and risk-seeking as to loss, then the lawyer's word choice, framing an offer positively as a gain or negatively as a loss, will impact the client's thinking. In Kahneman and Tversky's classic experiment, different subjects were given two sets of choices between alternative programs to combat an outbreak of a dangerous Asian disease expected to kill 600 people. The first group was asked to choose between Program A that would save 200 people and Program B that would have a 1/3 probability of saving 600 people and a 2/3 probability of saving no one. A second group of respondents were asked to choose between Program C, in which 400 people would die, or Program D that would have a 1/3 probability of no one dying and a 2/3 probability that 600 people will die.[92]

Professor Max Bazerman[93] later conducted a similar experiment in which participants were given parallel choices regarding a financially troubled, 6,000-worker company with three manufacturing locations. First, participants were asked to choose between Plan A that would save 2,000 jobs and one of the manufacturing plants, and Plan B that would have a 1/3 chance of saving all of the manufacturing plans and all of the jobs. Next, they were asked to choose between Plan C that would result in the loss of 4,000 jobs and two of the three manufacturing locations, and Plan D that would have a 2/3 chance of losing all of the manufacturing plants and all of the jobs.

In both experiments, the vast majority chose Plan A, and then Plan D. If you read the problem carefully, this makes no sense. Plans B and D are the more risk-seeking. So, internally consistent risk seekers should choose B and D. Plans A and C have certain outcomes. Those who prefer certainty should prefer these plans in both instances. Why do people choose inconsistently? The answer is in the framing: Plan A is framed around the positive—SAVING lives or KEEPING jobs, so it is preferred to B. But Plan C is framed around the negative—CERTAIN LOSS of lives or jobs—and so taking risk with plan D is preferred.

Thus, a key tenet of psychology's Prospect Theory is that an identified reference point determines the frame—whether you view an option as a loss or a gain—and that impacts your decision.[94]

Back to the Law

Your client has been offered $80,000 to settle her gender discrimination suit. In light of recent precedent, and the judge assigned to the case, you believe she has a 70 percent chance of losing the case on summary judgment and about a 55 percent, or slightly better than even chance of winning at trial. The likely damages range is from $70,000 to $250,000. Your client's last settlement demand was $120,000. You are convinced the $80,000 on the table is indeed the defense's final offer. You may frame the choice in one of these two ways:

> *This $80,000 offer is $45,000 lower than our last demand. I know it's far less than what you wanted coming in here today, but it might make sense to take it because our chances are not great.*

Or:

> *I am concerned about losing on summary judgment, which would mean you won't recover anything. Yes, there is a possibility you could get more at trial, but it is also possible that we could lose there, wait all that time, and still get nothing. Right now, the defense has put $80,000 on the table. That $80,000 would cover your basic expenses for at least a year, maybe two if necessary. It would be yours for sure—no rolling any dice. If you turn it down,*

it's as if you were giving that $80,000 back, for the privilege of taking a gamble.

Note that both characterizations are true. What might the difference in impact be?

Many mediators could testify as to the impact of framing rejection of a settlement offer as "losing" an opportunity," or "giving back" the settlement amount vs. rolling the dice. The actor-clients in hundreds of client-counseling sessions consistently report that a shift in positive or negative framing shifts their feelings about settlement. When the settlement offer seems like a loss, it is easy to turn down. The same is true if the amount of the offer means accepting "out-of-pocket" losses. When the offer on the table is framed as a certain gain (a check for bank deposit) vs. a roll of the dice, it becomes more difficult to reject. And they don't like to give up an opportunity for a sum certain that won't be available after summary judgment.

Lest there be any doubt that negative or positive framing of an offer or demand affects the way it is received, an experiment by professors Guthrie and Korobkin confirms the point. Subjects were asked to assume the role of plaintiff in an automobile accident case. In one version of the case, subjects were told that their Toyota, originally purchased for $14,000, had been destroyed, and they had medical damages of $14,000, entirely covered by medical insurance. An experimenter acting as their lawyer presented them with a $21,000 offer in one of two ways: as "less than" the total value of their losses," or "more than" their actual expenses. A far higher percentage of subjects who heard positive framing were inclined to accept the offer than were subjects who heard negative framing.[95]

Given the potential power of positive and negative framing for legal clients, a lawyer should not rely upon random, unintentional phrasing choices. This raises the question: Is it manipulative or dishonest to present only one frame—that most likely to lead to the lawyer's recommended choice? Readers must decide this one.

As a practical matter, experience suggests that your client will already have adopted one frame—from the reference point of his original hopes or expectations. The client will thus negatively frame an offer that is too low or a demand that is too high. The lawyer's role may be one of balance, recognizing the client's reference point, and suggesting the other.

Extra-Weightiness of Loss

It is appealing to think that a simple phrasing flip will work magic. Sometimes it does. Asking a client whether, if the settlement offer were deposited in her bank account, she would want to write a check in that amount to the defendant for the privilege of a gamble may have the intended effect.

However, research suggests that when losses are real—out-of-pocket-costs already expended—positive reframing has less impact. Both mediator experience and additional research by Guthrie and Korobkin confirm people's strong preference for restoring real dollar losses even when choices are reframed to highlight gains from a reference point.[96] We are loath to compromise if that won't cover what we've lost.

Reactive Devaluation

A well-known phenomenon in the psychology of decision-making, "reactive devaluation" occurs when we devalue a proposal or statement of worth as a reaction to its source, rather than to its apparent value.[97] It occurs when we distrust the offeror. Imagine that your client wishes to leave his employer and escape the full brunt of his non-compete obligation. With your client's approval, you have been negotiating on his behalf toward an agreement permitting him to sell within certain territories, and to maintain certain accounts, while abandoning claims to others. Your client is willing to sell or even give back a minority ownership share in the employer's company. He greatly dislikes and distrusts the principal owner of the company. Every time the owner offers to permit your client to sell within a particular area of the territory (otherwise off-limits under the non-compete), your client belittles its value, saying, "Sure, the businesses with high potential are further south."

Negotiation scholars note that reactive devaluation is not entirely irrational when we lack complete or balanced information. If I don't know the value of an asset offered, I might reasonably assume that the other side has chosen to offer what is less valuable. It is legitimate to seek information and verification.

Yet, the psychological tendency toward reactive devaluation can operate simply as a response to the other side. Progress toward agreement is difficult if your client devalues and rejects everything the other side offers. One classic remedy for reactive devaluation is involvement of a third-party neutral—a mediator. When the mediator suggests a proposal, or a new term, or another asset to add to the mix, her trusted neutrality should neutralize the devaluation.

When a client's reactive devaluation is slowing progress, the lawyer can play a constructive role by suggesting that the client privately identify what he values highly and why. Then, as offers or counter-offers are received, the lawyer can match these to the client's previous statements of value.

Matters of Equity, Fairness, and Self

Irrational but Real Resistance

We resist capitulation to power that is unfairly exercised. We resist accepting an offer that is economically rational, when the offer seems grossly inequitable, insulting, or disrespectful. In an "ultimatum game" played in many negotiation courses and workshops, people will reject very low offers and receive nothing, rather than permit the other side to realize disproportionate gain. Lawyers and mediators inevitably witness client's strong emotional reactions to "insulting" offers—on both the defense and plaintiff's side.[98]

This yields a few tidbits of advice:

- Even if a negotiation move will not be deemed sufficient, explanation of its rationale is wise, as it helps clients view the move as other than merely greedy, an exercise of power, or a tactical game. So, counsel your clients to provide reasonable explanations when they negotiate. Ask the other side for rationales behind offers, counter-offers, and demands.
- With your client's permission, explain to the other side why your client made various choices that seem to trouble them, at the table or away from the table. If appropriate, seek information or explanations to dispel client suspicions of the other party's intent to exploit or disrespect.
- Clients appreciate knowing that just as they have moved from an initial position and aspiration, so has the other side. Imagine that your client initially wanted to settle for no less than $200,000 but now sees the wisdom of settlement in the $150,000 range. It sounds a bit silly, but your client may feel better if he learns the other side entered the negotiations with a limit of $100,000 and has been pushed equally hard. As counsel, it's not ethical to create this fiction. But if you do learn it from opposing counsel, you would be wise to communicate it to your client. The same is true for defense counsel. We don't like to lose, but somehow, it helps if the other side is losing too.

The Unveiled Self—Fairness and Perspective

If only we had a nickel for every time a client said, "I just want what's fair!" Not at all coincidentally, your client's view of what is fair will likely inure to his benefit. When it's a "matter of principle," the chosen principle inevitably rewards the chooser.[99] Honest observers of people, from their playground disputes to their political positions, will acknowledge that our sense of equity tends to be self-serving. Thus, the wealthy may favor flat fees or a flat tax rate, invoking the principle that we should all pay an equal amount or an equal share. Those at the lower end of the income scale maintain that graduated tax rates are more fair as they more equally distribute the burden: a 10 percent rate for a low earner requires as much or greater sacrifice as a 40 percent rate for a high earner. Fortunately, in matters of ethics, politics, and social contract, some may transcend self-interest. However, self-serving bias in judgment of what is fair is all too common, particularly where there are many possible standards, choices, and arguments.

When the great political philosopher John Rawls wrote *A Theory of Justice*,[100] he described a "veil of ignorance" as needed for determining decisions about political, legal, and social policies. Rawls recognized that, because equity is self-serving, people will make policy decisions favoring their own interests. Fair policies and justice are achieved when decision-makers cannot predict impact upon themselves, as they remain ignorant of their own future stations in life.

Asking lawyer and client to transcend self-interest in search of a neutral vision of equity—to don Rawls's "veil of ignorance"—seems a tall order. It may also be inconsistent with the lawyer's obligation to advocate in his *client's* best interest—fairness *for his client*. Yet, your client may benefit from greater understanding of the other side's view of fairness. When your client sees ONLY his own position as principled, fair, and right, he views the other side as unprincipled, unfair, and greedy. Emotions run high. The other side is experienced as evil, illegitimate, exploitative. Your client does not want to engage, much less compromise with them.

If your client comes to recognize other legitimate perspectives on fairness, emotions may be calmed and reason possible. If she grudgingly understands the other side to be taking a different but somewhat principled and sincere stand, they will seem less evil.

Negotiation and compromise are not mere capitulation, but efforts toward reasonable resolution in your client's greater interests.

No Escaping Psychology

This chapter is long but surely not exhaustive, given that psychology enters all of our predictions, perceptions, memories, and decisions. Neither clients nor lawyers are machines in human form. To be human is to be sometimes inaccurate, forgetful, irrational, fallible, and unknowing of the future. Psychology forms part of our humanity. As long as lawyers and clients remain human, it is wise to be mindful of how psychology's tricks, traps, and tendencies predictably impact lawyer-client counseling.

Notes

1. "Paul Valery: Tel Quel (1943)," Wikiquote, http://en.wikiquote.org/wiki/Paul_Valéry (accessed May 27, 2011).

2. "Bobby Fischer Quotes," ThinkExist, http://thinkexist.com/quotation/i-don-t-believe-in-psychology-i-believe-in-good/532741.html (accessed May 27, 2011).

3. Without claim to exhaustive review of all Star Trek episodes, this capacity does come in handy. Gene Roddenberry, "Dagger of the Mind," *Star Trek: The Original Series*, season 1, episode 11, directed by Marc Daniels, aired November 17, 1966 (Culver City, CA: CBS Paramount International Television, 1994), VHS.

4. I strongly recommend decision analysis in general and litigation risk analysis in particular as invaluable for lawyers seeking to assess case value and for communicating with clients. I also recommend the Tree Age software, developed by attorneys Morris Raker and David Hoffer and originally designed for this purpose. The writings of the original expert, author, and trainer in this field, Marc Victor, are also excellent sources. I have also authored or co-authored various articles and chapters regarding decision analysis for lawyers and mediators, with a focus

on its use for communicating with clients in a mediation context. See Marjorie Aaron and Dwight Golann, "Evaluation and Decision Analysis," Chapter 8 in Dwight Golann, *Mediating Legal Disputes* (American Bar Association, Section of Dispute Resolution, 2009); Marjorie Aaron, "Finding Settlements with Numbers, Maps, and Trees," in *The Handbook of Dispute Resolution*, ed. Michael Moffitt and Robert Bordone (San Francisco: Jossey Bass, 2005) 202–218; Marjorie Aaron, "Evaluation in Mediation," in *Mediating Legal Disputes*, ed. Dwight Golann (Boston: Little, Brown & Company, 1996) 267–305; Marjorie Aaron and David Hoffer, "Decision Analysis as a Method of Evaluating the Trial Alternative," in *Mediating Legal Disputes*, ed. Dwight Golann (Boston: Little, Brown and Company, 1996), 307–334; Marjorie Aaron, "The Value of Decision Analysis in Mediation Practice," in *Negotiation Journal* 11, no. 2: 123–134 (1994). Numerous others have written on this topic, including (but not limited to): Jeffrey Senger, *Federal Dispute Resolution* (San Francisco: Jossey Bass, 2004), 80, 113–15; Louis Kaplow and Steven Shavell, *Decision Analysis, Game Theory, and Information* (New York: Foundation Press, 2004), 1–34; Jay Folberg, Dwight Golann, and Lisa Kloppenberg, *Resolving Disputes: Theory, Practice, and Law* (New York: Aspen Publishers, 2010), 151–155.

5. The acronym BATNA was first used and popularized in Roger Fisher and William Ury, *Getting to Yes*, 1st ed. (New York: Penguin Group, 1983).

6. As these endnotes suggest, this chapter draws upon a well-known literature in psychology and decision-making. I began reading that literature in the early 1990's, as my mediation practice and training work grew, and I was so often witness to the impact of psychological biases among mediation parties and lawyers. At that time, and through the 1990s, I was discovering books and articles by Daniel Kahneman and Amos Tversky, Edward Russo, and Paul Schoemaker, as well as colleagues Robert Mnookin, Jeffrey Rubin, and Max Bazerman at the Program on Negotiation at Harvard Law School. A comprehensive entry point into the social science was Kenneth Arrow, Robert H. Mnookin, Less Ross, Amos Tversky, and Robert Wilson, eds., *Barriers to Conflict Resolution* (W. W. Norton & Company, 1995). Professor Mnookin's "Why Negotiations Fail: An Exploration of Barriers to the Resolution of Conflicts," *Ohio State Journal on Dispute Resolution* 8, no. 235 (1993) served as an excellent summary of its application in legal disputes. The chapter on psychology by friends and colleagues law Professor Dwight

Golann and psychologist Helaine Scarlett Golann in Professor Golann's *Mediating Legal Disputes* also served as an important guidepost. More recently, I am indebted to author-professors Jean R. Sternlight and Jennifer K. Robbennolt for their excellent article: "Good Lawyers Should be Good Psychologists: Insights for Interviewing and Counseling Clients," *Ohio State Journal on Dispute Resolution* 23 (2008): 437. Though I had begun drafting this book before reading their article, I had not yet written this chapter. Their thorough work on how psychologists' insights merit attention in the client interviewing and counseling context served as an important filter for my decisions regarding what to include and what to omit from the broader psychology literature. While findings by Professors Russell Korobkin and Chris Guthrie, and the experimental and empirical work of numerous other professors examining decision making in legal contexts (cited extensively below) is not so recent, they were new, welcome, and valuable discoveries for me in the course of researching this chapter.

7. At the very least, as a mediator, spouse and mother, awareness of these tendencies encourages some skepticism regarding my own initial judgments. It also greatly enhances my capacity for patience when I see them operating in others.

8. Emily Pronin et al., "Understanding Misunderstanding: Social Psychological Perspectives," in ed. Thomas Gilovich et al., *Heuristics and Biases: the Psychology of Intuitive Judgment* (New York: Cambridge University Press, 2002), 646; Lee Ross and Andrew Ward, "Naïve Realism in Everyday Life: Implications for Social Conflict and Misunderstanding," in ed. Edward S. Reed et al., *Values and Knowledge* (Mahwah, NJ: Lawrence Erlbaum Associates, Inc., 1996), 103, 110–111. This definition of naïve realism is also quoted by Jean Sternlight and Jennifer Robbennolt in "Good Lawyers Should be Good Psychologists," 463 n. 88.

9. Kathryn Schulz, *Being Wrong: Adventures in the Margin of Error* (New York: HarperCollins, 2010). For an entirely accessible but more extended discussion of naïve realism, see pages 99–104.

10. Ibid., 99. The described experiment is an idea attributed to the philosopher Daniel Dennett and the results published by Austrian psychologists Heins Wimmer and Josef Perner in "Beliefs about Beliefs: Representation and Constraining Function of Wrong Beliefs in Young Children's Understanding of Deception," *Cognition* 13 (1983): 103–128.

11. Schulz, *Being Wrong*, 103.

12. Sternlight and Robbennolt, "Good Lawyers Should be Good Psychologists," 464, citing to Lee Ross and Donna Shetowsky, "Contemporary Psychology's Challenges to Legal Theory and Practice," *Northwestern University Law Review* 97 (2003): 1091.

13. Sternlight and Robbennolt, "Good Lawyers Should be Good Psychologists," 464–465.

14. Adam Galinsky et al. "Power and Perspectives Not Taken," *Psychological Science* 17 (2006): 1068, 1072, cited in Sternlight and Robbennolt, "Good Lawyers Should be Good Psychologists," 497 n. 246.

15. Schulz, *Being Wrong*, 80–81 (discussing Richard Nisbett and Timothy DeCamp's experiments, published in "Telling More Than We Know: Verbal Reports on Mental Processes," *Psychological Review* 84, no. 3 (1977): 231–259). This experiment is also described in William Hirstein, *Brain Fiction: Self-Deception and the Riddle of Confabulation* (Cambridge, MA: The MIT Press, 2005).

16. Schulz, *Being Wrong*, 106–107 (discussing the "bias blind spot," caused in part by the fact that we can only look into our own minds). Schulz quotes Princeton psychologist Emily Pronin and her colleagues' observations regarding a study of the bias blind spot that "we are not particularly comforted when others assure us that they have looked into their own hearts and minds and concluded they have been fair and objective." Emily Pronin, Thomas Gilovich, and Lee Ross, "Objectivity in the Eye of the Beholder: Divergent Perceptions of Bias in Self versus Other," *Psychological Review* 111, no. 3 (2004): 784. Thus, Schulz concludes (at 107) that "we look into our hearts and see objectivity; we look into our minds and see rationality; we look at our beliefs and see reality."

17. Garrison Keillor, originator, host, and star of Minnesota Public Radio's much beloved radio show (broadcast nationally through NPR), *Prairie Home Companion*, tells weekly stories from his Minnesota "home-town, Lake Wobegon, where the women are strong, the men are good looking, and all of the children are above average." Given Mr. Keillor's recent announcement of retirement plans, I cannot be certain that the "above average" quality of Lake Wobegon's children will be as universally recognized in the future as it is today. Schulz refers to this as "the Lake Wobegon Effect" in *Being Wrong*, 106; see also David Dunning,

Chip Heath, and Jerry M. Suls, "Flawed Self-Assessment: Implications for Health, Education, and the Workplace, *Psychological Science in the Public Interest* 5, no. 3 (2004): 69; David Dunning et al., "Why People Fail to Recognize Their Own Incompetence," *Current Directions in Psychological Science* 12, no. 3 (2003): 83–87 (describing research that indicates most people are not adept at judging their limitations and greatly overestimate their own talent and expertise).

18. Richard Klimoski, "Assessment from Nontraditional Points of View," in *Applying Psychology in Business*, ed. John Jones, Brian Steffy and Douglas Bray (New York: Lexington Books, 1991), 286 (citing Michael Harris and John Schaubroeck, "A Meta-Analysis of Self-Supervisor, Self-Peer and Peer-Supervisor Ratings," *Personnel Psychology* 41 (1998): 43–62.

19. On marriage: Ziva Kunda, "Motivated Inference: Self-Serving Generation and Evaluation of Causal Theories," *Journal of Personality and Social Psychology* 53 (1987): 637–640. On small business: Arnold Cooper et al., "Entrepreneurs' Perceived Chances of Success," in *Journal of Business Venturing* 3 (1988): 97, 100–107; Laurie Larwood and William Whittaker, "Managerial Myopia: Self-Serving Biases in Organizational Planning," *Journal of Applied Psychology* 62 (1977): 194–198.

20. Remembered conversation between Professor Marvin Bressler and the author, whose memory has faded as to its date and place, but places it certainly a long time ago.

21. Regarding schemas, see: Earl Hunt, "What Is a Theory of Thought?" and Stephen J. Ceci, Tina B. Rosenblum, and Eduardus DeBruyn, "Laboratory versus Field Approaches to Cognition," both in Robert J. Sternberg, ed., *The Nature of Cognition* (Cambridge, MA: MIT Press, 1999), 32 and 388.

22. Arien Mack and Irvin Rock, *Inattentional Blindness* (Cambridge, MA: MIT Press, 1998), 53–78. The gorilla story and the airline story are presented in Schulz, *Being Wrong*, 62–63.

23. The experiment was originally discussed in Daniel J. Simons and Christopher S. Chabris, "Gorillas in our Midst: Sustained Inattentional Blindness for Dynamic Events" *Perception* 28 (1999): 1059–1074. Their more recent relevant work is *The Invisible Gorilla* (New York: Random House, 2010). Interested readers can see this and related videos at http://www.theinvisiblegorilla.com/videos.html.

24. Daniel Simons and Daniel Levin, "Failure to Detect Changes to People During a Real-World Interaction," *Psychonomic Bulletin & Review* 5 (1998): 644–649.

25. Schulz, *Being Wrong*, 63.

26. Jeremy Wolfe, "Inattentional Amnesia," in *Fleeting Memories*, ed. Veronika Coltheart (Cambridge, MA: MIT Press, 2000), 71–94.

27. Charles G. Lord et al., "Biased Assimilation and Attitude Polarization: the Effects of Prior Theories on Subsequently Considered Evidence," *Journal of Personality and Social Psychology* 37 (1979): 2098–2099. See also J. E. Brophy and T. L. Good, *Teacher-Student Relationships: Causes and Consequences* (New York: Holt, Rinehart & Winston, Inc., 1974), 42–77.

28. Albert Hastorf and Hadley Cantril, "They Saw a Game: A Case Study," *Journal of Abnormal and Social Psychology* 49 (1954): 129–134.

29. David O. Sears and Richard E. Whitney, "Political Persuasion," in *Handbook of Communication*, ed. I. D. Pool et al. (Chicago: Rand McNally, 1973): 253–289.

30. James K. Sebenius, "Six Habits of Merely Effective Negotiators," *Harvard Business Review* 79, no. 4 (2001): 94.

31. See Zev J. Eigen and Yair Listokin, "Do Lawyers Really Believe Their Own Hype and Should They?: A Natural Experiment," *Yale Law & Economics Research Paper* No. 412 (July 12, 2011); Elizabeth F. Loftus and Willem A. Wagenaar, "Lawyer's Predictions of Success," *Jurimetrics* 28 (1988); Jane Goodman-Delahunty et al., "Insightful or Wishful: Lawyers' Ability to Predict Case Outcomes," *Psychology Public Policy, and Law* 16 (2010): 133–157.

32. Joyce Ehrlinger, Thomas Gilovich, and Lee Ross," Peering into the Bias Blind Spot: People's Assessments of Bias in Themselves and Others," *Personality and Social Psychology Bulletin* 31, no. 5 (2005): 680–692.

33. Ibid., 681.

34. Ibid., 681–682.

35. Austin Sarat and William L. F. Felstiner, "Law and Social Relations: Vocabularies of Motive in Lawyer/Client Interaction," *Law and Society Review* 22, no. 4 (1988): 740.

36. Randall Kiser, *Beyond Right and Wrong: The Power of Effective Decision Making for Attorneys and Clients* (New York: Springer-Varlag Berlin Heidelberg, 2010), 93.

37. Kiser, *Beyond Right and Wrong*, 93–94 (citing William L.F. Felstiner, Richard Abel, and Austin Sarat, "The Emergence and Transformation of Disputes: Naming, Blaming, Claiming" *Law and Society Review* 15 (1980–1981): 637).

38. Kiser, *Beyond Right and Wrong*, 93 (quoting Felstiner, "The Emergence and Transformation of Disputes," 641).

39. Sarat, "Law and Social Relations," 747.

40. In his discussion of attribution biases, Kiser cites *Wall Street Journal* writer Jeffrey Zaslow, and observes that "the instinct of self protection encourages people to blame others," but as Zaslow writes, ultimately blame "ruins everything, creating hostilities, scapegoats, and an avoidance of hard decision that could actually solve problems." Kiser, *Beyond Right and Wrong*, 96–97 (quoting Jeffrey Zaslow, "It's All Your Fault: Why Americans Can't Stop Playing the Blame Game," *The Wall Street Journal*, September 15, 2005, D1).

41. Ulric Neisser and Nicole Harsch, "Phantom Flashbulbs: False Recollections of Hearing the News about Challenger," in *Affect and accuracy in recall: Studies of "flashbulb" memories*, eds. Eugene Winograd and Ulric Neisser (New York: Cambridge University Press, 1993): Vol. 4, 9–31 (discussed in Schulz, *Being Wrong*, 72–73).

42. According to Schulz, "a group of cognitive scientists working together as the 9/11 Memory Consortium repeated and expanded on Neisser's study after September 11, with roughly the same results." *Being Wrong*, 73. See Ali Teckan et al., "Autobiographical and Event Memory For 9/11: Changes Across One Year," *Applied Cognitive Psychology* 17 (2003): 1057–1066; Marilyn Smith, Uri Bibi, and D. Erin Sheard, "Evidence for the Differential Impact of Time and Emotion on Personal and Event Memories for 9/11," *Applied Cognitive Psychology* 17 (2003): 1047–1055.

43. Sternlight and Robbennolt, "Good Lawyers Should Be Good Psychologists," 475 (quoting Ronald P. Fisher, "Interviewing Victims and Witnesses of Crime," *Psychology, Public Policy, and Law* 1 (1995): 738; Marcia K. Johnson, Shahin Hashtroudi, and D. Stephen Lindsay, "Source Monitoring," *Psychological Bulletin* 114 (1993): 3; D. Stephen Lindsay and Marcia K. Johnson, "False Memories and the Source Monitoring Framework," *Learning and Individual Differences* 12 (1997): 145; Karen J. Mitchell, Marcia K. Johnson, and Mara Mather, "Source Monitoring and Suggestibility to Misinformation: Adult-Age Related Differences," *Applied Cognitive Psychology* 17 (2003): 107.

44. Ulric Neisser, "John Dean's Memory: A Case Study," *Cognition* 9, no. 1 (1981): 102 (cited in Daniel Goleman, *Vital Lies, Simple Truths* (New York: Simon & Shuster, 1985), 94, and in Kiser, *Beyond Right and Wrong*, 100).

45. Attorneys with interest in this topic are advised to consult: Elizabeth Loftus, "Leading Questions and the Eyewitness Report," *Cognitive Psychology* 7 (1975): 560; Elizabeth Loftus and Guido Zanni, "Eyewitness Testimony: The Influence of the Wording of a Question," *Bulletin of the Psychonomic Society* 5 (1975): 86; Peter A. Powers, Joyce L. Andriks, and Elizabeth F. Loftus, "The Eyewitness Accounts of Females and Males," *Journal of Applied Psychology* 64 (1979): 339.

46. Loftus, "Leading Questions," 560, 566 (cited in Sternlight and Robbennolt, "Good Lawyers," 476 n. 150).

47. Loftus, "Leading Questions," 563–565.

48. Loftus and Zanni, "Eyewitness Testimony," 86; Loftus, "Leading Questions," 560.

49. Sternlight and Robbennolt, "Good Lawyers," 477 nn. 151 and 152 (citing David A. Pizzaro et al., "Ripple Effects in Memory: Judgments of Moral Blame Can Distort Memory for Events," *Memory & Cognition* 34 (2006): 550, 552–553, and Mark D. Alicke, "Culpable Control and the Psychology of Blame," *Psychological Bulletin* 126 (2000): 556. See also Mark. D. Alicke et al., "Culpable Control and Counterfactual Reasoning in the Psychology of Blame," *Personality and Social Psychology Bulletin* 34 (2008): 1371.

50. "To be uncertain is to be uncomfortable." QuotationsBook, http://quotationsbook.com/quote/5531 (accessed August 12, 2011).

51. "Eric Hoffer Quotes," BrainyQuote, http://www.brainyquote.com/quotes/quotes/e/erichoffer399157.html (accessed August 12, 2011).

52. Perhaps this overstates the case. Perhaps many client-to-lawyer questions yield simple, conclusive answers: a policy banning women from all high-paying jobs is unlawful; driving while intoxicated will justify your arrest; you may not punch your child's teacher (even if she deserves it). While these explanations may not be welcome to your client's ears, they are straightforward and simple to communicate. Thus, they don't require discussion in this book.

53. Research on lawyers and prediction has focused on the litigation context, but there is no reason to believe our predictive powers improve in other areas of practice.

54. Loftus and Wagenaar, "Lawyer's Predictions of Success."

55. Interestingly, lawyers on contingency fees exhibited particular bias. They had the same (misplaced) level of confidence (65 percent) about case outcomes as other attorneys, but they won only 42 percent of their cases, compared to an overall win rate of 56 percent. This is consistent with the study by Goodman-Delahunty, Granhag, and Loftus, cited infra note 56, and also cited in Randall Kiser's *Beyond Right and Wrong*. Kiser's broader finding that type of case is more highly correlated with win/loss rate than types of "actors" (lawyers) suggests an explanation. Kiser, *Beyond Right and Wrong*, 53. Kiser notes lower win rates for plaintiffs in case types in which contingency fees are common. Ibid., 56. So, while the cause of lower win rates—more prediction error by plaintiff's contingency fee counsel—could be more overconfidence, risk-taking personalities, or stronger partisan bias, I suspect the answer isn't that simple.

56. J. Goodman-Delahunty, P. A. Granhag, and E. F. Loftus, "How Well Can Lawyers Predict Their Chances of Success?" unpublished manuscript, 1998 (cited in Derek J. Koehler, Lyle Brenner, and Dale Griffin, "The Calibration of Expert Judgment: Heuristics and Biases beyond the Laboratory," in *Heuristics and Biases*, ed. Thomas Gilovich et. al., 705–706). These sources are also cited in Kiser, *Beyond Right and Wrong*, 56 n. 37.

57. Marc Galanter, "The Regulatory Function of the Civil Jury," in *Verdict: Assessing the Civil Jury System*, ed. Robert E. Litan, (Washington, D.C.: Brookings Institution Press, 1993), 81–83.

58. Roselle L. Wissler et al., "Decisionmaking about General Damages: A Comparison of Jurors, Judges, and Lawyers," *Michigan Law Review* 98 (1999): 751, summary discussion at 805.

59. Kiser, *Beyond Right and Wrong*, 42–46. The underlying study can be found in Randall L. Kiser, Martin A. Asher, and Blakeley B. McShane, "Let's Not Make a Deal: An Empirical Study of Decision Making in Unsuccessful Settlement Negotiations," *Journal of Empirical Legal Studies* 5, no. 3 (2008): 551–591. The study authors examined differences in case "context"—types of cases—and in "actors" through characteristics of the lawyers involved and concluded that, for the most part, *context* accounts for more of the differences in tendency be right. In other words, different types of cases, as well as numbers and types of claims within those cases, are more or less likely to yield plaintiff's

verdicts versus defense verdicts. (For this reason, I strongly recommend that ALL attorneys dedicated to accurate prediction obtain a copy of this study.)

Despite the way Kiser characterizes the study's conclusions, its method was NOT focused on attorneys' predictions. Indeed, neither attorneys nor clients were polled as to their trial outcome predictions. Instead, it compares the final reported settlement offers and demands to the trial results and analyzes "decision errors," defined as instances in which the trial result was "worse" for a party than the last settlement offer. Moreover, it does not differentiate between attorneys' and clients' views. Undoubtedly, in some cases, clients would have rejected an offer or declined to meet a last demand, counter to lawyers' advice. Thus, the study is not a *direct* measure of attorney predictions or judgment. Moreover, settlement offers and demands are NOT generally intended to BE the amount of a predicted trial verdict. Rather, they generally reflect a prediction of trial outcomes (or range of outcomes), roughly discounted for estimated risk and cost.

Using Kiser's characterization of decision error: given that defendants win—achieving a $0 verdict—51 percent or 52 percent of the time— defendants' AVERAGE decision error rate *should* be low (assuming the defense typically makes offers of $1 or more). Again, in Kiser's terms, if a plaintiff made a final demand of $80,000 and the trial resulted in an award of $150,000 to the plaintiff, the defense would be considered to have made a "decision error" in the amount of $70,000. On the other side, if a plaintiff turns down a last offer of $20,000 in the same case and recovers $0 in a defense verdict, the plaintiff's "decision error" would be counted as $20,000. In other words, all plaintiffs' losses are counted as decision errors as long as the defendant had made at least a $1 offer.

Yet, defendants' "decision error *cost*" eclipsed plaintiffs' decision error cost. The plaintiff's mean cost of error was $52,183 in New York, and $73,400 in California. However, defendant's mean cost of error was $920,874 in New York, and $1,403,654 in California—orders of magnitude higher.

60. Note Kaiser's discussion in *Beyond Right and Wrong* points to the underlying study results that plaintiffs "mistakenly" anticipate a win or fail to discount sufficiently for likely loss a bit more than half the time, which is somewhat more often than the defendants. However, in my

view, plaintiffs' lower "error *costs*" indicate that plaintiffs discount their final settlement demands greatly (even if not always quite enough) to adjust for risk. Defendants' VERY high mean error costs suggest rather dramatic failures to recognize how high the damages are likely to be, if and when plaintiffs will win on liability. Or, also probable, they fail to factor that higher damages risk into their settlement offers.

61. Kiser makes the point that this 78 percent agreement rate is higher than that of expert to expert agreement in many other fields. *Beyond Right and Wrong*, 18.

62. Neil Vidmar and Valeri Hans, *American Juries: The Verdict* (Amherst, NY: Prometheus Books, 2007), 149–151.

63. Michael Heise et al., "Juries, Judges and Punitive Damages: Empirical Analyses Using the Civil Justice Survey of State Courts 1992, 1996, and 2001 Data," *Journal of Empirical Legal Studies* 3, no. 2 (2006): 293. See also Vidmar and Hans, *American Juries*, 311 (citing a study by Thomas Eaton and Jennifer Robbennolt finding "that juries did not award punitive damages more often than judges and made similar decisions about the appropriate amount of damages.")

64. Wissler et al., "Decision Making about General Damages," 751. In this study, lawyers, judges, and citizens who had reported for jury duty were presented with the same set of hypothetical case facts and asked to estimate the appropriate level of damages to be awarded to the plaintiff. There was considerable difference among the awards by legal professionals (judges and attorneys) and less variation among potential jurors.

65. J. Goodman-Delahunty, P. A. Granhag, M. Hartwig, and E. F. Loftus "Insightful or Wishful: Lawyers' Ability to Predict Case Outcomes," *Psychology, Public Policy, and Law* 16, no.2 (2010) 133–157.

66. Ibid., 142. Interestingly, the study referenced above suggests some gender differences, with less overconfidence and hence better calibration of prediction to results among women lawyers than among male lawyers.

67. Robert E. Knox and James A. Inkster, "Postdecision Dissonance at Post Time," *Journal of Personality and Social Psychol.* 8, no. 4 (1) (1968): 319–323.

68. Research also indicates that imagining a possible event increases estimates of its likelihood. Amos Tversky and Daniel Kahneman,

"Judgment Under Uncertainty: Heuristics and Biases," *Science* 185, no. 4157 (1974): 1124–1131. See John S. Carroll, "The Effect of Imagining an Event on Expectations for the Event: An Interpretation in Terms of the Availability Heuristic," *Journal of Experimental Social Psychology* 14 (1976): 88–96. See also Edward Bowman and Howard Kunreuther, "Post-Bhopal Behavior at a Chemical Company," *Journal of Management Studies* 25 (1998): 387–402.

69. Nicholas Epley and Thomas Gilovich, "Are Adjustments Insufficient?" *Personality and Social Psychology Bulletin* 30 (2004): 447–460.

70. Kiser's results suggest that those with training as neutral mediators may be somewhat better predictors. Kiser, *Beyond Right and Wrong*, 86.

71. See Jennifer K. Robbennolt, "Attorneys, Apologies, and Settlement Negotiation," *Harvard Negotiation Law Review* 13 (2008): 349.

72. See Russell Korobkin, "Psychological Impediments to Mediation Success: Theory and Practice," research paper, University of California, Los Angeles School of Law, Los Angeles, CA, March 2005. See also Edward M. Bodaken and Kenneth K. Sereno, "Counter-attitudinal Advocacy, Ego- Involvement and Persuasive Effect," *Western Communication* 39 (1976): 236.

73. Of course, there are an enormous number of possible answers, many suggested by this and other chapters; several may be true for any particular client.

74. Tversky and Kahneman, "Judgment Under Uncertainty," 1128.

75. Max H. Bazerman and Margaret A. Neale, *Negotiating Rationally* (New York: The Free Press, 1992), 26–28.

76. Andrew J. Wistrich, Chris Guthrie, and Jeffrey J. Rachlinski, "Inside the Judicial Mind," *Cornell Law Review* 86 (2001): 777.

77. See Gretchen B. Chapman and Brian H. Bornstein, "The More You Ask For, the More You Get: Anchoring in Personal Injury Verdicts," *Applied Cognitive Psychology* 10 (1996): 519, 522.

78. Russell Korobkin and Chris Guthrie, "Opening Offers and Out-of Court Settlement, a Little Moderation May Not Go a Long Way," *Ohio State Journal on Dispute Resolution* 10 (1994): 1. For a summary of articles on anchoring, see Dan Orr and Chris Guthrie, "Anchoring, Information, Expertise, and Negotiation: New Insights from Meta-Analysis," *Ohio State Journal on Dispute Resolution* 21 (2006): 597.

79. As a professor who also teaches negotiation, the author cannot resist noting that extreme anchors are correlated with more competitively favorable negotiation results for the party casting the extreme anchor. However, opening with an unjustifiably extreme anchor also yields higher number of impasses and may damage the negotiator's credibility. Lynn M. Mather, Craig A. McEwen, and Richard J. Maiman, *Divorce Lawyers at Work: Varieties of Professionalism in Practice* (Oxford: Oxford Univ. Press, 2001), 128. Classic negotiation advice suggests opening with the most aggressive anchor that can be justified—it must pass a straight-face test. See Bazerman and Neale, *Negotiating Rationally*, 23–30.

80. Epley and Gilovich, "Are Adjustments Insufficient?," 447–460. Anchoring should be recognized either as a deliberate strategy, or as reflecting one's initial thinking about the case. As negotiators, we should resist the psychological impact of the other side's anchor and set our own.

81. Laura Beth Nielsen, Robert L. Nelson, and Ryon Lancaster, "Individual Justice of Collective Legal Mobilization? Employment Discrimination Litigation in the Post-Civil Rights United States," *Journal of Empirical Legal Studies* 7, no. 2 (2010): 175–201.

82. Daniel Kahneman, Jack L. Knetsch, and Richard H. Thaler, "Experimental Tests of the Endowment Effect and the Case Theorem," *The Journal of Political Economy* 98, no. 6 (1990): 1325–1348. Summary adapted from Bazerman and Neale, *Negotiating Rationally*, 36–37. The experiment was also described at length in Amos Tversky and Daniel Kahneman, "Loss Aversion in Riskless Choice: A Reference-Dependent Model," *The Quarterly Journal of Economics* 106, no. 4 (1991): 1039–1061.

83. For a discussion of status quo bias and its relationship to the endowment affect, see Tversky and Kahneman, "Loss Aversion in Riskless Choice," 1042–1043.

84. Dwight Golann, "Death of a Claim: The Impact of Loss Reactions on Bargaining," *Negotiation Journal* 20, no. 4 (2004): 539.

85. Amos Tversky and Daniel Kahneman, "The Framing of Decisions and the Psychology of Choice," *Science* 211, no. 4481 (1981): 454. These numerical examples are derived from their article.

86. Ibid.

87. For additional and accessible explanations of Prospect Theory, risk aversion and loss aversion, see Scott Plous, *The Psychology of Judgment and Decision Making* (New York: McGraw-Hill, 1993); Amos Kahneman and Daniel Tversky, "Prospect Theory: An Analysis of Decision under Risk," *Econometrica* 47 (1979): 263–291.

88. "No more than $60,000" may sound extreme, based upon the potential exposure in this case. However, the idea that a defendant might indeed stick at such a number is borne out by empirical research by Randall Kiser and his colleagues, indicating that defendants' last offers tend to be far, far lower than the damages awarded when the defense is unsuccessful. As discussed earlier, partisan perception is no doubt at work, as defendants most likely failed to assess the likely damages. But psychologists' insights into attitudes toward risk and loss suggest that this data supports the observation that defense litigants tend to choose greater (future) risk over certain and current loss.

89. The fact that the risked loss will take place in the future undoubtedly causes it to be discounted as well: Shane Frederick, George Loewenstein, and Ted O'Donoghue, "Time Discounting and Time Preference: A Critical Review," *Journal of Economic Literature* 40, no. 2 (2002): 351–401.

90. Chris Guthrie, "Framing Frivolous Litigation: A Psychological Theory," *The University of Chicago Law Review* 67, no. 1 (2000): 163–216.

91. Related research indicates that we tend to overweight the possibility of unlikely or improbable events, and underweight the possibility of more likely events. Perhaps we just simplify: it will happen or it won't. That makes us worry (almost) as much about airplane crashes—unlikely—as the more probable automobile accident.

92. Tversky and Kahneman, "The Framing of Decisions and the Psychology of Choice," 453.

93. Max H. Bazerman, "The Relevance of Kahneman and Tversky's Concept of Framing to Organizational Behavior," working paper, *Journal of Management*, Massachusetts Institute of Technology, December 1983, 1–3.

94. Kahneman and Tversky, "Prospect Theory," 263.

95. Russell Korobkin and Chris Guthrie, "Psychological Barriers to Litigation Settlement: An Experimental Approach," *Michigan Law Review* 93, no. 1 (1994): 131–133.

96. Two sets of subjects were given the same facts about their car accident case. One set was informed that their Toyotas—at the original cost of $14,000—had been destroyed—and they had medical damages of $14,000, for a total value of $28,000. Because their medical expenses were covered (and ignoring subrogation issues for the purposes of the experiment), the offered settlement of $21,000 represented a net cash gain. A second group was informed that their BMWs—original cost of $24,000—had been destroyed and medical costs were $4,000, also a total value of $28,000. The offered settlement was $21,000. Not surprisingly, far fewer BMW owners accepted the settlement. Korobkin and Guthrie then tried a follow-up experiment to test the impact of positive and negative framing. For some subjects, they deliberately framed the offer as a gain over a possible $0 recovery and over the previous offer. While the Toyota owners responded with higher acceptance rates, the BMW owners did not. Guthrie and Korobkin hasten to point out (and this author agrees) that reframing may be more difficult but not futile in real loss circumstances, but may take more time and skill. Ibid., 162–163.

97. Lee Ross, "Reactive Devaluation in Negotiation and Conflict Resolution," in *Barriers to Conflict Resolution*, ed. Kenneth Arrow et al. (New York: Norton, 1995), 26–43.

98. In yet another one of professors Guthrie and Korobkin's simulated legal negotiations, students were more likely to reject low settlement offers when given no explanation of a landlord's failure to respond to their requests for building repair. Presumably, the landlord's failure to respond was viewed as dismissive and disrespectful. When the landlord communicated the reason for his failure (though not a legal excuse), recipients were more likely to accept. Korobkin and Guthrie, "Psychological Barriers to Litigation Settlement," 143–147.

99. George Loewenstein et al., "Self-Serving Assessments of Fairness and Pretrial Bargaining," *The Journal of Legal Studies* 22, no. 1 (January 1993): 135–159.

100. John A. Rawls, *A Theory of Justice*, rev. ed. (Cambridge, MA: Belknap Press of Harvard Univ. Press, 1999).

How to Say It, and Why

A lawyer is a more strategic and effective counselor when fully informed as to the impact of language, meaning, emotion, and psychology on his client's capacity and willingness to understand and accept bad news and legal realities. Though there can be no single, immutable script for a lawyer-client counseling scene, the preceding chapters sought to provide insight into which lines are best avoided, and which are best to choose. They suggest deliberate ways to facilitate your client's emotional de-escalation, full comprehension, and robust cognition, and to build client trust and loyalty. They provide advice to lawyers for deriving alternative script strategies: on order, structure, frame, metaphor, and language to use within an inevitably improvisational lawyer-client counseling session.

That the lawyer's lines consist of accurate and well-chosen words is necessary. But it's not necessarily sufficient. The words alone do not determine their effectiveness. Watch the same actor deliver the same line with entirely different vocal pitch, volume, timing, physical stance, motion, and gesture. What he said will have an entirely different effect because of the way he said it.

The final four chapters focus on the delivery—"how to say it"—using voice and gesture for greater client understanding and acceptance, particularly in the face of complexity, uncertainty, and bad news. Opening the "how to say it" chapters, "Choices in Voice" suggests strategic shifts in vocal speed, pausing, and pitch. "Choreography of Counsel" offers research and advice on choices in body position, posture, and motion. "A Gesture to Clarity" discusses how gesture can enhance or undermine comprehension. The final chapter, "Channel Navigation Notes," suggests ways gesture and movement in the physical space between seated lawyer and client can strengthen client connection and trust.

Lawyers are not actors in a literary fiction. Our client communication occurs in the non-fictional world. But we are wise to borrow from actors and communication science for advice on how to clarify, convince, and connect when counseling clients on matters of legal reality.

6

Choices in Voice

"The voice is a second face."

—GERARD BAUER[1]

"You can spend all day getting ready and then blow the whole thing when you open your mouth."

—KATHLEEN TURNER[2]

Vocal choices—the ways we use our voices to speak—influence the effectiveness of communication more than the words we use, and most of our communication occurs in conversations or small meetings, rather than trials or public forums. Yet, law school and CLE trainings tend to focus on strategies of formal argument and persuasion. When it occurs, instruction on lawyers' use of voice is directed toward the court or jury or occasionally, large group presentations.

In all of my formal education and training, I recall no attention to use of voice when meeting with a client, colleague, or superior. Of course, if a lawyer or law student uses his or her voice incompetently—if his or her conversational speech pattern is incomprehensible or annoying, or suggests extreme lack of confidence, seriousness, or professionalism—successful job interviews are highly unlikely. If he hangs out a solo practitioner's shingle, it is hard to imagine a client retaining him as counsel.

Given that most of us are eventually hired by firms or organizations and retained by clients, it is fair to assume that lawyers, indeed most people, naturally use their voices more or less effectively. The emphasis here is on "more or less." Let's think back to a lawyer's goals for a client counseling session. One goal is to explain legal concepts so that a client understands them and to ensure that the client expresses his interests, concerns, and confusions. Another is to build trust and rapport through each conversation, strengthening the lawyer-client relationship. Finally, the lawyer wants to convey appropriate confidence, competence, and authority—"gravitas"—so that, to paraphrase a very old television commercial, "when the lawyer talks, the client listens." The lawyer's vocal choices—tone, pitch, and pattern of his voice—can contribute more or less to achievement of these goals. Skillful and strategic use of voice is no substitute for content, but it can help to ensure that the client fully understands and carefully considers the sound advice of his well-trusted lawyer.

Timing Is Everything

I am unaware of any studies that establish what percentage of lawyers talk too fast. For those of us who do, does awareness or feedback to that effect slow us down? Well, maybe sometimes. As a too-fast-talker, my embarrassment at watching my hyper-speed speech on video recordings may have led to somewhat more moderate speed in formal presentations. Perhaps becoming more confident enables us to slow down, as nervousness seems to stimulate the fast-forward function.[3] Let's assume that many people who speak quickly do so quite intelligibly. The rate may be fast but the enunciation superb. Why does this matter in a client counseling conversation?

The Need for Speed Bumps

When a lawyer speaks quickly, albeit with clear-as-a-bell enunciation, on a legal concept of some complexity and import, the client may hear all of her words but *lack time to process their meaning*. The more difficult the concept, the more difficult or technical the words chosen, the more time the client needs to process the meaning of a sentence.[4]

Clients also need time to process messages that cause emotional discomfort: risk of an adverse outcome, the opposition's view of his credibility, missing evidence or difficult precedent, unforeseen costs or delay, or a disappointing settlement offer or contract proposal. If the lawyer speaks quickly, and the client catches the negative import of the first phrase or two, his emotions may prevent him from absorbing the words that follow. Even if he technically hears them, he may be unable to process their meaning. As discussed in chapter 1, upon hearing life-altering news, people often enter what University of Wisconsin Sociology Professor Douglas Maynard calls a "noetic crisis" in which one is "unable to assemble sensuous appearances (noemata) into a coherent object." According to Maynard, "The noesis, consisting of ordinary acts of gestalt comprehension and involving perception, recollection, retention, and other 'modes of consciousness' as exhibited in embodied action and interaction, is at least momentarily blocked."[5]

Pausing frequently as you convey technical and particularly negative information is consistent with advice written for physicians who must inform a patient of bad news. Physicians are advised to "give information in small chunks," because "studies have shown that most patients fail to retain up to 50% of the information given, even if it is about something simple. . . . When the diagnosis is more serious, the information drop out may be more substantial."[6]

Advice for Fast Talkers—Use Simpler Language

Assume that a fast talker uses only words his client would recognize and define correctly on a vocabulary test. Some words will still require more cognitive energy to process than others. Think of the old camp song that conveyed the same meaning in two versions: "Indicate the way to my habitual abode; I'm fatigued and desire to retire" and "Show me the way to go home; I'm tired and I want to go to bed." While a client might know all of the words in the song's first version, each takes a moment or so to decode. The second version involves no delay. As soon as we hear the words, we understand them, no matter how quickly they were spoken.

Many of us understandably make "higher" language choices when speaking with a highly educated client. Technical legal jargon aside, no client wants his lawyer to speak down to him, and no lawyer wants his client to feel that he is doing so. If you are a speaker of moderate speed, with an educated professional client, you may choose to "indicate the way to the habitual abode." But if you tend to speak quickly, you should err on the side of language choices that "show the way to go home" where possible. With no time wasted on decoding language in a speedily vocalized sentence, all of the client's cognitive processing can be directed toward understanding the legal problem.

Pause In Compensation

Talking too fast involves two elements: (1) the rate at which words are spoken within a sentence; and (2) the length of pauses between spoken sentences or topics. Ideally, one could modify both. In my observation and experience, people find it extremely difficult to sustain a deliberately slower rate of speech than that which comes naturally. However, it *is* easier to train oneself to PAUSE between spoken sentences and paragraphs. The good news is that punctuating your speech with regular and sufficiently lengthy pauses largely compensates for talking too fast. Now let's talk about when to pause and for how long.

Regular Speed, Regular Pauses, with Time for Direct Glance

Effective pauses are in timing—frequency and duration—and glance. So, when and for how long? Of course, it depends. A regular-speed speaker conveying uncomplicated concepts that are unlikely to elicit a strong emotional response should pause naturally between clusters, facts, or ideas—where a new paragraph would begin if your comments were written. When you pause, LOOK at your client, take a breath. Create some time, and thus space, for a client question or interjection and for you to read your client's facial expression. Although this is indeed exactly what occurs in normal conversation, it is often forgotten when lawyers speak with clients. Moreover, "normal" conversational conditions—easily accessible concepts and little emotional impact—are not necessarily the norm in a client counseling session.

Speed Talkers, E-X-T-E-N-D Those Pauses

If you do tend to speak quickly, EXTEND ALL pauses. What seems like a natural, adequate pause to you is so fleeting, so quick, your client misses it without perceiving any break in your narrative.[7] Remember, when you speak very quickly, your listener needs some time at the end of each sentence or thought cluster to process the meaning of those quickly spoken words. If the pause is too quick, the listener-client never has a chance to catch up before you are on to the next sentence. The client may try to follow with compromised comprehension of the words already spoken, or the client may take an extra second or so to process that first sentence, and thus miss the first part of the next one.

Consider this metaphor, drawn from early morning runs in the neighborhood. A 10+-minute miler is jogging a three-loop course with her friend, a 9-minute miler. The slower runner expends some extra effort on the first half of the first loop so she can gab and catch up on gossip. After a bit, the faster runner pulls ahead and waits for her slower friend at the top of the hill. If the faster runner starts running as soon as the slower gets to the top, the slower will have had no similar chance to catch her breath. She won't be able to keep up much at all for the rest of the run. Bottom-line advice for runners and fast talkers who want to keep up the conversation: take longer pauses— even if the ideas being discussed are not overly challenging.

More Often Than You Imagine

Mindful that legal concepts are complex—the first year of law school wasn't easy—some lawyers give a careful, step-by-step explanation of every aspect of the legal process and relevant case law or statute, then pause and ask if the client has any questions. As she turns to convey the concept of summary judgment, the lawyer may implicitly or explicitly beg the client's patience while she explains all of the elements. A long pause at the end is better than none, but my strong advice is to punctuate your explanation with many, many pauses between subtopics or elements.

Failure to stop until the end prevents a lawyer from learning if there's confusion along the way. It calls to mind the frustration many of us felt when doing a long math problem with related and sequential subparts. If we made a mistake or applied a mistaken assumption in an early subpart, it carried through the rest of the problem. For the more verbally inclined, the analogy would be to a crossword puzzle, in which one wrong word throws off all others that intersect its boxes.

The lawyer may prefer to offer her perfect, logically-ordered, well-prepared explanation in sequence without interruption until complete. However, the client is likely to better understand the whole if permitted pause space along the way to absorb and process information, express any confusion, discuss what he's gleaned, or ask about its impact upon business or personal contexts.

Research provides strong support for the value of pausing to permit time for reflection and discussion, if listeners are to recollect and understand material presented. For example, in one experiment, groups of students listened to a series of videotaped lectures in three formats: (1) without pauses; (2) with pauses every seven minutes, permitting students to reflect or review notes; and (3) with pauses at the same intervals, but permitting students to discuss the material with peers. Results showed that students in both lectures punctuated by pauses performed better on a test of the lecture content than those who did not have the benefit of pauses. Students permitted to discuss the material performed best.[8]

A well-known and simple communication game yields further empirical evidence for the value of permitting discussion time. In that game, called "One-Way Two-Way Communication," a speaker is provided with a drawing consisting of a series of linked geometric shapes. He must describe the drawing to an audience so that each audience member will be able to replicate it. After explaining where the first geometric shape is placed on the page, the speaker generally describes each shape, beginning with how it is attached to the preceding shape.[9]

In the "one-way" version of the exercise, the speaker's description is uninterrupted. The audience cannot ask questions. In the "two-way" version, the goal is the same but the audience members are permitted to raise their hands and ask questions, which the speaker must answer before proceeding. Inevitably, a lower percentage of the audience replicates the picture accurately when communication is one-way. It is also less satisfying to the audience, though preferred by the speaker.

The two-way communication exercise takes more time, because of all those interruptions and questions. The speaker doesn't enjoy it as much, but the audience prefers it, and the pictures are far more accurate. These results bear out for lawyers and clients: two-way communication—pauses and discussion as you go—will yield greater client satisfaction and more accurate understanding.

Double the Extended Pause for Degrees of Difficulty

When a lawyer is explaining complex concepts, the pause time should lengthen *significantly*. I don't pretend to precision here, or a magic number of seconds—just a much longer pause, perhaps double the usual. Even where the lawyer has gone to great effort to choose clear language, explain underlying concepts, and avoid legal jargon, new and difficult legal concepts simply take time to grasp and process. That first year of law school extended over nine or ten months, and it included an entire course on civil procedure. How long does it take a law student to understand jurisdiction, summary judgment, motions notwithstanding the verdict, and standards for sufficient pleading? How long does a torts professor spend on contributory negligence, assumption of risk, the reasonable person standard, or foreseeable harm? What about liquidated damages or the statute of frauds in contracts class?

Assume that in order for your client to make an intelligent decision about his case or the terms of a contract proposal, he needs to understand one of the legal concepts referenced above, and he needs to appreciate how it affects his circumstances. Even if the lawyer is well-prepared and thus masterfully succinct with a description of the concept in a mere sentence or two (okay, maybe three), she is well advised to pause—several beats—to let the client process that description.

The second reason to pause is that it gives the lawyer an opportunity to learn whether the client is confused or perhaps unsure of his understanding. Pausing enables the lawyer to observe her client's facial response and elicit a question or comment.

This seems simple; so why do lawyers so often fail to pause? Why do they tend to move directly from one explanation, to an alternative explanation, or to provide more detail? When we try to explain a legal concept, we naturally listen to our own explanation as it emerges. Our internal listener—also the internal voice—worries whether that explanation was good enough. Perhaps it lacked specificity; perhaps a different metaphor would be helpful, and so on. We become concerned about whether the client really grasped the matter, because we did hear some potential ambiguity in our initial explanation. So we quickly add to it, and then again.

Many people use talk as filler when nervous or uncomfortable. Professor Stefan Krieger, who teaches clinical law courses at Hofstra, is "often struck by [his] students' knack for . . . talking incessantly when silence should be the most appropriate action. In an initial interview, for example most students in a law school clinic will . . . chatter on nervously while the client, frozen by the emotions of the situation, painfully pauses or remains silent in her recitation of her story."[10] The result is a long, unbroken string of explanations of the original and difficult legal concept, with nary a breath in between, and a lawyer who has *no* idea which, if any, registered with his client.

Instead, PAUSE for several beats after the first portion of an explanation. Really stop and look at your client. That pause will have created space for your client to give you direction. It's not generally necessary for you to take more air time to ask if your client has any questions. Just stop talking. Take a breath. Perhaps lean back a bit. Observe your client's face as he processes what you've said so far. He will either nod for you to continue, or look quizzical or confused. He may ask a question. If not, and you have noticed some confusion or hesitance—and there's been no signal for you to go on—then you might ask if he has questions. Now, when you move forward with your explanation of the concept, you can be comfortable knowing that it addresses your client's concern.

Another Multiplier in Negative Territory

Messages with strong, particularly negative emotional impact demand much, much, much longer pauses. It's not difficult for a client to understand the words: "If we lose at trial, and I believe that's a grave risk, the case will be over, and you will not receive anything." Nonetheless, it would be a mistake to go from the words "your case will be over and you will not receive anything" straight to "so I was heartened when opposing counsel indicated that he would be willing to negotiate a settlement." Your client just won't be ready to hear it.

If you pause and observe her face, you will see that she is coming to terms with the idea of possibly, maybe probably, losing at trial and what that means to her—undoubtedly on many levels. As discussed in chapter 1, a social psychologist would say that, if the idea of winning at trial was significant within her social world, then your message is disorienting, and she feels herself slipping into another world.[11] Wait, and wait some more. Give her time and space. If she is looking down, don't start talking. Her downward head indicates that she is not yet receptive to hearing, or she may be looking inward.[12] When she looks up, she may want to express frustration, sadness, anger, incredulity . . . or she'll be ready to move forward and hear you describe other possible avenues.

The example above—"your case will be over and you will not receive anything"—is an obvious one for a long pause. In fact, clients may experience emotional responses—not overwhelming, but emotional nonetheless—to various legal concepts that seem negative or unfair. Think of the idea of "precedent": a client may not like learning that his outcome will be affected by other cases. The idea of arguing to a judge before getting to a jury may create frustration or evoke suspicion about judges. Settlement may conjure feelings of selling out. The concept of punitive damages often elicits a sense of extortion on the defense side, just as relinquishing or recognizing the unlikelihood of punitive damages feels like surrendering righteousness for a plaintiff. One who is sued personally takes it personally, even if his lawyer can explain the other side's legally justifiable strategy. Referencing the "reasonable person" standard will raise hackles.

For lawyers, these are realities or hurdles to be surmounted. They provide opportunities for the lawyer to exercise intellectual prowess and advocacy skill. For the client, they represent barriers to, or uncertainty about, what fate he will be forced to accept. Thus, they may elicit strong emotions, and warrant a long pause. This is true even if you've forecast the bad news, as recommended in chapter 1, and have already explained (and paused after) the sources of the risk.

Exponential or Multiple Multipliers

Even the mathematically-disinclined will anticipate this advice: When you are speaking with a client about complicated legal concepts AND these will impact the client emotionally, stop for at least a triple pause or, for fast talkers, double pause to the power of two—quadruple!

Vocal Synchrony for Connection and Control

"Vocal synchrony"? The phrase is intended as an elegant way to refer to similarity in the tone, volume, and rate at which you use your voice when speaking. Research establishes that vocal synchrony can increase rapport and persuasiveness.[13] While arguably part of mirroring (discussed in chapter 7), synchrony seems the better word here, as voice occurs temporally.

People's lack of vocal synchrony—very different speech styles—has the opposite effect.[14] Have you ever witnessed a conversation in which one conversant spoke at hyper-speed, with a great deal of volume and tonal variation in each sentence, and the other's speech was slow, deliberate, and even-toned? Doesn't the conversation seem out of synch, sometimes to the point of being comical? If the conversants are good friends and recognize their disparate vocal patterns, it's no problem. However, in a lawyer-client relationship, lack of vocal synchrony can undermine comfort and rapport, even if neither recognizes why. Consider the lawyer who speaks quickly, using a wide range of vocal tones, working with a client who is always deliberate, precise, slow, and even-toned. Or, imagine the opposite pairing: a vocally volatile (somewhat hysterical) client and the hyper-cool (bordering on wooden) professional. This is the stereotype, perhaps reflecting the reality that legal problems ultimately belong to clients.

A vocally quick, emotional, and expressive client in conversation with a lawyer who is slow, measured, and even-keel may eventually become more frenetic—voice more exaggerated—as she fails to evoke an expressive reaction. To her, responses in slow speed and even vocal tones mean the lawyer "doesn't get it." Her speech may become even faster than before and vocal tones more emphatic. If the lawyer continues with a steady, expressionless voice, the client's vocal pattern may become yet more exaggerated.

Whatever your baseline speaking style, my general advice is to be attuned to your client's and shift in that direction. The good news is that people instinctively recognize each other's baselines. So, if you are normally low-key, and you increase volume and intensity just a bit in response to your client, that will likely be sufficient. You need not match your client's vocal speed, tone, or volume, but it is helpful to synchronize.

Vocal Synchrony = Empathy at the Hot Spots

Imagine your client narrates his sense of unfairness, woe, or humiliation, speaking quickly and with emphatically expressive vocal tones. His lawyer responds: "I understand what you mean" or "that must have been difficult." If the lawyer's voice is slow and wooden, without emphatic tone, these words will fail to communicate emotional understanding or empathy. The client may well snap back immediately with "*Do you really understand?* It was terribly humiliating and difficult!"

Now, imagine the conversation differently. Imagine that the lawyer responds: "*I DO understand what you mean!!*" or "*Wow! That must have been VERY difficult! What a mess!*" Because the client can feel, through the vocal tone, that his lawyer does understand or "gets it," he will not be driven to further repetition and greater vocal emphasis to communicate the severity of the circumstances and their impact.

Actors on stage in a state of high, shared emotion may intentionally achieve perfect vocal synchrony, fully matching each other's pitch, volume, and speed. In an unscripted and very real lawyer's office scene, when a lawyer fully matches his client's emotional tone, both of their emotions may escalate and intensify. If your client is deflated, his voice slow and low-energy, and you replicate that, you will both end up mired in slow and low. When your client is very angry, fully mirroring the anger in her voice makes you empathetic but ineffective at helping her think rationally.[15] Your client may trust you on a personal level but come to lack confidence in your strength as an attorney. Clients want lawyers to listen, understand, and respect the way they feel, but *also* to be stronger and cooler, more collected and reasoned.[16] When a client is under stress, the lawyer serves that client well by keeping his head and his voice under some control.

This is tricky, then. Sometimes, your calm, constructive voice in response to a client's emotionality—deep despondence and low affect or strong anger and high affect—are what's needed to bring your client to even keel. Confidence and connection are maintained as your client appreciates your professional role on his behalf. For many clients, the calm vocal middle ground may be the best first strategy. For other clients, your calm voice in response to their voicing deep emotion creates frustration, alienation, and disconnection. For these clients, I suggest a deliberate strategy of vocal synchrony to communicate empathy. Adjust your voice *closer* to your client's range—in pitch, volume, and speed—reinforcing that you do indeed "get" the emotional impact for your client. Then, and only then, you may attempt to transition into the realm of reason.

[Almost] Match and Then Shift for Control and Movement

Fortunately, mirrors or natural tendencies to synchronize work two ways. Most clients will also tend naturally to move toward your vocal style and patterns. The lawyer who uses this tendency strategically may be able to shift her client's emotional state during their conversation. To do so, as suggested above, the lawyer should ALMOST match the client's vocal tone. Then the lawyer should deliberately shift her vocal pattern toward a more constructive range.

For example, assume that deflation and despair aren't serving your client well. He can't seem to summon any energy toward resolving his legal problem. We know that his experience of some positive emotion in the interaction will likely assist his cognitive engagement and decision-making (see chapter 4 on emotion). You might try consciously pitching your initial vocal tone and speech close to your client's—low, but not quite as low. Then, over the next few sentences or paragraphs of speech, gradually and deliberately raise your vocal tone to more constructive energy levels. You are meeting your client in his vocal and emotional territory, and then lifting him with you, up and out. One word of caution: even as you inject a bit more energy or volume into your voice, be mindful not to go too fast. Studies indicate that speaking faster than the other person in a conversation can make that person feel pressured.[17] So, don't let your vocal speed get too far ahead of your client's along the way.

Occasional Dramatic Intervention Near the Top

For most of us, deliberate vocal synchrony at other end of the emotional spectrum seems much higher-risk. When a client is highly frenetic, agitated, or angry, speaking quickly and loudly, it is hard for a lawyer to enter the conversation at a pitch, volume, and speed initially close to the client's and then deliberately bring it down over the course of that sentence or the next. It contradicts the common wisdom that the lawyer should remain calm. Yet, doing so gives the lawyer dramatic control to shape the client's voice and emotion in speech that follows. While I fear this written assertion is less than convincing, demonstrations of this "trick" are compelling. Imagine the lawyer reaching up with his voice, capturing the client's voice and pulling it down with him. The client's voice then shifts to a lower tone, volume, and speed, at least for a while.

Let's refine the common wisdom: the lawyer should remain *in control* of his own voice and emotions, remaining inwardly calm. However, when a client's voice reflects high emotions, a lawyer may wisely use his voice in synchrony, and then, with his voice, move the client to a calmer state.

The Voice of Gravitas

In his *Three Laws of Motion* and the *Principia*, Sir Isaac Newton explained the laws of physics that cause apples to fall from trees and the moon to stay above the earth. He named that force gravitation (or gravity) after the Latin word *gravitas*, which translates into "heaviness" or "weight."

The good Dr. Goodword summarizes the meaning of gravitas as "earnestness, seriousness of tone, substance, or demeanor that elicits the respect of others." He observes that the word "generally surfaces during elections when voters become interested in the ability of politicians to appear eminent and statesman-like."[18]

Lawyers' gravitas enhances client respect for their legal expertise and judgment. As with all professions, different lawyers may have different analyses and reach different conclusions. Most clients know it is not wise to shop for the lawyer whose analysis and advice are most palatable. However, clients do want to be confident in their lawyer, particularly when his analysis is unexpectedly pessimistic or his advice constraining. A client (or colleague) is less likely to second-guess the analysis and advice of a lawyer perceived as having gravitas because, as the word suggests, his words carry more weight. The real question then is: how does a lawyer acquire gravitas?

Feel It First—Then Project It

Gravitas, much like confidence, must first be felt. If a lawyer is confident, she will communicate that confidence in the way she speaks, in her voice and gesture. If a lawyer does *not* believe her words should have weight, her conclusions are well-supported, or her

advice should be taken seriously, she will not communicate with sufficient gravitas.

Gravitas is acquired naturally with age, experience, and mounting
expertise. Yet, if you have participated in a professional meeting of
peers in age and status, you have no doubt observed that some people's words still carry more weight. This may be due to differences in
the quality of their reputations, comments, or perhaps timing within
the meeting. Clearly, however, a speaker's presence and manner of
speaking—the gravitas style quotient—also affects impact.

Assume that you have done thorough research and thought carefully about strategy and conclusions in a legal matter. You are justifiably
confident that your analysis and advice is sound. You can use gesture
and tone to project gravitas or, at minimum, to avoid "anti-gravitas."

How? Much can be gained from the discussion of vocal speed in
this chapter, as well as gesture and movement in the chapters that
follow. Not surprisingly, people with high-pitched voices should try
to speak at the lower end of their vocal ranges. A study by Ronald
Bond and others replicated earlier findings that higher vocal frequency (pitch) is negatively correlated with listeners' perceptions of
the speaker's competence.[19] In addition, you should avoid head bobbing, nodding, or frequent smiling as you speak. Enlarge and anchor
your physical presence by resting your elbows on the table. Gestures
should be controlled and purposeful.

Witnessing hundreds of client counseling sessions, including
many with older and younger practicing attorneys, has convinced
me of tremendous power in slow, controlled, confident speech.
Slowly delivered words contain an assertion that they are important
and valuable enough for the time taken. As discussed earlier, simply
pausing in a rushed stream of legal explanation may help with client
comprehension, but it's not enough for gravitas. For that, a lawyer
should also speak with slower, "deliberate speed" when presenting
important conclusions or advice.

Finally, perceived gravitas may also be influenced by the placement of vocal emphasis. Generalities about emphasis are of little

value, absent context. A communication expert could undoubtedly offer technical terms for variations in emphasis and volume, all used by speakers with a full quotient of perceived gravitas, yet it would be foolish to suggest that a lawyer must follow a scripted formula for her words to be given weight. (It would also be foolish to think that anyone would, in fact, follow such a formula, even if suggested.)

Nevertheless, I hope the reader will indulge one piece of advice relating to emphasis: Having now observed hundreds of lawyers and law students in vocal exercises for gravitas, I believe that we communicate our authority and weight by speaking more firmly and slowly when describing our contribution. Consider the sentence: "I have reviewed the documents and the law, and I have concluded that a motion *in limine* is unlikely to be successful here." Say the various parts of the sentence with consistent speed and emphasis, first somewhat quickly, then with moderate speed. Now, say it again, but really slow down when you say only the words: "I have reviewed" and "I have concluded" within the sentence. You may also choose to adjust the volume a bit. By taking time on these words, you are communicating the importance of your review. It also suggests that you were thorough and took some time on the task. Slowing to emphasize "I have concluded" suggests that your conclusion was carefully and wisely reached.

No lawyer should or would rehearse every anticipated phrasing of every formal or informal presentation with clients or colleagues. However, we benefit from being mindful of what gravitas looks and sounds like. In some situations, gravitas is particularly important, when impressions are formed on first meeting or when presenting important or unexpected analysis and conclusions.

Notes

1. "Gerard Bauer Quotes," ThinkExist, http://thinkexist.com/quotes/gerard_bauer/ (accessed May 26, 2011).

2. Kathleen Turner's quotation by Brad Gooch in his article,"The Queen of Curves," *Vanity Fair* (September 1986) was located in Robert Barton and Rocco Dal Vera, *Voice Onstage and Off*, 2nd ed. (New York: Routledge, 2011), 4.

3. Robert Barton and Rocco Dal Vera note: "[M]ost of us speed up when tense or excited." Ibid., 18.

4. Paul E. King and Ralph R. Behnke explain that "[a]s listening responsibilities accumulate, a cognitive backlog may occur that contributes to the deterioration of information processing capacity." "Effects of Communication Load, Affect, and Anxiety on the Performance of Information Processing Tasks," *Communication Quarterly* 48, no. 1 (2000): 82. Michael J. Beatty defines a cognitive backlog as "a function of continued and persistent inputs of information which is either difficult to assimilate into existing attitude structures or is input at an unmanageable rate." "Receiver Apprehension as a Function of Cognitive Backlog," *Western Journal of Speech Communication* 45, no. 3 (1981): 277.

5. Douglas Maynard, *Bad News, Good News: Conversational Order in Everyday Talk and Clinical Settings* (Chicago: The University of Chicago Press, 2003), 12 (internal citation omitted). See also Robert S. Adler, Benson Rosen, and Elliot M. Silverstein, "Emotions in Negotiation: How to Manage Fear and Anger," *Negotiation Journal* 14 (1998): 161–79.

6. Robert Buckman, M.D., *How to Break Bad News: A Guide for Health Care Professionals* (Baltimore: The John Hopkins University Press, 1992), 82.

7. Cf. Kevin Wheldall, Stephen Houghton, and Frank Merrett, "Natural Rates of Teacher Approval and Disapproval in British Secondary School Classrooms," *British Journal of Educational Psychology* 59 (1989): 38–48 (finding that teachers over-estimate the amount that they pause).

8. Kathy L. Ruhl, "Does Nature of Study Activity During Lecture Pauses Affect Notes and Immediate Recall of College Students with Learning Disabilities?" *Journal of Postsecondary Education and Disability* 12, no. 2 (1996): 16–27.

9. Frederick E. Tesch, Leonard M. Lansky, and David C. Lundgren, "The One-Way/Two-Way Communication Exercise: Some Ghosts Laid to Rest," *Journal of Applied Behavioral Sciences* 8 (1972): 664–73.

10. Stefan H. Krieger, "A Time to Keep Silent and a Time to Speak: The Functions of Silence in the Lawyering Process," *Oregon Law Review* 80 (2001): 199.

11. Maynard, *Bad News, Good News*, 4.

12. Allan Pease and Barbara Pease, *The Definitive Book of Body Language* (New York: Bantam, 2006), 194–195.

13. David B. Buller and R. Kelly Aune, "The Effects of Speech Rate Similarity on Compliance: Application of Communication Accommodation Theory," *Western Journal of Communication* 56, no. 1 (1992): 37–53.

14. See Pease and Pease, *The Definitive Book of Body Language*, 259.

15. In one experiment, clients tended to choose lawyers they perceived as competent, but were not skilled at perceiving competence. Surprisingly, in that experiment, lawyers scripted to use "sophisticated comforting skills" in a divorce case scenario were viewed as less competent by clients. The authors posit, however, that the personal nature of the case and "comforting" interventions at the beginning stages of an initial interview may have seemed inappropriately and uncomfortably intimate. I tend to agree, given the actual script used. David Dryden Henningsen and Iona Cionea, "The Role of Comforting Skill and Professional Competence in the Attorney-Client Relationship," *Journal of Legal Education* 57, no. 4 (December 2004): 530–538.

16. Kristin B. Gerdy summarizes several formal and informal studies of what characteristics clients most want in their attorneys, with empathy often high on the list. "Clients, Empathy, and Compassion: Introducing First-Year Students to the 'Heart' of Lawyering," *Nebraska Law Review* 87 (2008): 1–61. Similarly, studies in the medical field have shown that patients often want doctors delivering bad news to show empathy as well as confidence and control of the situation. See Linda F. Smith, "Medical Paradigms for Counseling: Giving Clients Bad News," *Clinical Law Review* 4 (1998): 396.

17. Pease and Pease, *The Definitive Book of Body Language*, 259.

18. Dr. Goodword [aka Robert Beard, PhD, Lingusitics], "Gravitas," alphaDictionary.com, http://www.alphadictionary.com/goodword/word/gravitas (accessed July 19, 2009).

19. For example, Ronald N. Bond et al., "Vocal Frequency and Person Perception: Effects of Perceptual Salience and Nonverbal Sensitivity,"

Journal of Psycholinguistic Research 16, no. 4 (1987): 335–350. Note that there is also a connection here among gender, speech, and power. See Cathryn Johnson, "Gender, Legitimate Authority, and Leader-Subordinate Conversations," *American Sociological Review* 59, no. 1 (1994): 122–135.

7

Choreography of Counsel

"Movement never lies. It is a barometer telling the state of the soul's weather to all who can read it."

—MARTHA GRAHAM[1]

"Good choreography fuses eye, ear and mind."

—ARLENE CROCE[2]

Why think about choreography—body position and movement—in client counseling, if your language is clear and you listen well to your client? Isn't that enough? In fact, research consistently indicates that when we speak, our listeners receive less than 10 percent of our spoken messages through the words alone, approximately 30 percent through voice and tone, and at least 60 percent through body language. The accompanying nonverbal cues are often far more important than the words themselves. Nonverbal cues are particularly salient in communicating confidence, rapport, and emotion.[3]

Complexity aside, a lawyer's choices in body position and movement can also enhance or undermine her client's perception of her confidence, authority, and effectiveness. These perceptions matter; they affect the client's decision to retain a lawyer as well as the lawyer's ability to represent her client well. The client who doubts his lawyer's effectiveness or authority is less likely to listen carefully to the lawyer's explanations when patience is required, and less likely to consider the lawyer's counsel when it differs from his instincts or preferences.

Finally, the way a lawyer sits and moves in a client meeting influences his ability to establish connection, rapport, and trust. Why consciously think about body language for greater rapport in a client meeting, when you've undoubtedly and naturally built robust, connected relationships without thinking about it? The answer is that conscious, intentional use of body language can strengthen these natural abilities when needed most. When is that? When we meet with a potential new client for a short time or with a known client now facing difficult legal circumstances. The client who feels disconnected or wary of his lawyer is less likely to confide openly and completely, and less likely to raise business or personal circumstances that may bear upon choices made. He may resist the lawyer's opinion and advice and withhold candid expression of concerns or confusion. His mind may become closed to difficult concepts or to considering your counsel.

This chapter provides an introduction to selected insights from the study of body language that are easy to incorporate and directly relevant to client counseling. Readers who find the body language material in this chapter of particular interest are encouraged to read more broadly. Thus, the chapter notes include references to selected sources on body language in professional contexts.[4] With awareness and intentionality comes the opportunity to use position and movement to enhance client confidence and trust.

Body Basics

Without so much as skimming an article on the topic, most people know much about body language as expressed through body position. We know that leaning back may indicate detachment, lack of engagement, confidence, or relaxation (and some of these may be related). Most people know to interpret a posture of arms crossed over one's chest as defensive or closed—non-receptive.[5] We sense that lack of eye contact may reflect lack of interest or engagement. When someone is fiddling with an object, we sense nervousness or discomfort. As the late journalist Edward R. Murrow once observed: "[A] blur of blinks, taps, jiggles, pivots and shifts [is] the body language of a man wishing urgently to be elsewhere."[6] Your client's (or your own) leg jiggling typically means you're aching to get up and walk away.[7]

Size Matters in the Distance

We all know that people are comfortable speaking across a certain distance, whether seated or standing. That distance varies some-what by culture and personal versus professional contexts.[8] For most western cultures, *The Definitive Book of Body Language* describes a "personal zone" of eighteen to forty eight inches, the distance we stand from others at friendly social gatherings, and a "social zone" of four to twelve feet, the distance we stand from strangers.[9] In gen-eral, these distances are somewhat reduced between two women and increased between two men. Within cultural limits, people who like each other do sit closer, even in professional settings. People of equal status also sit closer than people of unequal status.[10]

Given that comfortable social zones are not set distances, but rather ranges, a lawyer is well advised to consider physical size when deciding where and how to sit in a client counseling session. A client may feel somewhat threatened when a larger lawyer approaches the edge of a generally comfortable distance, but less so if the lawyer is of average or smaller size. In the courtroom, larger lawyers are gen-erally advised to keep greater distance from witnesses, particularly on cross-examination, lest the jury view them as intimidating the witness. Lawyers who are shorter and more slightly built (and per-haps more soft-spoken) can approach quite close to the witness stand without risking jury backlash.[11]

Courtroom wisdom translates to seated lawyer-client interac-tions. In the actor-client counseling sessions observed and recorded by the author, client-actors report greater comfort and ease when larger lawyers are seated a bit further away. Closer tends to feel intimidating, making it difficult for the client to concentrate, dis-cuss, and feel self-possessed. Sitting at a somewhat greater distance also permits space for the lawyer to lean forward toward the client to indicate engagement and connection or to emphasize a point, without invading the client's comfort zone.

Start from Neutral

What then would be a "default" or neutral position from which to start a lawyer client meeting? If a lawyer is to use gesture, from what seated position should these gestures begin? It seems clear that neutral would be the attorney sitting more or less upright, at an appropriate distance across from the client.

A well-known interviewing and counseling text recommends that an interviewing lawyer face the client squarely, with an open posture, lean forward a bit to indicate engagement, establish good eye contact, and appear relaxed.[12] The acronym SOLER (Squarely facing, Open position, Leaning forward, Eye contact, Relaxed) is offered as a mnemonic as you arrange your office chairs and then as you sit down at the client meeting.[13]

SOLER is backed by solid research of academics in communication and psychology. When you face someone squarely, with an open body posture—no arms crossed—you are perceived as open, receptive, not defensive, and ready to listen. People who make more consistent eye contact are perceived as warmer and more likeable (though constant, uninterrupted eye contact can feel threatening).[14] In fact, other experiments have confirmed that eye contact correlates with how much people like each other. Not surprisingly, a speaker feels more powerful when he receives eye contact, and women generally make more eye contact when listening and speaking than most men do. Listeners who lean forward are also perceived to be more interested, and a generally relaxed position—without fidgeting or other distracting motion—reinforces the idea that one is attentive.[15]

Of interest for lawyers working with clients is a 1962 study in which an experimenter deliberately engaged in "warm" and "cold" non-verbal behaviors with subjects who were asked to perform a word association exercise. When acting "warm," the experimenter more frequently smiled, refrained from finger tapping, made more eye contact and leaned forward to a greater degree. The cold experimenter did the opposite. When the experimenter was warm, subjects successfully produced more words in the exercise. This result is significant for lawyers seeking their client's active participation in an interview or counseling session.

To encourage your client to speak, be comfortable, and feel trust: sit openly, resisting any urge to cross your arms, fiddle, or fidget; look directly as you listen and speak; and lead forward a bit to express engagement.

For Some, Elbows on the Table

Like it or not, in our culture, the larger person, the broader shoulder, are often equated with authority. As with the expression: "A giant among men," or a "giant in his field," we use language related to size to express power and accomplishment. Yes, this is in part a gender issue, given that the average woman is smaller and has less shoulder width than the average man. In fact, rather extensive research has established that height affects the way all people are regarded. Taller people are more likely to convince and persuade others because they are perceived as more convincing and persuasive—more effective.[16]

No doubt, shorter readers will resist. All readers can easily cite examples of many powerful, well respected, and authoritative colleagues who are short. In fact, as I write this, two very short men and one short woman come to mind—a rabbi, an attorney, and a scientist—each highly effective, persuasive, accomplished, and respected. When they talk, people listen! The research simply establishes that if two speakers deliver the same presentation, in the same manner, most listeners' *initial* subjective impression will be to find the taller speaker more effective. We are wise to understand that a lawyer's other physical characteristics, including age (or youth), gender, voice, and speech patterns may also influence clients' intuitive subjective impressions of authority and thus their willingness to be persuaded.[17] Such subjectivity may influence an initial client meeting and perhaps a client counseling session, depending upon how much the lawyer and client have worked together.

Fortunately, impressions often shift over time and experience. When a lawyer is expert, highly articulate, and a skilled communicator, his physical characteristics should not determine client perception, particularly after speaking a sentence or two.

So, what's a not-so-tall or not-so-big lawyer to do when sitting and speaking with a client? For all lawyers who are relatively short, small or slightly built, experienced actors' advice is to sit with both elbows to forearms on the desk or table. This body position immediately makes your shoulders squared and larger—your outline commands much more space in the visual frame. Observation of hundreds of counseling sessions confirms that the seated lawyer's simple shift from forearms under the table to fully on the table has powerful visual impact, creating the appearance of greater authority and confidence.

The point is to increase the space you occupy in a visual frame. Never mind polemics on gender, size, and power. Here's my advice to other-than-giant and, particularly, younger lawyers: sit forward just a bit, and let your elbows and forearms rest on the table. Some form of jacket—with structured shoulder—is important. Even if the dress code is casual, wear that jacket over your polo shirt!

More physically imposing lawyers need not be tethered to the table top. However, if you feel more comfortable with elbows on the table, place your chair a few inches more distant from your client, to avoid intimidation. In fact, elbows on the table—or one elbow at a minimum—tends to reduce excess, nervous movement, such as shoulder shaking and head-bobbing, as discussed below. All of us should avoid crossing arms defensively. Keep arms and hands relaxed and open—no clenched fists.[18]

Try to Take it Standing Up

Particularly if you are relatively short, slightly built, young, or female (or some combination) and concerned about perceived effectiveness with a particular client, consider taking opportunities to stand up. Assume you are seated, with perfect SOLER, conducting a rapport-filled lawyer-client conversational update on the status of this client's case. When it comes time to walk your client through an explanation of his options, or to explain relevant legal constraints and advice, try standing up. An easel or white board or prepared exhibit can assist client comprehension and provide a natural excuse for you to stand while speaking with your client. In *The Complete Book of Body Language*, authors Allan and Barbara Pease recount their consultation with a five-foot-one-inch female senior manager in a predominantly male firm who complained about constant interruptions in management meetings. When she employed a strategy of walking over to the coffee table and returning to stand at her seat while presenting her thoughts, she was amazed at the lack of interruption and apparent gain in authority.[19]

An Aura of Authority in (Lack of) Motion—Do's and Don'ts

Watch the Nods

Imagine an experiment in which pairs of people are told to talk with each other while standing on a stage. One person of each pair is instructed to nod or bob his head as he talks and the other to keep his head still. Then observers from a distance are asked which person in each pair has greater power: it won't be the head bobber.[20]

As listeners, we often nod and smile toward the speaker. Nodding is described and understood as a positive social behavior—recommended for building rapport. Psychology and communication scholars identify listeners' nodding as "backchannel responses"—short vocal responses indicating attentiveness, including comments such as "hmmm," "uh-huh," "yeah" or "right."

While it may be friendly, nodding is also characterized as submissive, with its origin in bowing—a lowering of the body. A listener's nodding affirms the speaker's status in a conversation. It communicates the desire to go along with and please another—the one with perceived power. The idea of nodding as submissive is confirmed by a study that placed observers in college classrooms and found that students nodded more to professors than they nodded to their peers.[21] This was consistent with earlier findings from workplace studies indicating that the workplace subordinate—male or female—in a conversational pair nods more frequently than the superior—the boss. Not surprisingly, research does suggest a gender issue: women generally nod, smile and employ more back-channel responses in conversation than men. Even in peer-to-peer conversations, women listeners tend to nod more than men. [22]

Limit Your Listener's Nod

Does this mean lawyers should forswear from the friendly nod? NO! Nodding and smiling are positive expressions. Likeable people— likeable lawyers—nod and smile. More important, the client feels encouraged and comfortable when his lawyer nods and smiles. Thus, for lawyers seeking to build rapport and trust, some[23] nodding and smiling when listening to clients is helpful, appropriate, and natural. We want to be viewed as serious, confident, and competent, but not as unfriendly, wooden, or unresponsive. We do want to create a positive emotional environment. On the other hand, if you are concerned lest a particular client perceive you as subordinate or less authoritative, consider fewer head nods even as the client is speaking.

The best advice is to become your own observer as you listen to clients (or others) speaking. Do you find yourself nodding a great deal? If so, are you nodding to express genuine agreement or to encourage an uncertain speaker who is seeking your approval or assent? Then let the listener nods continue. However, if you find yourself nodding and smiling because of a felt need to please; if your nods are to a more powerful speaker; or if you feel unequal status: hold that head still for a while!

Banish SPEAKER's Head Bobbing

Head bobbing is my pejorative term for notable, energetic nodding *when we speak*. Head bobbing seems to reflect excessive concern that what we say be "pleasing," or just plain nervousness. Paradoxically, some people bob their heads in an exaggerated way when conveying bad news—as if an up and down head motion could negate their very unpleasing message.[24] The speaker who keeps her head relatively still is perceived as speaking authoritatively, and thus as more of a leader. James Bond speaks with his head still, always in control.[25] It is remarkable to observe the contrast when the same person speaks the same words, first with a lot of head bobbing and smiling, and then again with head deliberately still and much less facial expression. Bobbing head and smiling appears uncertain, less confident, too eager. With the head kept still and facial expressions moderate, the speaker appears far more authoritative and confident.

The bottom line advice is: "banish head bobbing" when *you* are speaking to a client, and anyone else whom you would like to impress with your authority and competence. Of course, you need not alter every natural head movement or gesture. Over the next few days, make a mental note when you find yourself nodding, smiling a great deal, or otherwise moving your head as you speak. When you notice it, try holding your head still. If you must, use occasional slow, controlled nods to punctuate and emphasize positive aspects of the information conveyed. This will communicate continued interpersonal engagement, with confidence and authority.

Save That Smile

Research on smiling largely parallels that on nodding: people with power smile less in conversation; subordinates smile more in conversations with superiors; and women smile more in conversation than men do.[26] Research isn't necessary to know that we often nod and smile at the same time. My advice regarding smiling is also parallel. Become aware of when and why you smile in client interactions. Smile naturally as part of establishing friendly rapport. Smile (and even nod) to make your client more comfortable when he is speaking. But avoid the nervous smile or the smile to please; these undermine serious messages and the authority of the lawyer who conveys them. As discussed in chapter 1, a nervous smile while delivering "bad news" can confuse, anger, or alienate a client who interprets your smile as insensitivity to its impact for him.

Mirror, Mirror and Your Client

Communication research reveals that mirroring helps create positive emotions, feelings of rapport and trust in the other. To mirror is to reflect or imitate the other's style or affect—vocal tone, body position, and ways of moving. Referred to as the "Chameleon Effect,"[27] when two people engage in a sustained, face-to-face discussion, some "behavioral" mirroring—mimicking of body motions— occurs naturally, even among strangers. When speaking with someone whose style is more animated, with free and dramatic hand gestures, and a wide and expressive vocal range, to mirror is to adopt a similar, animated style. It's well established that people mimic words, accents, rate of speech, tone of voice, syntax, and facial expressions.[28] People who measure high on social intelligence scales are particularly and naturally adept at mirroring.[29] Logically, when two people of very different styles converse, and both have at least normal social intelligence, their gesture, body language, and vocal tone will gravitate toward the middle.

Mirror, Mirror for Rapport and Connection

Deliberate mirroring can profoundly influence perceptions of rapport, expressed as interpersonal closeness or likeability. In one research study, when experimenters conducting a fictional marketing test consciously but unobtrusively mirrored participants' postures and behaviors, they received higher scores in participants' ratings of interpersonal closeness.[30] In another study, four trained experimenters were enlisted to engage in one-on-one discussions of various photographs with volunteer student participants. During half of these interactions, the experimenters purposefully mirrored the behavior mannerisms of the participants; in the other half, they used only neutral body language. Participants were then asked to complete a questionnaire regarding how much they liked the experimenter and the smoothness of the interaction. Participants whose movements were mirrored experienced the interaction as having gone more smoothly and reported liking their experimenters significantly more.

Thus, to reinforce rapport and connection, lawyers are advised to mirror their clients' gestures, body posture, and vocal style, as well as language choices and degree of formality. As the lawyer, your speech and movement must remain professional, but there's considerable room within that professional range. If your client is very casual, using slang or profanity, with large gestures, you might meet him part way, by speaking more informally, with expressive hand motions. (This is consistent with the discussion of vocal mirroring in chapter 6.) Of course, mirroring should not be done in an obvious way, lest it be experienced as annoyance or mockery. For that reason, it's best to delay a bit and not to mimic precisely.

Move to Affect Your Client's Position—Literally

Perhaps surprisingly, research indicates that the *client's* body position may affect her ability to absorb information communicated by her lawyer. In one study, volunteers instructed to sit with their arms tightly folded across their chests during six different lectures retained far less than students instructed to sit and listen with legs uncrossed and arms unfolded, in casual, relaxed sitting positions. These results replicated earlier research indicating those with closed posture had 38 percent less retention and more negative views of the speaker and his lecture. [31]

Thus, to the extent that the lawyer can influence a client to assume a more open posture, he may enhance the client's ability to absorb complex or nuanced information and advice. For the client whose arms are crossed,[32] the lawyer should make sure his own position is open and non-threatening. The lawyer might consider changing topics for the time being, or asking the client if she has any concerns. The lawyer might also consider using a prop to open the client's arms by sharing a chart or photograph to review or asking the client to point out the most important issue on a posted agenda. Or he might suggest a stretch break.

Shifting through Choreography

When literary characters become shape-shifters, transforming themselves to another species or gender, the new shape often affects mind, emotion, and experience.[33] While not as dramatic or complete as shape-shifting, when we adopt the posture, position, and motions of confidence, authority, and openness, our perceptions and realities are shaped. Lawyer and client will find that open body posture makes each feel more receptive to the other. Mirroring to foster a client's feelings of connection contributes dynamically to the interaction, yielding greater ease for both. Lawyers are known to be masters of the verbal, of argument, of persuasion with words. But we are also wise to observe and to choreograph body and motion for hearing and communicating.

Notes

1. "Quotes by Martha Graham," Dance Quotes, http://www.dance-quotes.net/martha-graham-quotes.html (accessed April 21, 2011).

2. "Choreography Quotes," Dance Quotes, http://www.dance-quotes. net/choreography-quotes.html (accessed April 21, 2011).

3. One widely quoted statistic is that communication is 93 percent nonverbal and only 7 percent verbal. This derives from a study by Albert Mehrabian and Susan R. Ferris. Albert Mehrabian and Susan R. Ferris, "Inference of Attitudes from Nonverbal Communication in Two Channels," *Journal of Consulting Psychology* 31, no. 3 (1967): 248–252. David Lapakko criticizes this statistical "urban legend" and argues that the Mehrabian and Ferris study is very limited in its applicability and was never intended to establish the relative importance of verbal and nonverbal communication. "Three Cheers for Language: A Closer Examination of a Widely Cited Study of Nonverbal Communication," *Communication Education* 46 (1997): 63–67. See also David Lapakko, "Communication is 93% Nonverbal: An Urban Legend Proliferates," *Communication and Theater Association of Minnesota Journal* 34 (2007): 7–15. Peter A. Andersen cites other estimates but concludes "all these estimates are a bit bogus; the relative importance depends on the task and the context." *Nonverbal Communication: Forms and Functions*, 2nd ed. (Long Grove, IL: Waveland Press, 2008), 4. Moreover, channels of communication may not be "additive," in the sense that the total message is the sum of its parts. Timothy G. Hegstrom, "Message Impact: What Percentage is Nonverbal?" *The Western Journal of Speech Communication* 43 (1979): 134–142. And some have suggested that interpersonal communication cannot be separated into separate verbal and nonverbal components. See Stanley E. Jones and Curtis D. LeBaron, "Research on the Relationship Between Verbal and Nonverbal Communication: Emerging Integrations," *Journal of Communication* 52, no. 3 (2002): 499–521. But Anderson cites many studies that find nonverbal cues are more salient than verbal cues in communicating messages about the relationship between interlocutors. Peter Andersen, *Nonverbal Communication*, 4.

4. See, e.g., Carol Kinsey Goman, *The Nonverbal Advantage: Secrets and Science of Body Language at Work* (San Francisco, CA: Berrett-Koehler Publishers, 2008); Joe Navarro and Toni Sciarra Poynter, *Louder than Words: Take Your Career from Average to Exceptional with the Hidden Power of Nonverbal Intelligence* (New York: Harper Business, 2010).

5. Arm crossing can be an attempt to create a defensive barrier between someone and someone or something else. People also take the arms crossed position when they disagree with something that has been said.

Barbara Pease and Allen Pease, *The Definitive Book of Body Language* (New York: Bantam, 2006), 91–94.

6. "Edward R. Murrow Quotes," ThinkExist, http://thinkexist.com/ quotation/a-blur-of-blinks-taps-jiggles-pivots-and-shifts/632064. html (accessed April 21, 2011).

7. Pease and Pease, *Definitive Book of Body Language*, 210.

8. Ibid., chapter 9 (esp. 201–205).

9. Ibid., 195.

10. Supporting the intuitive notion of relationship between size, proximity, and threat or comfort levels, Barbara and Allan Pease, in *The Definitive Book of Body Language*, report upon a six-foot-eight-inch chemical salesman in England who perceived that customers were threatened by his height. His sales increased by 62 percent after he began giving sales presentations while seated rather than standing (324); see also Albert Mehrabian, *Nonverbal Communication* (Rutgers, NJ: Transaction Publishers, 1972), 20–21.

11. The impact of gender differences in size and their impact on comfortable distance in witness interactions is discussed in Stanley L. Brodsky et al., "Attorney Invasion of Witness Space" 23 *Law & Psychology Review* 49 (1999): 52–53.

12. Robert F. Cochran, John F. DiPippa, and Martha M. Peters, *The Counselor-at-Law: A Collaborative Approach to Client Interviewing and Counseling* (Newark, NJ: Lexis Publishing, 1999), 29–30.

13. Gerard Egan, *You & Me: The Skills of Communicating and Relating to Others* (Pacific Grove, CA: Brooks/Cole Publishing Company, 1977), 114–116.

14. Mehrabian, *Nonverbal Communication*, 22 (citing various studies by Exline and Eldridge).

15. Ibid., 24 (citing the results of a 1962 study by Reece and Whitman).

16. Timothy Judge and Daniel Cable, "The Effect of Physical Height on Workplace Success and Income: Preliminary Test of a Theoretical Model," *Journal of Applied Psychology* 89 (3): 430, (citing studies by Baker and Readding (1962) and Zebrowitz (1994)).

17. For discussion of the impact of attorney characteristics on jurors, see Peter Hahn and Susan Clayton, "The Effects of Attorney Presentation Style, Attorney Gender, and Juror Gender on Juror Decisions." *Law and Human Behavior* 20, no. 5 (1996): 533–554.

18. Goman, *The Nonverbal Advantage*, 26–27.

19. Pease and Pease, *The Definitive Book of Body Language*, 322.

20. Plenary session demonstration at ABA Section on Dispute Resolution Conference, Atlanta, GA, spring 2006.

21. Marie Helweg-Larsen et al., "To Nod or Not to Nod: An Observational Study of Nonverbal Communication and Status in Female and Male College Students," *Psychology of Women Quarterly* 28 (2004): 360.

22. See Judith Hall and Gregory Friedman, "Status, Gender, and Nonverbal Behavior: A Study of Structured Interactions Between Employees of a Company," *Personality and Social Psychology Bulletin* 25, no. 9 (1999): 1082–1091 (suggesting significant subtleties in interaction between gender and status). Hall and Friedman note earlier research suggesting links between approval-seeking and status, including H. M. Rosenfeld, "Approval Seeking and Approval Inducing Functions of Verbal and Nonverbal Responses in the Dyad," *Journal of Personality and Social Psychology* 4 (1966): 597–605 (studying student dyads).

23. Pease and Pease, *The Definitive Book of Body Language*, 230. It is sometimes associated with gender, with women thought to engage in more of it than men.

24. This is based upon the author's observation of between four and five hundred students in client counseling sessions with client actors, as well as observation of counsel in real mediation settings.

25. Pease and Pease, *The Definitive Book of Body Language*, 347.

26. Marianne LaFrance and Marvin A. Hecht, "Gender and Smiling: A meta-analysis," in *Gender and Emotion: Social Psychological Perspectives. Studies in Emotion and Social Interaction,* ed. A. H. Fischer (Cambridge, MA: Cambridge University Press, 2000), 118–142; see also Marianne Schmid Mast and Judith A. Hall, "When is Dominance Related to Smiling? Assigned Dominance, Dominance Preference, Trait Dominance, and Gender as Moderators," *Sex Roles* 50 no. 5/6 (2004): 387–399.

27. Tanya L. Chartrand and John A. Bargh, "The Chameleon Effect: The Perception-Behavior Link and Social Interaction," *Journal of Personality and Social Psychology* 76, no. 6 (1999): 893–910.

28. Summarized in Rick B. van Baaren et al., "Mimicry for Money: Behavioral Consequences of imitation," *Journal of Experimental Social*

Psychology 39 (2003): 393–398. This article describes a number of the underlying experimental studies.

29. Chartrand and Bargh, "The Chameleon Effect," 905.

30. Richard E. Maurer and J. H. Tindall, "Effect of Postural Congruence on Client's Perception of Counselor Empathy," *Journal of Counseling Psychology* 30, no. 2 (1983): 158–63; Christopher F. Sharpley et al., "Standard Posture, Postural Mirroring and Client-Perceived Rapport," *Counseling Psychology Quarterly* 14, no. 4: 267–280.

31. Pease and Pease, *The Definitive Book of Body Language*, 91.

32. It is arguable that lawyers could or should become adept at the full range of body language signals and what they mean, to better understand client feelings, not to mention proclivities for truthfulness or deception. While I might agree, that is not the central topic of this book. Recommended resources on body language are: Albert Mehrabian, "Inferences of Attitudes from Nonverbal Communication in Two Channels," *Journal of Consulting Psychology* 31, no. 3 (1967): 248–252; Albert Mehrabian, *Silent Messages: Implicit Communication of Emotions and Attitudes*, 2nd ed. (Belmont, CA: Wadsworth, 1981).

33. See, e.g., Sarah Grubb, "Vampires, Werewolves, and Shapeshifters," in *True Blood and Philosophy: We Wanna Think Bad Things With You*, ed. George A. Dunn and Rebecca Housel (Hoboken, NJ: Wiley, 2010), 215–227.

8

A Gesture to Clarity

"It's a rather rude gesture, but at least it's clear what you mean."
—KATHERINE HEPBURN[1]

Watch an effective professor lecturing on philosophy or history, a charismatic clergyman recounting a parable or moral choice, a talented trial lawyer summarizing events and characters, or a popular financial advisor laying out complex investment issues. Watch as a ship's captain advises his crew of strong currents and rocky shoals ahead and presents the navigation choices. Don't you see these speakers gesturing with their hands and arms as they convey a strong message, clarify a point, emphasize an insight, or minimize trivial or unwarranted concerns? People use gesture naturally. For some of us, trying to talk without hands is just about impossible.

A speaker's gesture can amplify or detract from direct spoken meaning or intended emotional impact. The ship's captain who wishes to convey confidence to his crew in the face of rising storm swells is well advised to refrain from frenetic hand wringing when reviewing the navigational course. No Ph.D. in communication is required to know that words of warmth and welcome are strengthened by a gesture of open arms and hands, and undercut by a tight, clenched fist on the table. Jabbing at the air suggests that all is not under control, even if words were chosen to reassure.

This book does not pretend to survey all ways that gesture influences communication, nor does it intend to render the reader self-conscious about gesturing in normal interactions or simple presentations. For that, many articles and books on gesture and body language are recommended in this chapter's notes. Instead, we'll focus on a few sets of gestures toward the fully-informed client—the client who clearly understands her lawyer's communication of legal concepts, consequences, and choices as necessary to make good decisions on her own behalf.

Consistent research findings support the role of gesture in enhancing listeners' understanding and retention. When a speaker presents information, an explanatory lecture, or a story without accompanying gestures, the audience absorbs and remembers less.[2] In one study,[3] one group of participants watched a videotape of an actor using speech and gesture to tell a vignette, while a second group only listened to the actor's vignette, without accompanying gesture. The group that heard and watched the actor recalled significantly more detail about the vignette than the group that only heard the actor. In another experiment, college students were randomly assigned to watch sets of "Speech Only" and "Speech + Gesture" videos. They were asked to write their recollections immediately after the simulation and again thirty minutes later. Students who watched the lectures with gesture recollected more and retained it better.[4] Similar results were obtained when audiences listened to comical narratives, with and without gestures, to illustrate running, jumping, and other actions, events, and places in a cartoon story line. In yet another study, the group watching their narrator gesture as he told a vignette recalled significantly more detail than the other group whose narrator did not gesture.[5]

When listeners are less proficient in the language of a presentation, gestures become even more important. One study compared understanding and retention of lessons presented in English, with and without gesture, both to school children who were native English speakers and to school children with less English proficiency.[6] Not surprisingly, the lessons with accompanying gestures were far better understood and retained, particularly by those with less English proficiency.

Why does this matter if you and your client are adults who speak English fluently? Consider that the language lawyers use and the legal system's constructs and procedures are foreign to many. Even if a lawyer takes pains to translate technical legal terms, the lawyer's professional language is generally less familiar to the client.[7] The non-native school children in the study described above did speak some English, but their vocabularies were less extensive. So too with clients, who may understand most of the words lawyers use, but not recognize terms of art, the framework of reasoning from precedent, or the role of procedural motions. Gesture may therefore be more important for clients unfamiliar with the legal system and thus challenged to fully decode and understand a lawyer's explanation and counsel.

Location, Location. . .

Place and Then Keep New Mexico in New Mexico

Using deliberate gestures that "place" events, objects, or ideas in consistent locations can help your client keep them straight, while haphazard or inconsistent gesture can create confusion.[8] Imagine that you are talking with your client about whether to incorporate in New Mexico or Ohio. It will help your client remember the New Mexico considerations if, when you talk about them, you always gesture toward a location in one direction. Advantages and disadvantages of incorporating in Ohio should be located by gesture in another, clearly different location.

This advice applies not only to geographic areas, but to different courts (even if they happen to be located in the same physical public square) and to different clusters of concepts or options. When speaking about the reasons to file in state or federal court, gesture toward one place for the state court and toward another for the federal court. Gesture to distinct locations to help your client keep straight the anticipated testimony of one witness versus another, as well as helpful and unhelpful facts found in discovery, or positive and negative case precedent.

Many, perhaps most, people locate and separate concepts by gesture quite naturally. So why is this advice important? Because failure to be mindful leaves us apt to be careless and thus to unintentionally confuse the client-listener. Having placed the federal court on the left and the state court to the right, the lawyer who later refers back to them and gestures to opposite places will *interfere* with his client's ability to process the information spoken.[9] It's as if a small voice will enter the client-listener's mind to say: "Huh? I thought that was over there. Those related concepts are there too; which ones come with it? I can't follow this."

If you were to try an experiment with a small audience, gesturing to place "the good guy" in Michigan and "the bad guy" in New York, and later switch the location of your gestures when referencing "good guy" and "bad guy," you would observe confusion on people's faces. Eyes would squint; heads would cock quizzically or shake a little bit. It's also true that if you DID maintain consistent gesture locations for the "good guy" in Michigan, switched topics entirely for a while, and later asked the audience where the good guy was, they would all reflexively point to Michigan.[10]

Watch Out for and Avoid Random Gesturing

Many of us gesture a great deal, especially as we embark on a difficult task of explaining complicated information or concepts. Particularly when tensions are high and consequences important, we may tend to wave arms, jab with fingers, or point toward risk. That is precisely when a lawyer should take care to avoid unwittingly placing a concept or idea in space and then neglecting or changing its location.

Of course, after deliberately placing an idea at a particular spot in space or on the table, we must beware of later returning to random expressive but unrelated hand movements in that same space.

Gesture for Transition or Movement

Imagine you have spoken to your client about whether to file suit in state or federal court and have explained that one benefit of state court is an expedited calendar with more efficient motion and trial process, but that one drawback is less careful judicial scrutiny of preliminary motions. You described federal court's slower speed and longer backlog, but likely more careful judicial reasoning. Now you want to talk about possible mediation. You might gesture toward the state court spot, remind the client of the attribute of speedier process, and then move your hand deliberately from the state court to a mediation "spot" nearby, as you explain that mediation may offer even faster resolution while maintaining client control over the outcome.

Anchors, Waves, Floaters, and Flyers

Anchor What Is Weighty[11]

A boat's anchor creates a stable resting place by virtue of its weight in the water. To convey a concept as important and real, gesture to anchor it: place it firmly on the table or solid surface by pressing your hand there. Once there, it must be reckoned with. Place it in front of you, between you and your client, and it cannot be ignored. Place it deliberately to the side, and it remains important, but to be dealt with after the topic at hand.

If you are seated and you want to describe summary judgment as a significant hurdle, place your hand at a particular place on the table when you describe it. Imagine talking with your client about a dollar offer—money that is "on the table." When you say those words, touch the table firmly with the flat of your hand. Describe the terms of the offer in some detail, as well as their potential impact, keeping your hand anchored there or gesturing toward where you anchored it on the table. Ask your client if she wants to "walk away from that and leave it *there*?" on the table or—gesturing up into the air—"Let it disappear?" You might even observe that to turn down the offer that now "belongs" to your client is, in effect, to give it back to the other side. Take the hand anchoring those settlement funds in front of your client and move it (and thus the funds) *away* from your client and toward the other side of the table.

Now imagine the same discussion, but this time when you talk about money on the table, just make a gesture in the air. When you describe the other terms offered, make a little wave when you mention each term. Wave the same way when saying that she is free not to take the offer. If you go through these motions as you talk, it is easy to feel which presentation will tend to make your client carefully consider the settlement. Obviously, if your client is comfortable rejecting the offer, placing it deliberately on the table will not change her mind. However, if she is at all uncertain, it is more likely to make her stop and think for a moment.

In sum, when referring to something important, anchor it firmly on the table. Each gesture back to that anchor reinforces its weightiness and importance.

Wave Away—The Anti-anchor

When referencing an unimportant or unlikely event, if you wave it away—up high and off the table—your client is less likely to focus on it, or to consider that it is or could be real. This is fine, if its likelihood is indeed remote or its consequences insignificant. "Well yes, some court costs would be added to the hundreds of thousands of dollars" seems appropriate for a high-handed wave motion when these costs are small compared to others and would not affect litigation decisions. Assume you are in a favorable jurisdiction and your client is asking what will happen if your summary judgment motion is granted. Your response might be—hand firmly on the table—"the case will be over!" Then, wave your hand high when you say: "They could always appeal, but I don't think the plaintiff will be able to afford it, and the chances of that appeal being successful with the judges in this circuit are slim." You are communicating, with your wave of the hand (as well as with words and, undoubtedly, voice) that there is little cause for concern.

Waving away what is unlikely or unimportant is a natural gesture. Even if you did the opposite—anchored with your hand to the table when talking about something insignificant—no harm would be done. It might give your client pause. He might take a moment to ask about the appeal. Or, he might interpret your hand's firm landing on the table as emphasizing your confidence in the assessment of minimal risk.

Take Care with Real, Floating, and High Flying

There is danger in a waving hand motion when you *want* to communicate real risk or high importance. Imagine yourself gesturing to a client when saying, "the award against you could be very, very high!" Or, "if their motion were granted, most of our best evidence would disappear!" Or, "if the injunction were granted, they would stop you from working 100 miles from here." In all of these instances, your natural gesture might be to raise your hand, indicating "high" damages. You might wave high to indicate "disappearing" evidence, or put your arm out and up to emphasize "100 miles from here."

Some of us naturally gesture high to emphasize points, or express great concern or large consequence. Large motion indicates big impact. That's fine. Inadvertently, however, when you stop waving and move onto the next topic, it's as if the problem has vanished— as waved into the air. It doesn't seem real. There has been no grappling with its concrete impact. It somehow becomes equivalent to a myriad of other vaguely bad or not-so-terrible things that might or might not ever happen. Assume that, in fact, the threatened non-compete radius of 100 miles *would* seriously affect your client's ability to earn a living; the predictably high damages award *would* likely exhaust his company's credit limits; or excluding the evidence *would* dramatically reduce your client's chances of winning and thus, the level of any subsequent settlement offer. As counsel, all of your communication—by word and by gesture—should support your client's careful consideration of these events as *real* possibilities.

Advice to the Arm Sweeper

After a natural and appropriately dramatic, emphatic gesture, slow it down and bring it to the table. You might say, with your arms wide and high, "The injunction could go as far as 100 miles and last two years," and then pause, bring your hands to the table, and say, "Let's talk about this: what if it were 100 miles?" As you spread your hands some distance apart and anchor them on the table surface to give the event weight and concrete reality, you ask: "How many potential customers are inside that range? How many outside? Will you be able to manage the driving for two years?"

For the client whose case is threatened with a serious motion *in limine*, you might first put all of the important evidence on the table in separate clusters, and then push the targeted evidence away and off the table to illustrate the motion's potential impact. You can then gesture toward what (little) evidence will be left supporting the case.

When High Flyers Are the Downside

The "high damages" award example poses a somewhat subtle problem. Conventional wisdom suggests high hands for high numbers and low hands for low numbers, particularly when setting forth a range. But, haven't we said that an idea placed in the air instead of on the table may seem less real, thus less threatening? Important here would be *not to wave*, but rather to deliberately *place* the high damages number at a high spot and let your hand pause there. If appropriate, you might place the company's annual profits or credit limits somewhat below it. Having placed the damages number high, you can anchor the idea of the damages award as a real threat by moving your hand down and placing it on the table, inviting discussion of that possibility and the business consequences.

Ode to the Easel, Pad, or Computer—USE THEM!

Consideration of gesture should not be interpreted to devalue the power of writing. The opposite is true: if you find yourself repeatedly gesturing and pointing to many steps and paths of possible choices or uncertainties, it is time to take out the pad, the easel, or the laptop and start writing.[12] You may wish to mark a series of events in order and indicate time intervals between them. In fact, when you anticipate the need to discuss many complex issues, options, or events, your preparation should include a paper or electronic chart or list. At minimum, a blank easel, pad, or laptop should be handy. Our actor-clients unanimously agree that they *very* much appreciate it when their lawyer has prepared a chart or outline for them.

Many people avoid the easel pad, white board or laptop projection as somehow artificial or only for students. We may feel uncomfortable in what seems like the role of a classroom teacher. But, the lawyer-counselor may have much to teach before the client is sufficiently informed for a wise decision. If so, before your client arrives, *do* take some time to list concepts or sketch a diagram on an easel pad, white board, or laptop that you can view or work on together. Later, you will naturally gesture to what is written there.

The Hand-Off

Gesture provides power to reinforce or undermine communication. Don't squander that power or employ it haphazardly.

Notes

1. "Katharine Hepburn Quotes," Brainy Quote, http://www.brainy-quote.com/quotes/quotes/k/katharineh114447.html (accessed on June 7, 2011).

2. Ruth Breckinridge Church, Philip Garber, and Kathryn Rogalski, "The Role of Gesture in Memory and Social Communication," *Gesture* 7, no. 2 (2007): 151 ("[G]esture rich with semantic content that elaborates on speech content may help to strengthen memory traces and consequently strengthen memory for speech."). For descriptions of additional research, see Robert M. Krauss, Palmer Morrel-Samules, and Christinga Colasante, "Do Conversational Hand Gestures Communicate?" *Journal of Personality and Social Psychology* 61, no. 5 (1991): 744.

3. See Judith Holler, Heather Shovelton, and Geoffrey Beattie, "Do Iconic Hand Gestures Really Contribute to the Communication of Semantic Information in a Face-to-Face Context?" *Journal of Nonverbal Behavior* 33 (2009): 73–88. The authors note, however, that the communicative efficacy of gesture depends in part on the type of information sought to be conveyed.

4. Judith Holler and Geoffrey Beattie, "The Interaction of Iconic Gesture and Speech in Talk," cited in *Gesture-Based Communication in Human-Computer Interaction: 5th International Gesture Workshop, Selected Revised Papers* (2003): 3853–3885.

5. See Holler, Shovelton, and Beattie, "Do Iconic Hand Gestures Really Contribute," 73–88. The authors note, however, that the communicative efficacy of gesture depends in part on the type of information sought to be conveyed.

6. Ruth Breckinridge Church, Saba Ayman-Nolley, and Shahrzad Hahootian, "The Role of Gesture in Bilingual Education: Does Gesture Enhance Learning?" *Bilingual Education and Bilingualism* 7, no. 4 (2004): 303–319.

7. See chapter 2, "Translating the Terrain."

8. For example, a study by Laura Wagner and others found that young children, when explaining brief cartoons to listeners, used explicit gestures even when told not to and even when their listeners could not see them. The authors suggest that the children's pointing to aspects of the

cartoon aided their cognitive processes during story-telling. "Children's Use of Pointing to Anchor Reference During Story-telling," in *Proceedings of the 29th Annual Boston University Conference on Language Development*, ed. A. Brugos, M. R. Clark-Cotton, and S. Ha (Somerville, MA: Cascadilla Press, 2005), 639–650. See also Wolff-Michael Roth and G. Michael Bowen, "Decalages in Talk and Gesture: Visual and Verbal Semiotics of Ecology Lectures," *Linguistics and Education* 10, no. 3 (2000): 335–358. Roth and Bowen studied students' comprehension of university ecology lectures in which the lecturer used graphs. They argue that gesture foregrounds and thus reinforces intended meaning, whereas asynchrony between gesture and speech is likely to confuse a lay audience in particular.

9. For example, see David McNeill, Justine Cassell, and Karl-Erik McCullough, "Communicative Effects of Speech-Mismatched Gestures," *Research on Language and Social Interaction* 27, no. 3 (1994): 223–237. The authors had participants watch videos of other people telling vignettes based on cartoons. The videotaped narratives contained a range of mismatches between narrator gesture and language. A control group only listened to audio narration of the vignettes but did not watch the video. Each participant then retold the vignette to another person based on memory. Those exposed to a mismatch were far more likely to include the mismatch in their retelling of the vignettes. Some participants who were unable to resolve the conflict between the mismatched gesture and language simply omitted that portion of the vignette. Other researchers have suggested that "conflicting gestures may hinder speech comprehension because they direct comprehension *away from* the meaning of the spoken message and toward other meanings (specifically, those meanings conveyed in the gestures). Intuitively, one might expect such conflicting gestures to hinder comprehension," particularly where the spoken message is more complex and thus requires more cognitive resources. Nicole M. McNeil, Martha W. Alibali, and Julia L. Evans, "The Role of Gesture in Children's Comprehension of Spoken Language: Now They Need It, Now They Don't," *Journal of Nonverbal Behavior* 24, no. 2 (2000): 134, 144.

10. I am indebted to John Bromels, an actor and playwright in Cincinnati, OH, for introducing me to the wisdom of keeping "New Mexico in New Mexico," and "bad deeds far away from good deeds." Mr. Bromels and Rocco DalVera, professor of drama at the University of Cincinnati's College Conservatory of Music, have provided invaluable

further elaboration of locating and anchoring concepts through gesture. Intentionally buried in this endnote is their observation that lawyers may confuse witnesses or juries by gesturing to different and inconsistent locations when referencing the opposing lawyer's or witness's ideas.

11. Negotiation scholars and students know the concept of anchoring in the literature of psychology and negotiation: an initial number—even if extreme or injected from an unrelated source—tends to function as a psychological anchor, drawing negotiators' subsequent offers in its direction. See Amos Tversky and Daniel Kahneman, "Judgment Under Uncertainty: Heuristics and Biases," *Science* 185, no. 4157 (Sep. 27, 1974): 1124–1131. Marianne Gullberg discusses anchoring gestures as helpful to distinguish visually what is not easy to distinguish verbally. "Handling Discourse: Gestures, Reference Tracking, and Communication Strategies in Early L2," *Language Learning* 56, no. 1 (2006): 162.

12. Long before writing about client counseling, this author used decision analysis and wrote of its effectiveness in mediation practice. In fact, one of the great powers of a decision tree is that it "maps" the twists and turns of the litigation path and encourages careful discussion of each step—each junction or possible event.

9

Channel Navigation Notes

"Connections are made slowly, sometimes they grow underground."
—MARGE PIERCY[1]

Observe a successful interaction between two people sitting at a desk or table: you can almost see a channel of connection in the airspace between them—a channel through which words, eye contact, and facial expressions are exchanged. Speak, nod, listen, and gesture into that channel and you reinforce or diminish connection—depending upon your movement and the message communicated. Protect the channel as shared, sacred space. Try not to gesture and place within that channel a fact, idea, or issue discordant with your client connection.

Advice for the Privileged

An important application for this advice arises when you must describe the attorney-client privilege and its exceptions. Speaking and gesturing into that channel while explaining to your client that "communication between us is generally confidential and protected" is wise; it reinforces trust and rapport. However, exceptions to the privilege are another matter. Explaining the circumstances under which confidences might or must be disclosed can be uncomfortable, as they reference either unlawful client behavior or future conflict with the client. Perhaps for that reason, survey research done by Fred C. Zacharias, a professor at the University of San Diego School of Law, found that, of lawyers who inform their clients about confidentiality, 72.1 percent admitted that they tell their clients "only generally that all communications are confidential."[2] Only 27.8 percent acknowledge to their clients that any exceptions exist. Of the clients surveyed, only one recalled any mention of specific exceptions.[3]

Although the exceptions may be relevant only for the exceptional client, the exceptional does happen. Clients do utter surprising and unwelcome words. Thus, best practice would logically be to include the existence and general nature of exceptions when first describing the attorney-client privilege. Yet it is easy to understand why so many lawyers fail to do so. Early in an initial meeting, when establishing rapport and trust, it feels inconsistent, indeed jarring to say: "If you tell me you are about to commit a crime or cause someone serious bodily harm, then our conversation would not be protected."

So what's a lawyer to do? Clearly, the particulars of the attorney-client privilege can and should be set forth in a document provided to the client, preferably before your meeting. Plain language in the document may make it safe to reference the exceptions, rather than describe them in detail. But, recognizing that many people do not read such documents easily or carefully, how can you build the client's trust and the comfort that the privilege should afford, when referencing or describing the exceptions?

Sideline the Discord: Place It Outside the Channel

When you speak, deliberately use gesture to place references to those discordant exceptions outside of the communication channel. Imagine that you met your client a few moments ago and have engaged in initial small talk or ice breakers. The client seems reasonably comfortable. In response to your question about what brought him to your office, your client characterizes it as a problem with a live-in girlfriend, business partner, or a credit situation. The representative of a corporate client might speak of an environmental issue or a securities law problem. You explain that before addressing the particulars, it is your practice to review the attorney-client privilege, and you ask if he is familiar with it. He responds: "Well, I've heard the phrase, but not really." You and your client are facing one another across a desk. There is good eye contact, clear communication, and the beginning of rapport. You explain that the attorney-client privilege means:

> *When you, a potential client, come in to talk with me, I am legally obligated to keep what you tell me confidential. It is privileged under the law and I cannot talk or testify about it. There are a few exceptions, which are described in this pamphlet. I'd be happy to go over them in more detail if you have questions, but generally they mean . . . .*

Now, envision yourself looking at and gesturing to your client while facing right into that communication channel and saying:

> *So if you were to tell me that you plan to commit a crime or do something that will cause serious harm to someone, I would have to disclose it.*

The words sound terrible—they sound as if you could indeed imagine this person committing a crime or doing harm. It is particularly jarring when these words are spoken and directed inside that channel where trust and positive communication were flowing just a few moments ago.

My first advice is to change your language to the third person, perhaps referencing another lawyer (hypothetical or real) and another client. You might say:

> *If my partner down the hall meets with a client who tells him that he's going to rob a bank the next day or if a client tells him he's going to hurt someone, my partner would have to disclose that.*

Or, you might explain it in a lighthearted way, using characters from a movie. Just this change can make referencing exceptions to the privilege less awkward.

Now, imagine using the revised language and directing your gestures *outside* of the channel as well. Avoid placing the lawyer-client confidentiality and criminal activity disclosure issues in shared, trusted space between you and your potential client. Wave it off high and to the side to communicate that you don't perceive it as a real threat, but an abstract concept unlikely to apply. Then, return your direct gaze and your open hands toward the client to hear his legal problem within that channel.

Language Still Matters, Channeled or Not

Imagine a serious personal injury case in which you believe the defense will accuse your client of exaggerating the pain and disability caused by her soft tissue injury and unjustifiably extending her time away from work. Your client needs to understand this, as it affects the range of possible damages awards.

Consistent with the advice above, when introducing the defense allegation, don't lean forward. Sit in a straight, neutral posture or even lean back slightly and direct your gestures outside the channel.

Be sure to use phrasing that clearly identifies the defense or defense counsel as the source of the allegation. Don't say: "There's an issue about whether your injuries were so serious." "There's an issue" suggests that you might agree. Instead, do say, "The defense attorney is questioning the extent of your injuries."

Deepening your client's feelings of insult or anger will further diminish any positive client emotions in your meeting and prove counter-productive for settlement discussions, now or in the future. Thus, language choice matters. You must alert your client to the risk, or perhaps explain why another medical examination is necessary. Note, however, that your choosing to say "they are questioning" or "they don't have outside confirmation" may not insult your client as much as "they are accusing you of malingering, saying that you're actually exaggerating and just want to stay home longer then really necessary."

It is often helpful, appropriate, and accurate to normalize the circumstances. Imagine that your client seems offended by the insurer's request that she be examined by an independent physician. You might lean back a bit and gesture somewhat to one side and say:

> *Undoubtedly, every year, people trip and fall in movie theaters and aren't badly injured but decide the large movie theater company would be an easy target for a quick settlement. The company knows that, and to make sure they are paying only for injuries that are serious, they ask that all claimants be examined by a doctor they have selected.*

Then, lean forward, face your client, and say (within that channel):

> *We have your x-rays and MRI scans that show your ruptured and bulging disc, and we have lots of other evidence of your serious injuries.*

Beyond Confidentiality and Malingering

In general then, staying outside of the channel is important whenever a lawyer must articulate a perspective the client will find offensive—views or legal theories that challenge a client's credibility or identity. For example, when a lawyer explains to a defense client that "the plaintiff is saying you purposely set him up for failure because of his race," the lawyer's accompanying hand gestures are best directed outside of the channel between him and his client.

When the lawyer's words shift to "Let's talk about how we can deal with this accusation," his gaze and hand gestures should be back within that direct communication channel, affirming an untainted client connection.

Not all bad news or negative words need be directed outside of the channel—just words that seem incongruent with the relationship. Indeed, there may be times to anchor a difficult problem on the table, exactly in that channel, as a problem "we have to address and overcome, together."

Motion Toward a Touchless Connection

With due respect for differing cultural sensibilities, most would agree that it is risky and unwise to touch your client, even to express sympathy.[4] Yet for many of us, touch is natural when another human being tells a heart-rending story of victimization, recounts extremely difficult personal or professional travails, describes debilitating injury and pain, or expresses great fear and uncertainty. Our natural impulse is a hug, a pat on the back, a squeeze of the shoulder. It's awkward to sit motionless when a client's eyes tears up, or chin trembles while struggling to control emotions. We don't want to appear wooden and unmoved; indeed, we are moved by our client's distress. Even if a touch might theoretically help the client's emotional state, it is generally a bad idea. Unintended consequences of a hug aside, the client needs a lawyer who is professional and in control.

One way to express emotional connection, without touching, is to move your hand forward on the table, bringing it closer to your client, within the channel, but without touching. Imagine saying, in response to your client's raw distress, "I know this is hard,"—and at the same time, putting your hand on the table, and sliding it forward, closer to your client. Your hand motion communicates that you are indeed moved, you do feel connection, and your impulse as a human being might be to touch. But restraint is best in the professional context. As your hand approaches or enters the client's

personal space—the intimate zone—it reinforces emotional connection, without being invasive or threatening.[5]

Notes of Affirmation and Disconnection

Noteworthy Is Important

To many lawyers, note-taking is a natural way to capture details,
protect against imperfect memory, and help maintain focus. Before
working with actor-clients in repeated client counseling simulations, it hadn't occurred to me that note-taking might elicit strong
positive emotional reactions. Thus, I was surprised when the actor-
clients expressed appreciation when their student-lawyers' took
notes. To paraphrase one actor-client: "Whenever my lawyer takes a
note, it makes me feel that I said something important."

But Take Note of Shift in Focus

While note-taking may foster client confidence, it also detracts from
eye contact and interpersonal connection. The note-taker looks
down at a note pad or computer rather than at the client listening or
speaking. The National Institute for Trial Advocacy (NITA)[6] admon-
ishes lawyers not to speak from notes and not to look down at notes
toward the end of a phrase to check on the next topic. Instead, the
lawyer should finish his thought speaking directly to the jury, then
pause and check his notes before moving on to the next topic (and
putting notes aside again).

The same advice unequivocally holds for lawyers in a cross-table
session with a client. Whether speaking or listening, the lawyer's
glance at the note pad renders her unable to focus on the client's
face. Some client-actors report feeling frustrated at their lawyers'
sustained break in eye contact while they are speaking. Some express
annoyance that their lawyer seems more concerned about having
perfect notes than listening to their story.

Micro Misses Matter

Many books and articles describe various micro-expressions that reveal a range of emotions. Without summarizing them here, it's notable that emotional micro-expressions occur quickly—often for only 1/15 of a second[7]—yet observers register and respond without being conscious of them.[8] Micro-expressions can indicate deception but can also reveal uncertainty, mixed emotions, and repression of a strongly felt emotion.[9] Listeners of normal social intelligence pick up on these micro-expressions.

When a lawyer looks down to take notes, he misses his client's subtle micro-expressions, not to mention less subtle, full facial expressions. Micro or full, these reflect emotional content and meaning. They carry important cues for a lawyer as listener, indicating when to ask a follow-up question and when to probe in a particular direction. They can be particularly important when the client's vocal tone is relatively flat, or intentionally measured.

Ironically, the lawyer who maintains scrupulous eye contact while conveying oral paragraphs of information or advice, but then glances down to check the next topic, will miss her client's facial expression when it is likely to be most telling. After all, at the end of the oral paragraph, the client is processing information and realizing its importance. As an observer, I often see the client's most revealing facial expressions in the moments *after* the lawyer has completed an explanation or a piece of advice. The client's eyes squint or blink, lips purse or form a fleeting grimace—signs the lawyer would notice *if she were looking in her client's direction*. Thus, the lawyer should retain eye contact for a moment or two *after* she has finished speaking, and then, and only then, glance down to make or check a note.

Avoid Loss by Laptop

Note-taking on a laptop offers great advantages and disadvantages. Clients may feel even stronger validation when their lawyer records their words on a computer.[10] Notes entered into a computer present no deciphering challenges, require no subsequent transcription, and are retrievable through a text search function.

Unfortunately, typing behind a laptop screen makes you seem more disconnected than writing on a note pad. Particularly when the laptop screen is up, it physically breaks into that channel space between lawyer and client. Connection flows between the laptop user and the device. Any observer of a class in which laptops are used will report less interactivity, even if students are *not* surfing the web. They are engaged in the space between eyes, fingers, and screen, and less so beyond. A recent video shows a well-known and wonderful mediator taking notes on his laptop during a mediation session. Students watching the video often comment that the laptop note-taking is distracting and makes the mediator seem less engaged. While the mediator is extraordinarily skilled and successful, this is despite the laptop, not because of it.

Have Your Notes and Connection Too

As usual, there's a dilemma: take notes to record details and communicate that the client's words are important, but miss facial expressions and break connection; or, forego note-taking to maintain eye contact and read micro-expressions, but miss or misremember important details. So, what's a lawyer to do?

At the beginning of the meeting with your client, explain that you want to be able to listen and converse during the meeting but that, in order to remember details, it's your practice to make notes. Let the meeting proceed, with a laptop or note pad well off to the side. Periodically, or just after the client mentions something significant, ask the client if you can take a minute to make a note "because that's important" or "because I want to get the details right," whatever is fitting. Then do just that, write on the note pad, or type on the laptop without guilt. When you're finished, look up, put the note pad or the computer to the side, and continue with the meeting: full eye contact, full communication.

The quality of the interaction remains undiminished. It is simply punctuated with pauses in which you take notes. These pauses can be helpful for you and your client, providing time and space to break, consider, and regroup.

Transparency Transcends the Dilemma

An additional plug for transparency: When you let someone know what you're doing and why, you dispel suspicion or speculation.[11] Assume that you are meeting with a client and it is important that you discuss a particularly difficult legal topic, about which you made some notes. Or, it's important to cover a technical set of questions about the way his company is structured. The conversation is headed toward the legal issue or it is nearing an end and you are concerned about having missed something. You just want to look at notes you made prior to the meeting. All too often, our instinct is to "just take a peek" at the notes, perhaps slowly move back the corner of the first page to see if what you seek is on the second. You don't want to interrupt your client, and you *are* still listening.

Avoid the temptation—be transparent. Furtive glances at notes and shuffling of papers is distracting and makes you seem uncertain. A client may worry about whether you are focused on her case or rifling through papers to look at something else. She may wonder whether what she's saying seems trivial or redundant. Or, she may think you are disorganized. Wait for a natural pause— or interrupt politely, and then explain: "I made a few notes before you came in about topics we needed to cover; let me just check and make sure we haven't missed anything." This communicates to that you viewed the meeting as important, you prepared for it, and you are intent upon discussing all that might matter to your client.

Notes

1. Marge Piercy, "The Seven of Pentacles," in *Circles on the Water* (New York: Knopf, 1982).

2. Fred C. Zacharias, "Rethinking Confidentiality," *Iowa Law Review* 74 (1989): 386.

3. Ibid.

4. As Roberto Aron, Julius Fast, and Richard B. Klein put it, touch in the lawyer-client relationship "must be at the right time and in the right way, and it must take into consideration the sexes of the lawyer and client," as well as their relative social status and power. *Trial Communication Skills* (Colorado Springs, CO: McGraw-Hill, 1986), 72.

5. Barbara Pease and Allan Pease, *The Definitive Book of Body Language* (New York: Bantam, 2006), 194–195.

6. David Ball, *Theater Tips and Strategies for Jury Trials*, 3rd ed. (Notre Dame, IN: National Institute for Trial Advocacy, 2003), 3–5, 234.

7. Anne E. Beall, "Body Language: Reading and Responding More Effectively to Hidden Communication," *Communication World* 21, no. 2 (2004): 18–20.

8. Ulf Dimberg, Monika Thunberg, and Kurt Elmehed, "Unconscious Facial Reactions to Emotional Facial Expressions," *Psychological Science* 11 (2000): 86–89. Study participants subjected to quickly-flashed facial expressions (not consciously noticeable) tended to mimic the unconscious stimuli. Thus, the brain was registering the expressions.

9. Also notable is the work of Paul Ekman, focusing on detecting deception through recognition of micro-expressions. Paul Ekman and Maureen O'Sullivan, "From Flawed Self-Assessment to Blatant Whoppers: The Utility of Voluntary and Involuntary Behavior in Detecting Deception," *Behavior Sciences and the Law* 64 (2006): 673–684. See also Paul Ekman, *Emotions Revealed: Recognizing Faces and Feelings to Improve Communication and Emotional Life* (New York: Owl Books, 2007), 214.

10. I have not tested this hypothesis, as my students are not permitted to use the laptop in the counseling skills exercise. However, my chief actress confirms the instinct.

11. "[T]ransparency helps to assure that the parties are clear about the process, about its goals, and about their role in it . . . . [T]ransparency provides others with a window into the mediator's thinking, analysis, and process decisions." Michael Moffitt, "Mediation 'Transparency' Helps Parties See Where They're Going," *Alternatives to the High Cost of Litigation* 16, no. 6 (1998): 81–91.

Final Thoughts

Much of the world is not rational, reasonable, or well-informed. Yet lawyers encourage reasonable and wise client decisions. We ask our clients to squarely face the reality of choice and risk and the workings of law and process, and then weigh their options on a true scale.

The more "difficult" client sustains real harm when he jumps from that cliff and his wings fail, as rational analysis of their construction would have predicted. When deal negotiations break down due to a business client's angry rejection of a contract term, his business continues to unravel. The bank predictably calls in its line of credit. Bankruptcy and foreclosure are devastating for him, his family, and his employees. For the litigation client, the real weight of the evidence has a habit of tipping the scale toward the heavier end. The judge's decision or jury's verdict is all or nothing.

The client's lament is sad: "If only I had understood how it would work. If only I could have seen this coming. If only I could have imagined the impact, I wouldn't have decided this way."

It is also casts doubt upon the lawyer, even if he tried mightily to counsel the client through bad news and legal realities. Unless the lawyer's efforts enabled the client to understand complexity, consider choices, accept risk, and envision possible consequences, he was never fully informed. He never processed the bad news; he never weighed the choices; he didn't see reality coming; he couldn't imagine it.

When lawyers counsel using advice from client science—research and observation of human perception, communication, cognition, memory, emotion, and social meaning in a legal context—that sad client lament is less likely. The fully informed client will generally make wiser decisions.

Informed by client science, we meet the highest standards of practice for lawyers-as-counselors. Our clients deserve nothing less.

Index